PRAISE FOR

READING JANE

The best book I've read in years. The alternating spirals of love and distancing between an adult daughter who sought warmth, and a mother who just couldn't deliver it. Elegant and beautifully written.

— **David Bodanis**, best-selling author of *The Art of Fairness: The Power of Decency in a World Turned Mean*

· · · · ·

Reading Jane is a beautifully told story of a mercurial, larger-than-life mother whose choice to end her own life while still in her prime sets her daughter on a quest to understand her mother's inner world by reading her diaries. A fascinating tale of mother-daughter love shot through with longing, enmeshment and disappointment. I found myself rooting for the author to free herself from her mother's grip and rejoiced when she did. By turns intriguing and repellent, the glamorous, eccentric Jane kept me reading late into the night and stayed with me long after I closed the book. *Reading Jane* is a triumph both as a literary memoir and as a contribution to the ongoing right-to-die debate in this country.

—**Zoe FitzGerald Carter**, author of *Imperfect Endings*

· · · · ·

Reading Jane is a brilliant memoir. It opens the door for each of us to truly consider what our family life (or lack of it) has meant to whom we have become. Kennedy reads her mother's journals after her mother's intentional end of life. What she learns and how it informs her own developmental history is presented in vivid, poignant, reflective terms. Her use of metaphor and shifts in time and space create a relational portrait of transgenerational and extended family experience that is both heartbreaking and invigorating. It is a gift to clinicians and non-clinicians alike.

— **Dr. Harriet Wolfe, M.D., President, International Psychoanalytical Association**

· · · · ·

Reading Jane is an extraordinary memoir of family secrets, love, loss, and a daughter's quest to understand how her mother's twisted history and death by suicide shaped her own life. Susannah Kennedy, raised the only child of a single mother in the kaleidoscopic days of the late 20th and early 21st century, writes with clear-eyed, sometimes brutal honesty. Her experience of other cultures—summers in Italy, life on multiple continents—informs and enriches the tale. Kennedy uncovers, in this deeply personal story, more than a few universal truths. A gifted first-time author, she leaves us wanting more.

—**Fran Moreland Johns**, board member End of Life Choices California, author of *Marshallville Stories, Dying Unafraid* and *Perilous Times: An inside look at abortion before – and after – Roe v Wade*

· · · · ·

Wow! was my first reaction on finishing Susannah Kennedy's breathtaking memoir, *Reading Jane*. This is a book that can be read on many different levels: It is a courageous exploration of Susannah's relationship with her charismatic, difficult, and troubled mother. It is an unflinching look at suicide and its effect on those left behind. And it is a bravely drawn picture of a woman's struggle to build a healthy life in the face of sometimes overwhelming odds. Brava to Susannah Kennedy for allowing us to accompany her on this fascinating journey.

— **Susan Buckley**, author of *Eating with Peter* and *Turning 15 on the Road to Freedom* with Lynda Blackmon Lowery

. . . . .

This excerpt "is some of the most honest, heartfelt, beautiful creative nonfiction I have ever read, both as an editor and as a reader."

— **Liza Olson**, former editor of *(mac)ro(mic)* literary journal

. . . . .

READING JANE

A Daughter's Memoir

SUSANNAH KENNEDY

Sibylline
PRESS

AN IMPRINT OF ALL THINGS BOOK

Sibylline Press
Copyright © 2023 by Susannah Kennedy
All Rights Reserved.

Published in the United States by Sibylline Press,
an imprint of All Things Book LLC, California.
Sibylline Press is dedicated to publishing the brilliant work
of women authors ages 50 and older.
www.sibyllinepress.com

Distributed to the trade by Publishers Group West.
Sibylline Press
Paperback ISBN: 978-1-7367954-7-7
eBook ISBN: 978-1-960573-02-5
Library of Congress Control Number: 2023935656

Book and Cover Design: Alicia Feltman

READING JANE

JANE

A Daughter's Memoir

SUSANNAH KENNEDY

To Niels, Julian, Dylan and Leah

Give sorrow words; the grief that does not speak
Whispers the o'er-fraught heart and bids it break.

—WILLIAM SHAKESPEARE,
Macbeth ACT IV. SCENE III

Probably Never

ALL THROUGH MY CHILDHOOD, my mother settled once a day to chronicle her life. Her diaries were factory-made, squarish, embossed with the year on the cover, the date printed onto the page, thin lines regulating the number of words allowed for emotions, events—no more, no less. A page per day. She wrote ceremonially, as if she were hiding secrets, lost in thought, available only with a distracted "hmm," to me.

"Not now, I'm writing in my diary," she'd say.

It was her private place, her room alone.

"Mommy, can I read your diaries?" I'd often ask.

She started off saying "Someday," and then she changed to, "When you are the age I was when I wrote them." One time when I remembered to ask as an adult, she said, "Maybe," then, "No, probably never."

I think I would have been fine never having read them. But then she chose suicide.

The grieving has taken place in phases. First there was the shock, the numbness, the nausea. Then there was the activity, and as her only child, I was the only one responsible. Identifying her body in the morgue, organizing her memorial, that weird shock of Robin Williams' copycat suicide; tearing up her self-written, visionary obituary; sponsoring a bland, adulterated version just to have something, anything, in *The San Francisco Chronicle*. Hiring a catering firm, booking hotel rooms for out-of-town relatives, booking a hotel for us—although she hadn't died there, her apartment still held the outbreaths of her last days—writing my version of a silent eulogy in two parts, one for her and one for those she left behind. Making it through the memorial gathering, listening to mawkish tributes to *la Principessa* from women whose friendships with my mother had always seemed more self-serving than intimate. My eyes stayed dry. Our three children, silent, dressed in black, watching the crowd. Until Carol appeared at my side—my childhood best friend, whom I hadn't seen in twenty years. She tapped me on the shoulder and, without a word, offered me her open arms, there amongst the crowd of San Francisco's ladies-who-lunch in their pearls and hats, and I began to cry and couldn't stop.

A month later, hiring a speedboat out to the middle of the bay, choosing the right words to accompany the box of ashes down into the saltwater currents. Cleaning out her apartment with my friend-since-high-school Melanie; taking silk blouses to the posh secondhand store on Polk St. with Diane; gleefully discovering Mom's full-length mink coat. Meeting with the lawyer, realizing the extent of my inheritance and the mess Mom left me, she who was so deliberate and calculated in her plans. And then the attention of women whose mothers had also killed themselves, chance encounters, acquaintances at parties. How could this be? So many of us? And their concerned eyes inquiring whether I was getting help. And my momentary self-questioning: *Do I need help? Am I not coping just fine?*

I was sure that I'd be okay. After all, my mourning was not dire, my suffering more extended and existential than acute. There were the three years after her death, when I resumed my life far away, returning to my therapist's office yet again, churning through the "ending" to my mother and me. And eventually, the decision to move us all permanently to California, which we should have done ten years before—had she not lobbied against it so harshly. I wish she had wanted me closer.

I wish she had said, "Oh, please come." Would that have made a difference?

I kept thinking of the small books lined up in the wooden chest.

Lipstick

March 2014

IT WAS THE LIPSTICK. *Pink.* A tawdry, hooker kind of pink, drawn small like a geisha bow. And the peculiar package of her knees, body draped by too many sheets, as if they had never straightened her out. Here in the back of the battleship gray Hall of Justice down on Bryant Street.

Those were the day's worst details. The ones that still cause a cringe. Worse even than finding myself standing in front of a thick window as the clerk at the medical examiner's office parted a drab curtain to reveal my mother's body on the other side of glass. She hadn't wanted this—an autopsy and an ignominious showing, the required "identify the body" that followed the discovery of her remains, head in large plastic balloon, helium tube attached, sedative jars in a row on the motel bathroom sink.

She had intended to set a poetic example, a healthy person's #BetterOffDead—protestation against America's industry of old folks homes and Alzheimer's and feeding tubes.

But when you clean out your house and organize your papers, when you write your goodbye emails and sneak your black chaise lounge down the kitchen stairs to the car, when you move into the cheap room where you stayed as a young mother, then tape up signs saying "Stop! Don't come in. Call the police!" so the maids in the morning won't have to be the ones to find you, when all these things happen, the rest of the world takes over.

And they call your only child on the phone and summon her into this hall with its glass cubicles like a passport line in the airport and the showing room in the back. "I'm sorry, ma'am, but this is the way it is done."

That's what happens, Mom, when you dream your own death, when you wait for the applause.

The Diaries

June 2014

A FEW MONTHS AFTER HER SUICIDE, hearing I couldn't enjoy spending time in my mother's apartment, a once in a lifetime apartment that now belonged to me, my friends organized a "Daughter Power" day to take back the space. Six of us met there one morning bringing every healing ritual we could think of. We told stories, shared poems and sayings, sprayed lavender in every drawer, and in every corner of every room. We ate delicious farm-to-table food. We swept the threshold of each entry, banged wooden logs, made a fire, and we sang.

It was amazing. It was beautiful.

But still.

I remember pausing at the linen closet drawers, the ones with doors that hinged down to once reveal my mother Jane's orderly sheets and towels. Empty. I'd given all the contents to Goodwill. I glanced at them again. Hmm.

I wasn't sure it was enough.

I peeked into the closet again. "Don't you think we should smudge in here, too?"

Five pairs of eyes stared back at me. My friends were game for anything. Women with a flair for superstition. But by now their cheeks were drooping with strain.

"Susannah, listen," Lizzie said, putting her hands on her hips and looking up at me. She was my most feminist, most incense-knowledgeable pal. "From what I understand, your mother was a powerful force. I don't think she'd choose to hide her spirit in the towel drawers."

I laughed. The tension was broken. She was right. I had to let superstitions go. "Come on, let's have some lunch."

In the afternoon, we got to work on the papers. We went through the plain wooden secretary, once housed in the boat house in the Hamptons, which Jane had retained after the divorce. We went through the closet with an extra bolt lock where she had stored her valuables when she went away for the summer. One by one, the stack of white bankers boxes we'd brought with us dwindled, each unfolded and filled with tax information, old checks, letters, and school district lawsuit business.

"What's in this chest?" my friend Terry asked, her hands running over the intricately carved dark wood of the Asian trunk in the living room.

"Probably my old baby clothes."

I knelt down next to it, pushed the bronze locking mechanism. The others gathered around. The chest top hinged up to envelop us in the smell of mothballs. Inside were not clothes but rows of little books, spine side down, the years marked in chronological order.

Slam. I let the heavy wooden lid free-fall shut.

I scooted violently back on the carpet. Maure and Reba looked sideways at me. "What? What's wrong?"

"Her diaries," I said.

It was as if the books were covered in anthrax dust.

My mother had said she'd given up journaling when she retired, fourteen years ago. I hadn't thought about them in years.

I sank back onto the white wool, put my feet up on the coffee table. My heart pounded, loud in my ears. *Why is it only in my right ear?* As if my heart had migrated upwards.

Terry and the others continued packing away the files from Jane's desk, chatting mildly all around me. I could tell they were giving me space, honoring something. *But why would I need it?*

My body leaden, the carpet thin under my shoulders, I stayed quiet.

After a while Diane nodded at the rest of the group. "We'll pack up the diaries and you can decide later whether to throw them away or read them."

Forty-five volumes of my mother's words.

Did she leave them for me to read, wanting me to tell her story to the world? Did she intend to convince doubters of the moral rightness of her plan? Was I supposed to be her interpreter or, worse yet, her confessor?

It's All Good

March 2014

My kids and I were sitting with my mother in her sun-filled living room overlooking San Francisco. It was supposed to be a special weekend of togetherness with three generations: Nonna (her chosen nickname), me, and her three grandchildren.

Leah was perched on the sofa, winding fluffy blue and purple yarn around her needles, homework for her fifth-grade handwork class on the following Monday.

"Nonna," she asked, "why didn't you sit with us last night?"

My mother had invited "us women" to the San Francisco Ballet. High culture with Nonna was always a slightly nerve-racking adventure when we visited. Our children were more at home in our rural farmhouse in Germany. They were used to being loud, with dogs and chickens and a forest to run in. Visits to Nonna emphasized comportment and diction, table manners and deferential conversation. When we visited, I always made sure the children had emergency outfits that fit them, tan slacks and white shirts for the boys, a dark blue dress with white tights for Leah. My rebellious side hated it. But I couldn't be released from the wish that my children would also grow up comfortable in symphony hall seats and coats and ties. Who knew where their lives would take them?

We had enjoyed dressing up yesterday. Leah had been excited about seeing a real ballet in a fancy opera house. We had gone to dinner at a restaurant with lots of other dressed-up ticket holders. Leah had held my hand tightly in anticipation as we walked up the broad stone steps and through the arched doorways of the War Memorial Opera House. But as we got to our seats, my mother had eased into a seat behind us instead of in our row.

"What are you doing?" I had asked.

"I'm fine here," she had said. It had been weird.

Now my mother deadpanned to Leah. "Those just happened to be the tickets I had."

I didn't believe her. She was a master season ticket buyer. We always sat together. Even then, not yet knowing, it had felt eerie. Like we were being framed, held in time. Being recorded. Now I realize from her perch behind us, she had watched us watching the dancers on stage.

"Wasn't Cinderella splendid?" She followed to Leah, "It was a beautiful thing to see you and Mama so enthralled and looking so fine."

"The best was the horse-drawn carriage," Leah said. She seemed hesitant.

"Did you catch those see-through tights," I added, trying to even out the mood. "And that the Prince's name was Tiit?"

Everyone laughed.

Today, after lunch, my mother had taken all three grandchildren to the Bay Club to work out. Julian and Dylan had played basketball. Leah had hung about while Nonna swam her mile of laps. Nonna swam every day. Had done so for thirty years. She also did what she called "my exercises" every day. Her relationship to her body, and by extension, to my body, was complicated. I remember when I was in junior high school, she began to joke, "I am like a foal and you are like a calf." I knew the secret message. Horses were beautiful, and their foals were thin and elegant. Calves were baby fat cows, knobby-kneed and goofy.

Now back in the living room, Leah took up her knitting project, finishing her purl and turning the needles. Dylan was prone in his favorite position on the window seat, watching the boats on the distant bay and listening to Tupac and Eminem on his headphones. Julian approached with a tray from the kitchen.

"So where are we all going to stay?" he asked.

A college sophomore, he was thinking ahead to organize our summer plans. We had just received the invitations to cousin Shea's wedding at her parents' rustic ranch house in Mendocino. Julian wanted to check in with his girlfriend about travel dates. There weren't many extended family events anymore and they were usually lots of fun.

I have a large Irish extended family. My mother had 25 first cousins, and all my life, we had visited some of them every summer. Like a butterfly alighting on a flower, she had pulled her favorites to her, with me, her shy little girl, in tow. By default, cousins twenty years older became my first cousins, too, rather than the aunts and uncles they actually resembled. It was a strange generational disconnect. It meant that in my young adulthood they had been middle-aged, so weddings and births had been few and far between. The last big wedding had been fifteen years before. I was really looking forward to a gathering again, to introducing my children to the extended family I had once known well.

"So, what do you think about Shea's wedding? We plan to rent an Airbnb up there," I said, reaching for nuts and turning to my mother. I expected her to be eagerly awaiting a gathering, to have already made plans. She was usually planning her summers by March.

"Are you going to stay on the ranch?" I asked. The ranch meant an old farmhouse with slanted floors and a huge fireplace in the living room and a bunkhouse up the hill with a hand-made outdoor shower and toilet. It wasn't fancy. It wasn't at all clear where we would all be sleeping on the wedding weekend.

My mother was holding the balls of yarn for Leah, next to her on the couch. She didn't respond. She didn't even seem to consider the question. A few seconds passed, a few seconds too long. I looked up.

My mother exhaled.

"I will not be there," she threw into the room.

Just a few words. But their force felt like a sonic boom.

Leah's reaction was the quickest. She raised her sweet blond head, suddenly staring intently at her grandmother. "What do you mean, Nonna?" she said, plowing right in with a speedboat's sure direction.

I felt a swell of pride for my little girl. As a child, I would have remained silent. I learned early to muffle my intuition. But Leah had no qualms about piercing unspoken friction.

"I'm not going because I will not be here anymore," my mother announced.

Plain words. They could have meant nothing. But the harsh "anymore" floated in the air, overtaking the room like skunk spray wafting through a window.

Leah looked at me, her yarn and needles dropped to her lap. Dylan remained in position listening to music. Julian fiddled with his fingers. Nobody said anything. There was a sound of tourists shouting to each other down below on the street.

My mother stood up. "Well, I'll go start dinner." She picked up her glass of wine and strode toward the kitchen. I looked at Julian. What had just happened? He seemed calm. Why were my insides icy? After a moment, Julian nodded after her, silently beckoning me to follow him.

I obeyed, suddenly grateful for movement.

"Mom, what did you mean?" I said when we entered the kitchen. She was already sitting on the tall counter chair tearing lettuce for the salad.

"You know I have always said I don't want to live past 75. I have made my plans. It will all come to pass before Shea's wedding."

I leaned against the kitchen sink, the Bay visible through the window behind me, boats plying their normal way across the gray March tides, seagulls, sea lions barking in the distance. A car horn tooted nearby. All was as it had been.

"I have everything organized. Do you want to know the details?"

Julian was a statue beside me. Two statues listening to a crazy lady.

"No." I stood ramrod still. My mind felt as if it was stuck in clear resin. "I don't want to know anything, Mom." *What was happening?* "What are you saying?"

She continued to tear lettuce, as if lost in thought. "I liked the story of your women's group," she said. "The 14th Moon ceremony. I've thought a lot about that. This will be a rite of passage we will share."

Confused, I flashed to the recent gathering; women dressed in red, girls in white, the older honoree—the elder—in black. I remembered telling her about it. My friend Lizzie had invited me into her New Moon group on this trip to California. My anthropologist brain and my German countryside life had sparked my curiosity. The crone ceremony sounded strange but in Lizzie's world drew its roots from a nourishing wish to honor female elders, once considered wise healers and teachers and mediators, able to accompany women at birth and at death.

Maybe that is what my mother meant.

We had dressed in our colors, we had sung pretty songs and sat in a circle and honored the woman's life. She had happened to be a midwife, which had added a special symbolism to the evening.

"I'm probably going to live to be over 90," my mother continued. Now aged 75, she cocked her head as if watching herself ironically. "Physically fit and healthy, that's what they'll all say."

Her eyes narrowed. "But not psychologically." She shook her head. "I'm so angry at Alan and Fritz that they lived so excessively and then popped off in an instant. God, I'll most probably linger and suffer even though I have lived a healthy life."

I could see her eyes clouding over. Fury in her shoulders.

I tried to sort through my images of Fritz, who was my husband Niels' father. Yes, Fritz and my own father, Alan, had both smoked and drunk to excess. They had never done yoga or lifted weights or swum long laps. They had both died in a moment, each at age 67, a heart attack and a stroke. I knew her protest intimately. Their deaths had been easy when they should have suffered. They indulged and were not punished. Instead, *she* would be punished. She had cared for herself well, would live long and become old. She would become frail and dependent — the worst fate of all. That their excesses—the fraught codependencies, the conflicts, the mixed-up grief following sudden death—had brought their own repercussions played no role now in my mother's calculations.

Illness and growing old had become an obsession of hers. Maybe even a fetish. She gathered suffering friends like a shepherdess with a flock. She took care of them and *tsk-tsked* afterward. She was generous to each of them, and then complained to me what a waste it all was. I had heard her opinions for years. My grandmother. My great uncle Ed. My great-grandmother. A cousin. An old friend. A neighbor. *All wasting away,* she'd trumpet to me. Yet still she would send a check or call daily. It felt like a mother's warmth turned inside out.

Her obsession had always unsettled me. Was it a disconnection between public and private? After all, she had always said, "Don't do as I do. Do as I say." Perhaps I was the only one who even felt this as a disconnection. Maybe those she helped were just happy for the care. Like a nurse writing a tell-all when she goes off duty, it doesn't matter to the patient.

But it mattered to me.

It didn't feel like real empathy. It felt perverted.

A mother's words can be like water drops on a stone, over time wearing into a toxic groove. The only way to stop the effect is to either cleanse the toxicity or build a protective roof so the drops splatter to the sides. It took me a long time to build a roof. Even now I wasn't sure how solid it would remain. Time was slowly marking me with her obsessions, her calculations and worries transferring onto me. Was I doing everything I could to live well? If I swam a mile a day, would that be enough? If I did calisthenics every morning, would that be enough? I had to follow her example. Surely, I didn't want to drop dead at 67 like my father.

The telephone rang in the back bedroom, one, two, three rings, and then went to voicemail.

"Most of my friends will be shocked and very, very angry," she continued now.

Her voice became monotone, strong, righteous.

"You must remind them *always* that I wanted to do this, and I am very proud of my choice. I refuse to be a deer in the headlights of aging."

She took a sip of her water. "When the dust settles, they will view me differently. I know that someday it will be celebrated to do what I'm doing."

Paralyzed, I said nothing. I recalled her bemoaning to me on the phone about her friend's husband who was "being kept alive" on machines, and about the neighbor's wife who was unable to feed herself.

She shook her head. "You don't know what it is like to live my life."

I suddenly worried about Julian, his arm against mine as we both faced her.

"Mom," I said. "Stop." He shouldn't have to listen to his favorite grandmother talk like this.

"I have instructions for you," she went on. "There is a folder all ready to go. In it are the cards I've written out for those who don't have email or need a personal note. My obituary is there. The list of addresses and bank accounts, passwords. My lawyer has all my legal papers and all you have to do is call him."

Obituary? She'd written her own obituary.

"I've worked it all out. My body will go to the UCSF medical center. It will go directly there. You don't have to be involved. The coroner's office will inform you. There's no way around that. But everything else should be simple."

Body to medical research? No burial. No ashes. No tombstone. No trace.

As if she'd never existed.

We stood there, Julian and I, his arms crossed, mine by my side. I think now, perhaps I should have sent him out of the room. What good would it do for him to hear all this at age 19? A mother must protect her children. But I felt no disquiet from him, no angling to get away. And I was in need of his strength, so I wouldn't have to be the only witness. To be able to say, *See, this is the way she really is.*

He says now he doesn't remember this conversation. Maybe I urged him away to check on his brother and sister. Or maybe he left quietly on his own. In my mind he was there next to me, but I know memory can sometimes be an unreliable narrator of details.

"Do you have questions?" she asked. "I'm happy to tell you."

"No, Mom, I don't have anything to say."

Suddenly a feeling came unbidden, remembering other hints. How she went for hour-long swims in the ocean, leaving me on the beach alone to search the waves anxiously for the return of her bathing capped head, her long arms breaking evenly through the water in her elegant backstroke.

"Don't be silly, Susannah. It is perfectly safe," she'd say, when I begged her not to go out into the surf.

To me, my pre-teen hands digging down into the wet sand, it meant waiting and watching nervously for Mommy to be back. I was never quite sure.

Suddenly, standing here in the kitchen, I didn't want to worry anymore. *Go on and do it, then. Stop threatening me.* She probably didn't mean it all anyway, as during our estrangement when Julian was little, when we found ourselves together at cousin Bree's wedding, and she broke her silence to seek out Niels and me after lunch. "I'm going for a walk in the hills," she had announced, a foreboding tone in her voice. All afternoon I had worried. *Let her be. She's just walking. It's getting dark. A gun, a noose?* She had returned in the shadows. I had been silly to worry. All that energy and fretting.

I felt like a pawn in her game.

My mother pulled open the refrigerator. "Then let me prepare dinner." She seemed relieved. "Why don't you have the kids set the table?"

In my memory, Julian placed his hand on my back, guiding me out to the living room. Life resumed. I didn't want to alarm Leah and Dylan. I guess both Julian and I tried to pretend all was well. Maybe it was. Maybe it had never happened.

Later, I would read in her diary that she found our talk pleasurable. No words on the psychology of death by suicide, its effects on family members, and why she was standing on that precipice at all. Instead, she anticipated relief, projecting onto us a shared wish for her to be gone. Satisfied, she could then settle calmly into a mundane evening. Her diary reads:

I now realize my death will be liberating. The sword of Damocles bugs them and my efforts at deliberate preparation of their emotions are misguided. I fixed a ham dinner and afterwards watched everyone play Scrabble. Then Susannah, Leah and I settled down with a Shirley Temple film. Julian and Dylan had good-natured recourse only to streaming on their computers. (March 15, 2014)

For me, it was another story. Adrenaline coursed through me all night. Conversations floated. The steam heater cracked and banged as it always did in my childhood bedroom. I was comforted by Leah's deep breathing in the other twin bed.

When light peeked through the shutters, I got up. Mom was sitting in the kitchen, fruit and a cup of coffee in front of her.

"Good morning." She seemed totally normal.

"Mom, I barely slept." I returned to my place by the sink.

"Yes, it is a tough thing to hear. My plans. But I feel optimistic now. I think it will all be fine. You will be fine."

In the darkness, I had tried to come up with some way of comprehending her story. Maybe it was all a fanciful delusion. I felt tired, as though wrinkles were forming too quickly.

"Mom, what are you doing?" I filled a mug with black coffee.

She smiled. "What time does Julian have to get to the airport?"

I had been planning on driving him there, for his return flight to New York, spring break over. It was only Sunday. Dylan and Leah and I had the rest of the long weekend to get through. I had to think of something to say.

"Mom, why don't you want to be in our lives anymore?" It came out slowly. It felt like the real true question.

It felt like that was all I had wanted, had brought us over here to be near her, to try to repair what she didn't want to repair.

She placed her hands around her coffee cup. I could see the dark liquid but no steam.

She spoke calmly, as if narrating a play from the sidelines. "You are so innocent." Maybe she had been thinking about it all night, too. "You didn't have to suffer through Helen, and then Mother's death. Your father just popped off quickly, as will I. You are lucky."

I didn't feel lucky. I didn't even register what she said about her sister Helen.

"But, Mom," the words came quietly. "Don't you want to see your grandchildren grow up?"

I was offering up my most sacred card.

She said nothing for a moment. Her eyes filled with tears. A surprise. Another few seconds.

"You are so—" her tone was observational, as if she were taking scientific notes on the character of someone unrelated. "—emotional." She located the word, like choosing from a list.

Emotional. The worst fate.

I stood there a little longer. She sat, her long thin legs crossed. Her gold bracelet resting halfway down an arm. The refrigerator hummed. Her eyes turned to mine, as if she were giving herself an instruction to look at me. But there was no one there I recognized. She had already left.

I returned to my bedroom and lay there until Leah awoke. Gradually, the boys stirred, and the bustle of breakfast began. I forced myself to appear calm but felt jittery. If I pretended enough, maybe I could protect us all and it would end up being just a nutty Nonna story someday.

Is this what good parents do? They play-act for their children, knowing children take their cues from parents? If I'm calm, they will be calm?

As the time approached to drive Julian to the airport, I went out to fetch the parked car farther up the hill. To get my coat, I opened the hall closet, squishing something soft under the hall runner. What's that? I lifted the carpet.

A clear plastic hose. Plastic hoses and helium to inflate a balloon bag over the head. Snippets of her Final Exit conversation years before came back to me: Pills to sleep and helium to kill.

If I were a cat, hair would have risen on my neck.

Once up the red steps and into the fresh air, I breathed more even-ly. I called Niels, nine hours ahead in Hamburg, getting ready to join us in California for his spring vacation, timed for his birthday. It was evening for him, after a week full of patients.

"She's talking about suicide. She's telling the kids." My voice turned into tears of exhaustion. "What am I going to do?" I had another day and night to manage at her house. "She is weird, distant."

I started pacing as I summarized the last 24 hours. "What am I supposed to do for her?"

Niels listened and spoke calmly, a doctor. "When I get there, I will talk to her. Right now, you need to take the children and get away. They shouldn't be exposed to her nonsense. Just go."

I stopped my pacing. Yes, it made sense. Yes, I'd do that. Of course. We could all drive to the airport and then just keep driving south to Santa Cruz, our home for the semester.

Yes. Run away. I felt like a teenager again. It had taken me over-long to run away from my father's house back then, too.

My mother seemed relieved. She made no effort to keep us another day. We quickly packed. Then, standing by the big oak door with the creaky hinges, she became a sentinel, hugging each of us, one by one, as we passed. She wished us a good trip home. Her grandmother greet-ings had always been spectral rather than toasty, arms barely touching our bodies, more a token than anything. This time they lasted just a few seconds longer. I couldn't bear the suspense. *Out of here. Out of here.*

That evening she wrote in her diary that she was relieved at the way the weekend had gone. She had successfully communicated her plans to me and was relieved of guilt. I had listened, as she knew I would. Now I would know what would happen and all would be well.

Safe travels for all ... They have each other, a huge comfort to me as I walk alone the next days, *una donna sola.* I busied myself with setting all to neat-freak order and doing laundry

> and going for a swim on this gorgeous warm Sunday afternoon. Peggy [a friend] came for supper bringing tasty tacos. Watched Netflix. (March 16, 2014)

All the way home down Highway 1, choosing the scenic route with the solace of a Tom Petty soundtrack and ocean vistas, Julian on the plane back to college, Dylan and Leah watching quietly out the car windows, I tried to make sense of what had happened. I felt drawn to her, as always. A pact. A whispering into my baby ears, calling in her chits. As if every time my little hand had held hers, every time her eyes had rested upon me with laughter or listened to my childhood stories, she had been passing out an expectation that someday I would be required to repay.

To hold a deathwatch, waiting, waiting.

As we approached Santa Cruz, we stopped at Natural Bridges Beach. It was a beautiful day. I felt easier now, with a lifting of dread the farther from her I got. We stopped for a while in the sand, watched the waves. The kids goofed around together. Normalcy returned. On occasions like this when her full power blasted down upon me, I felt how much strength it had taken me just to get away.

Yet still, as soon as I am away, I yearn for her presence. I become once again a satellite to her sun.

That evening I couldn't stop myself from writing her an email. I should have been angry. I should have focused on myself. Instead, I worried about her. Would she be agonizing about us? Would she be regretting her words?

> It seems kind of silly to think I should check in with you and let you know we got back to Santa Cruz fine. Spent a couple of hours at the beach, and Dylan and Leah went bodysurfing in their wetsuits. Beaches were very crowded today. Julian also got back home fine. ... (March 16, 2014)

Her answer:

> It is not silly. I love the thought of Julian having had a week of California sunshine and family togetherness, and Dylan and Leah in wetsuits body surfing is the best. The surf was high, according to news reports. You know that vapid New Wave saying, "It's all good"? ... Well, sometimes it just feels right. (March 17, 2014)

It didn't feel right. Nothing about it felt right at all.

The Concert

March 2014

THE DAYS FOLLOWING MOM'S ANNOUNCEMENT, I waited. Confiding in a few friends and Niels, I waited. What else could I do? Niels, a psychiatrist, confirmed what we all knew. If we reported her, even tied her arms together and transported her bodily to a mental hospital, even a good one like those in Germany, there was no psychiatrist or judge in the world who would keep her on a closed ward. She could charm anyone.

"What are you talking about, doctor? I just had a root canal done last week. Why would I do that if I was planning to kill myself? My family just exaggerates."

Niels called her when he landed in California. "Jane, we are not okay with this."

She told him how happy she was that she informed me of her plan so easily. "I'd like to meet you in Half Moon Bay for lunch so I can hand over my personal papers. That's a good halfway point, easy for us both. I can explain my wishes again."

As if that is all we were waiting for. As if clarifying what was in her safe deposit box would exonerate her.

It felt dirty. She was making us complicit in her plan. "No, Jane. I'm not going to meet you so you can hand over your papers as if this were some sort of business meeting," I heard Niels say.

I could hear the tone of her voice. She seemed distant, repeating some of the things she had said to me in the city, how nobody should feel sorry for her. Niels offered to talk if she needed help. He had often offered insight. That's what therapists did; they offered the chance at insight. Whether people took it or not was what made the difference between healing and continuing to suffer. Therapy only works for those who are ready to understand and change.

Niels and I had talked about it when he arrived from Germany this time. It was very unlikely she would want to change her mind now. She seemed serious. But we knew she could still be playing with us. She might go to all this trouble and then announce plans to go to Lake Como for the summer and never mention her suicide wishes again. Jane was very capable of gaslighting. "You're so sensitive. Don't take me seriously all the time."

But here we were, in Santa Cruz, in the days following her announcement. After a few more sentences on the phone, I noticed Niels stand up quickly. I moved closer to eavesdrop on her words.

"Susannah won't ever have a mother who's a *Better Off Dead*," I heard her reciting to him. "But she'll never understand, I wager. You've given her a family full of love. Our life experiences are so different."

"Jane, you know we all love you and we want to continue to have you in our lives," Niels responded.

"I have long-lived DNA, I would live way into my 90s most likely. I see no common sense in that." I could hear her clearly now, my ear pressed close to his shoulder.

"Jane," he repeated, trying to get her attention. "Stop this. I'm happy to find somebody for you to talk to."

I could tell he was irritated. It had been so many years of mother-in-law subterfuge. She wouldn't respond to his words. She never had. There had been moments in our lives together when she had actually asked him a real question, when it felt she might be on the brink of something curious, like, "Does your work *really* help people?"

And he'd say, "You seem to have a lot of doubts about that, Jane."

Each time she would pause and seem to think. I would hold my breath. I would hope, maybe this was it. Maybe she would reveal something. Maybe we could find a way to actually talk.

But always she would pivot. "Nah, I'll just stick to my laps and my city routine." And another chance would be gone.

Sometimes she'd add a sting: "All that matters are clean sheets and a good bank balance."

I rarely pushed back anymore. I knew how far she'd go. I'd be ghosted, one would say now. Years, as she'd done in the past. No, if I wanted any contact at all, she had always made clear it was going to be on her terms. Niels didn't push back either. He saw early on that the benefits of keeping in touch for me and for the grandchildren always outweighed the cruelty she sometimes meted out.

"Life is going to be good when I'm gone, you'll see," I heard her volleying.

Niels flung the phone receiver across the room as he hung up. "Bye, Jane," he muttered. I don't know whether she even heard him.

At a certain point, talking makes no more sense.

She wrote in her diary that day:

Of course, I take joy in the moments of togetherness but the hours, days, weeks of real life have no hold on me anymore. ... I went to Target for a helium tank to practice. (March 20, 2014)

The days stretched into weeks. My nights were uneasy. I tried to remain calm. Niels tried to enjoy his vacation, and Dylan and Leah had their daily lives. Julian was at college. Every day I was on edge.

When the calendar showed March 30, a chill arrived along with a nervous energy and I was unable to concentrate. March 30 was exactly 3/4 of the way through her 75th year. Seventy-five was 3/4 of a century.

She would choose today! Or she'd joke about it later, mocking my intuition. "How silly you were to take me seriously."

The kids played a little tennis in the park. We went for a walk along West Cliff Drive and had some salad for lunch. I lay down for a nap, Niels beside me. I couldn't rest. Agitated. Mind racing. Imagining. A jump from the Golden Gate Bridge. A drive to the ocean. Guns. Pills. Always, always, with the thought she might just show up on our doorstep for dinner, pretending all was well. That it had all been a trial run of something in the distant future.

A text came through from our neighbor in Germany: Our cat Caesar had died. Poisoned. Her dog had found him in the shed. Had Jane traveled around the world to kill our cat? The air churned around me. I couldn't rest. Whirling air. Lightspeed. I usually had a rational mind. I had never felt like this. Like gravity was loose. Like the ceiling and walls of my bedroom were porous. "Niels, I can't rest. I feel odd."

We rose, got ready for the afternoon concert put on by Leah's Waldorf school. Normal life. Familiar faces. Classical music in a neighborhood church. Smiles as we gathered to listen.

My phone was vibrating. *Brrrrz. Brrrrz.* Why didn't it stop? Polly, who had been Dylan's first violin teacher, was in the midst of a Rachmaninov piece up on the altar. Sunshine lit the stained-glass windows, tall and wide and side lit. *Brrrrz. Brrrrz.*

I looked down. My linen dress was wrinkled.

"Unknown Number."

All these past weeks I had jumped whenever a telephone sounded. Anticipating. Worrying. Would my mom tell me it was all a big misunderstanding? Would the Coast Guard call, having found her body adrift near Baker Beach? Each call, though, had been mundane. "Oh, Hi. Sure, I'll bring a salad to the potluck."

Brrrrz. Brrrrz. I knew this was it. Piano notes. I suddenly remembered to breathe. The little boy in front of me squirmed. The copper designs behind the altar held my eyes. Organ pipes. Where was the organ? The phone blipped once. A message. Niels glanced at me. I looked straight ahead.

Just another twenty minutes. Just another small segment of time to sit here, quiet and bored on this apricot-cushioned chair, surrounded by peaceful parents watching our children. Violin, cello, viola, piano. Familiar music, memories of the smell of leather in my grandfather's white Jaguar, stories of my great grandmother Muddie's piano concerts. A bridge in time, in this room, between my children's music and theirs.

Twenty minutes to be still. Before everything changes forever.

After the applause, we all filed out.

Outside the entrance, I turned to the side, pressed the voicemail button, caught the sound of a man's voice. "This is the San Francisco Medical Examiner's office."

Niels saw my body tense, saw me turn away, nodded to my friend Lizzie. People know in moments like this. "Come with me, let's go play with Isabel and Ida." Lizzie put her arm around Leah, leading her away in the opposite direction. A glimpse of my daughter's puzzled concern. I had to focus. A quick bob of my head confirmed to Niels, who took my arm so I wouldn't stumble on the way up the hill. Why was the sky so vast?

I tried to concentrate on the number the message said to call, tapped the phone screen. Ringing.

A man answered. "Office of the San Francisco Medical Examiner."

"Hello. This is Susannah Kennedy." What was I supposed to say again? "I just got a message."

The man's voice slowed, the timber lowering. "Are you the daughter of Jane Kennedy?"

A tiny "Yes." A squashed whimper. That's not me.

"I'm sorry to have to tell you this, but the police were called to the Pacific Heights Inn this morning where they found your mother's body." I flashed to the red sign on Union St., had passed it by a thousand times. It was the first place I'd lived in San Francisco, at age six, with my father and mother. We had moved from Manhattan, a start at a new life. A cheap motel room, flashes of a brown kitchenette. They had been apartment hunting. I had started a new first grade.

I began to shake. Why there? What was she telling me? Why? I was the only person alive who would recognize that connection. A private secret message just for me.

"Could you please confirm your full name. We need you to come in and identify your mother." A few beats went by. I could hear the other parents in the lower parking lot.

"What? Are you sure?" This wasn't right. She had been so deliberate with her planning. "She wanted her body to go directly to UCSF."

"Ma'am, when someone is found deceased alone the body cannot be released without an autopsy."

I was having a hard time comprehending all of this.

"But—but she killed herself!" *Breathe.* It sounded like I was trying to convince him of something. *Was I? Breathe.* "She made her plans known." Guilt. *I should have prevented it. I am in trouble.*

"Yes, there is no doubt, ma'am." He hesitated. "It says here there were signs in the room and on the bathroom door as well as a note on her body indicating her wishes. But this is procedure."

Niels was leading me over to a grassy knoll. His hand was warm on my skin.

The phone voice continued. "Come to the San Francisco Hall of Justice, ground floor, around the back, the medical examiner's office."

"Yes, sir."

The sky was whirling. Roiling. A hurricane circle. A still day invaded by wind. It makes no sense, but this is the way it was. A comet, a spirit ghost *whhhrrred* by. An arc, and then whoosh, it was gone, a cacophony silenced, an aperture in the air closed shut.

"Mommy!" A little girl's voice erupted from me.

The eucalyptus trees kept watch; the gravel crunched.

Then I crouched down. And wailed.

This was her last diary entry:

May I be successful in this awesome venture and may news of my death be quick and sweet. (March 27, 2014)

La Principessa

2014

THE GRIEVING BEGAN WITH THE SHOCK, the numbness, the nausea. I couldn't eat my dinner. I speared a bean with my fork but the whiff of cooked food turned my stomach. I left it on the plate. I sat. Niels, Dylan, and Leah made small talk about the concert. I tried to pay attention. I slumped. "Susa, I know you want to just sit here," Niels said gently. "You have some decisions to make."

As her only child, I was the only one responsible.

I rose from the table and dialed her closest cousin, Trevor, with the landline. He answered.

"It's Susannah," I said.

"Greetings," he began. "To what—."

"She did it," I said, interrupting him.

There was a pause. "No. Oh, no."

"Yeah."

It was quiet for a moment.

We had anticipated this conversation, he and I.

Trevor was her most loyal fan, always taking her side during our mother-daughter estrangements and always needling me for not being as funny, as thick-skinned, as look-at-me as my mother.

Now his usual stage tone melted. "Oh, Susannah, I'm so sorry."

And I heard his grief. He loved her. She had been his most loyal fan, too, his ally, the first cousin to really accept his gayness at a time when coming out had been a lonely risk.

"Should I call Fionna?" he offered.

Surprised, I noted a mini ray of comfort, a slight retreat of pressure around my head. "Yes, please. That would help a lot." Maybe I didn't have to do all this alone.

"Could you call any other cousins you think should know right away?" I watched the water boiling for tea on the electric stove. This was going to be a long evening.

"What about Peggy?" he asked. Peggy had been in my mother's circle of women friends for years. She was always exquisitely and formally dressed and wore oversized thick dark glasses, which made her eyes inscrutable. She blended perfectly into my mother's luncheons with the shrimp salads and Champagne and silver table settings. She spoke loudly and commandingly, her gestures calling to mind Shakespeare's Gertrude declaiming to Hamlet. .

I remembered the first time Peggy became my mother's official next-of-kin.

"Peggy will be in charge of what happens when I die," my mother had told me one day when the children were young, and we were visiting San Francisco. We had just said goodbye to Peggy after lunch. The children had galloped downstairs to play Ping-Pong in the building's communal basement room.

Surprised, I had tried to fend off any reaction. But I felt my face sliding into a sullen expression. I didn't like this whole topic.

I wanted to think about playgrounds and birthday parties, not plan for her death.

On the edges of my comfort zone nudged hazy details. No, it's true; I didn't want to take care of my old ill mother. I didn't want to make a decision about when to *pull the plug*. I imagined her lying in an ICU neon-lit bed, attached to cords, machines beeping, the doctor saying, "The coma is temporary." What would I do? How long is temporary? 10 days? 100 days? In my nightmare vision, my mother awakens and finds out she can't walk. She is furious, betrayed. It would be my fault. *Ugh.* Let Peggy be the one. Then, *no.* Though the thought of illness shallows my breathing, I don't want anyone else near my mother.

I felt like prey being dragged into the fox's den whenever I thought of that scenario.

My mother had gone ahead with her revised estate plan. She had named Peggy as her power of attorney for health care and ever after that there had been something about Peggy's proprietary familiarity with my mother that transmitted this wasn't just about Do Not Resuscitate from a coma.

Peggy had once approached me in the hallway like an espionage brush contact at the United Nations. "Here," she had whispered, handing me a small piece of paper with her name and phone number. "Keep this in case you need to get me."

For years, I had felt a shiver when I thought of the two of them.

"I'll call her," I told Trevor now.

Peggy picked up the phone right away. "Peggy, it's Susannah."

There was a moment's silence. We both knew there was only one reason I would call.

"She did it," I said.

There was a pause.

"But I am supposed to be the one they call." Peggy seemed nonplussed.

"Yeah, well, they didn't. They called me."

The next morning, Niels, Dylan and I drove up to the city to the morgue. Dylan had asked if he could come. Was he too young, at fifteen? No, maybe it was time. Niels agreed. Germans are not as afraid of death. As we drove, my thoughts surged. If Dylan could see her, could be part of the experience, he would be spared the gnawing fear inside me. He could learn to approach the topic of death calmly. He could grow older and find the right words when sorrow came to his friends. He could be calm. He could be safe and bolstered, like a Tibetan Buddhist.

In the car Dylan was silent, steeling himself.

But then we arrived at the reality of the gray-walled San Francisco Hall of Justice. The morgue clerk had no sympathy.

"No. You are only allowed one support person in there with you."

I glanced at Niels. I needed him with me. There was no doubt.

"If you want your son to see her, you need to book a funeral home like everyone else," the clerk said. There was a sudden sniff of appraisal in his glance, as if he suspected I was trying to cheat the system. *More people?* It was just my son.

Dylan was sitting up straight on the bench by the wall. He was ready. His older brother was at college. His younger sister was too young. He was up for the task. But now it was a no. What a mess. All this way we had driven together, and a no at the end. "Please sir, he wants to see his grandmother."

"No." The clerk moved his head right to left and back.

Afterward, Niels, Dylan and I exited the gray monstrosity silently. My shoulders felt like they belonged to toy soldiers in the Nutcracker. *Hut. Hut.* I did not even hear the loud talk of the men standing in line at the run-down bail store on Bryant St. *Bail Bonds* read a yellow sign in black letters, windows half-covered and a homeless person's tent outside. It turned out they didn't care about us. Nobody wants to bother someone coming from the death house.

Maybe the clerk knew best. Maybe he knew it wouldn't be nice for a fifteen-year-old to stand behind that smeary glass in the back room looking at an old lady with pink lipstick. Dylan walked quietly beside me. I felt bad, for both supporting that he see her, and that it didn't work out.

I was angry with her for making all of us, Niels, me, Julian, Dylan and Leah, adjust and react and take care of her once again. Actors in her story even after death.

After we left the Hall of Justice, Niels, Dylan and I drove to my mother's apartment on Russian Hill. I had the round key that I've always had, kept with me around the world. I remember how touched I had been when I discovered Niels had had a key to his parents' house on his key ring, too. Maybe a lot of adult children have this, a voucher of legitimacy, an "I belong here."

I unlocked the loud brass bolt and the door creaked open as it always did. We were enveloped by the scent of parquet floors and plaster walls that identified a San Francisco apartment built around 1900. After her death, I discovered that scent is an identifiable real estate marker. While she was alive, I just thought it was the familiar smell of my mother's home.

Everything was normal. The double-hung kitchen window was shut, ready for her to slide it up as she always did, letting in the footsteps and conversations of people walking by on Greenwich Street and the foghorn on Alcatraz. The counters were clean, the television remote placed on a lower shelf. The clock on the stove showed 1:15. In the master bedroom, her wooden, four-poster bed was serene, made as always with her four lacy cream-colored pillow shams, matching ruffle and duvet smoothed flat without a wrinkle. As I walked into the dining room, the swinging door fell back behind me. The glass table for eight was sparkling, free of smudges, an empty silver punch bowl in the middle and the formal chairs with her hand-needlepointed seats pushed precisely underneath.

I felt like we were trespassing, as if it were a stranger's house rather than where I had lived, where I had brought my own children to visit.

Niels called me from her office, the room that had once been my bedroom. It still had twin beds, though now with black lacquered Chinese frames and meticulously ironed bedspreads. The walls were no longer the green fern wallpaper I had begged her for in the 1970s. Her white Apple MacBook was closed on her desk. There was a printed note titled, "Where things are kept," and instructions to look in the small bureau to the left.

I flipped open the manila folder on top of the pile there. A white page had a quotation.

'You've been feeling tired,' said the stranger.

Instantly, my eyes smarted in recognition. *Watership Down* had been our treasured summer book when I was eleven, the one we carried in our suitcase that second summer in Italy—humidity and the sounds of Venetian water against the stones below our window. We had settled into our reading like cats settling into a spot in the sun. We read to each other every day, either during the siesta or before going to dinner. I had adored that book about rabbits, about wisdom and heartbreak, about the human condition. I had been old enough to know it was something special. She praised my reading aloud and thereby I learned to read aloud well. I had kept that very same book in my library at home and had picked it up a couple of times to read with my children, but the magic had not reappeared for them, and I had put the book away.

Now I read the rest of her photocopied lines: *It seemed to Hazel that he would not be needing his body anymore, so he left it lying on the edge of the ditch.*

Tears welled up and my heart squeezed tight.

Like her choice of motel, only I would know the nuance of this excerpt. It was a message directly to me from beyond the grave.

We three drove back to Santa Cruz that afternoon, back to sanity and the busy business of post-death. It is amazing how much work needs to be done. Get an appointment with her estate lawyer, cancel credit cards, call Medicare, get jewelry out of the safe-deposit box, contact her housekeeper.

Relatives called. Friends called. Urgent. Desperate. Sad. "Jane was so proud of you. She loved you so much." I could feel a fixed mask smile getting etched onto my face. Every day it got deeper. Who was I to correct them in their mourning? Some were shocked, needing comfort. I said some words. Niels said some words. I nodded and shrugged my shoulders. Some praised her as if she were a saint: "Jane was one of a kind, so elegant, vibrant, principled and authentic." They were the worst.

I was angry. But if I said I was angry I received kindly new-world nods. "Of course, dear, grief takes many forms." No, I wasn't grieving. I was angry. I was furious.

The days passed.

Leah and Dylan watched me carefully as I slumped at dinner moving my food around the plate. Especially little Leah. We had to have some sort of gathering to mark Jane's passing. We all felt unmoored.

Death needs recognition. We, those who had known her best, needed to come together soon. Her body was not yet at the crematory, delayed by a backlog at the morgue. But something was needed. In the end, Niels and I decided her apartment best signified her life for all of us. We would organize a reception. We sent out an email message—a gathering at the apartment she loved, the following weekend. Her friend Alexandra knew of a catering company. They would provide an elegant buffet lunch. Her estate would pay for airline tickets for extended family. I booked the hotels in Fisherman's Wharf at a group rate. We would gather and drink and eat and talk and then go home before sunset.

Nobody wanted to stay in her apartment after dark. Whether through a general fear of proximity to death or because of how she had died, the rooms felt spooky. Some cultures gather the outbreaths of life. They keep a corpse close, bathe and talk to it and around it. They honor the passing of a spirit and release her to a new life or wherever that energy goes. But death in my California family was always more fraught, a quick affair, the details handled by professionals, and bodies turned quickly to ash.

It wasn't the best way. Travel and my study of anthropology taught me alternative customs. In Germany, our friend Freya had invited us—honored us—to spend time with her husband a few hours after his passing. It had been the first dead body for which I had ever kept a vigil. Jens, always thin and wiry, had been a skeleton from illness by then. As I sat, I wanted to pretend he was made of plastic and would be hung back on a classroom wall. I had not been comfortable at his bedside and had been happy to leave, but I saw the sacredness in Freya's act: the passing from life to death to be honored and witnessed and accompanied. Freya had kept Jens at home with their two young teenage sons a few more days, until the funeral home urged her "*Es wird Zeit.* (It's time to go.)"

Back then, I couldn't have imagined organizing such a thing. But it rang true to something old and wise, and I took note for the future.

The next weekend, many relatives came from the East Coast and from Southern California. Cousin-sisters who hadn't spoken to each other in a decade came. San Franciscans came. Teacher colleagues and neighbors came. There was standing room only when the eulogies began. Some speeches were funny, and some were mawkish. My uncle Steven related the story of Jane in Jerusalem, fighting with a taxi driver over the fare, then hurling her suitcases from the trunk in the middle of the road. Everyone roared with laughter at his telling. Typical Jane. What a troublemaker. Georgianne talked about many things, how Jane helped her when she was ill and how Jane confided in her about being a single mother to a teenage daughter. I wondered briefly whether I should get to know Georgianne. Cynthia talked about their shared volunteer work lobbying PG&E to underground the haphazard telephone poles lining San Francisco streets. Most memorable of all was Peggy, quivering, sweating, truly in public mourning, calling out "*La Principessa*" with tears flowing down below her dark glasses, her urgency ringing through the room.

Niels and I watched and listened and held silent counsel. Julian, Dylan and Leah, dressed in black, were quiet for hours, watching the crowd. They barely spoke with the guests. They barely spoke with each other. Later, I discovered that Leah had written a message in the leather-bound guest book. "If my Grandma would have been a little more understanding and less always having to be right, then I think she would have been one of the best Grandmas in the *World*!"

After everyone went home, after the letters were gathered and the flowers distributed, her apartment—my apartment—stilled again. What were we going to do now?

It wasn't over. She had wanted to leave no body behind. But we had a body.

What were we to do with her?

In Germany, funerals are formal events with socially accepted timelines.

Guests wear black and gather at a cemetery chapel. A service is held, big or small, gentle or grim, depending on the deceased's personality and the leanings of the pastor in charge. Hymns are sung from an old-fashioned hymn book. There are readings from the Bible and a formal eulogy. There is a casket, which is closed. There are graveyard workers dressed in black suits who, donning white gloves, lift the corners of the casket onto a wheeled trolley. Then comes a procession through the cemetery, another prayer, and each guest files one by one past the gravesite. Each person pauses, looks down. Men grasp the shovel, fill it with dirt from a silver bucket and toss it down to land with a *thunk* onto the wood six feet below. Women grasp a handful of rose petals, or sometimes a single rose and its stem, to toss onto the wood with no sound. More recently, I noticed women opting for the dirt. Since we lived in a small village, I had been to quite a few funerals. It is common courtesy for neighbors to attend, even if they are not close.

I had been to just a few American funerals. All of them had been cremations. The most recent was my grandfather's in 2000. Used to German ways by then, I had been surprised that many Californians there wore flowered sundresses and cargo pants. I had also been surprised that my cousin fundraised for her IPO at the reception, and that my grandfather's wife brought a date. I suspect he was there for her emotional support, but it was strange to see her leaning on the arm of a handsome older man as she walked into the Stanford chapel.

None of that was what I wanted for my mother.

It took weeks for her ashes to be ready. I imagined refrigerated rooms in the bottom of that gray building, bodies in a row, waiting their turn for an autopsy and release to a funeral home. What kept the crematoriums from burning any old body and handing the dust over to the family? Who would know? This haunted me, until I read about a "witness cremation." The body is allowed a witness as it is put—alone—into a large furnace. It turns out crematories do burn one body at a time. It takes hours for the bones to be incinerated.

Gross. I put that thought aside and kept trying to figure out something to do with whatever pile of dust I would receive. I'd heard of people keeping the urn with them, talking to it, placing it on the fireplace mantel. "Imagine having my mother looking down on me even from death," I told a friend, a shiver coming unbidden. "No, I have to come up with a plan. I can't just *not* do something with her."

We could bury the ashes. But where? My grandparents were both mixed into the soil of their Portola Valley land, soil that I would have been happy to inherit and build a life upon. Neither my mother nor Uncle Steven had wanted that for me. Then that soil had been uprooted by backhoes and tractors and the house demolished and a French Riviera mansion built in its place by a Silicon Valley CEO. I doubt the new tech owners had kept the beautiful rose garden.

We could have an ash-spreading in the waves. I thought of the celebrations of life, the circles of people dressed in white that I sometimes saw in Santa Cruz at the beach. Guests tiptoeing toward water like sanderlings at the foreshore, back and forth, then into the waves, where they would stand, white robes billowing in the water, leaving flowers and ashes floating out past the wave break. No. The chance of swallowing a smidgeon of unknown dead person already made me reluctant to swim in the Pacific Ocean there. The surf is wild, the currents strong. But still.

During our discussion about finding a place for her ashes, Leah looked at me with her mouth pulled into the exact grimace I felt. "Here in Santa Cruz?! Please don't do that, Mom."

Yeah, we could never swim here again if we did. We had to have her far away from us.

Should we carry her to a cliff somewhere, maybe Big Sur? We could empty out the urn and gravity would accompany the dull gray particles to some sort of resting place. "Haven't you seen *The Big Lebowski*?" Niels laughed. "The wind whips around and the ashes fly back onto his face!" I instinctively pulled back. Plus, what did my mother ever have to do with Big Sur, or the mountains? She loved Italy. But no, I wasn't going to carry her with me on any transatlantic flight. Visions of me digging my hand into a box and spreading the contents at Lake Como made my skin crawl. I remembered our dog's ashes we buried in our German garden. They were smooth with little pebble pieces, like digging my hand into the pile of gray ash under a fire pit at the beach. I didn't have this horror with our dog.

Because our conversations always circled around Jane's love of swimming and water, we eventually settled on the San Francisco Bay. It felt fitting. She was, after all, an admiral's daughter and a passionate swimmer. And she had no wish to be buried in a specific spot with a marker.

There were still hesitations. Would she swirl out the Golden Gate and down the coast to mingle with our DNA at the 26th Avenue beach in Santa Cruz? I reassured myself that the Pacific was a mighty ocean, and she would never find us here. Even Leah deemed those 70 miles along the wild coastal cliffs far enough away.

On the appointed day, Leah, Dylan, Niels and I drove up to Sausalito to Captain Dave's sleek motorboat docked at the harbor behind the indoor model of the Bay. I had loved that huge 3D model as a child. Captain Dave's boat was clean and just the right reassuring size with comfortable benches in a U at the stern. It didn't look like it would capsize and leave us to mingle with the ashes. He knew what he was doing. "I'll turn the boat against the wind. Don't worry, the ashes won't land on you," he said.

I laughed. I guess a lot of people worry about that.

We invited cousin Brianna and her husband Rob who lived close by to join us. Julian was back at college, and I wanted extra family witnesses. I had asked my mother's friend Alexandra to pick up the ashes at the crematorium. I didn't want to enter that building. She kept them for me overnight. All I had to do was swing by. I had given instructions that the ashes were to be placed in a biodegradable box guaranteed to disintegrate in the water. Nobody was going to find a pod full of my mother on some diving trip somewhere. I imagined her bouncing along the bottom of the Bay with the current, to be discovered several years hence.

It was a beautiful brisk day with a blue sky. Pictures of us show somber faces. I spent some time trying to find the right words, knowing she had wanted none of this. Knowing she believed in nothing. She had once been a devout Catholic, and she and I had attended Roman Catholic Mass every Sunday for the eighteen years I lived at home. That part of the puzzle confused me, too. What would that God have said? Catholics believe suicide is a mortal sin. In olden days, suicides were banned from burial in a church cemetery. Though my mother no longer went to church, she had mentioned occasional visits to Zen centers and a San Francisco Hindu temple. Perhaps she had been searching for something meaningful again.

But what it felt like now was a disappearance into nothing.

When we arrived close to Angel Island, around the southern side so we had a view of San Francisco, Dave slowed his powerful white craft to an idle. He turned to us in a perfect polite and respectful tone: "Okay, I think this will be a good place. Anytime you want. Take your time." The six of us rose to our feet and gathered together close to the stern. The sun was shining. It was a beautiful day.

I had been nervous about this moment, worrying all morning how to create a ritual without any roots in tradition, the bubbles in my stomach the same as if I were going to be called upon to make a speech at an event with strangers. I should say something meaningful, but I had nothing to say. She wouldn't have wanted any of this. I didn't want any of this. Nobody did. Then, I remembered the Native American prayer that the New Moon circle had often incanted.

I grasped the box with her ashes. Movement is good. Holding the box with both hands I turned to each direction. "Prayers to spirits of the East, to the West, to the South and to the North." It felt ceremonial without being religious. Dylan and Leah watched me. Niels stood close. My cousin's red hair whirled in the breeze. She held a basket of flowers, all colors and shapes. I looked at Niels and nodded to her.

After one inquisitorial glance at Captain Mike and his comforting nod, I leaned over the railing and tossed the box onto the water. It splashed and then floated. We tossed flowers in to add to the color on the water. I pulled a card from my pocket. I had written some words, not really knowing or feeling what was right to say.

"Ashes to ashes, dust to dust.
From water all life arises.
To water we give her back.
May Nonna Jane's spirit flow
To the waters of healing,
To the waters of eternal peace."

The box bobbed for a bit and then sank. The flowers floated.

Later, as we drove back down the coast, I realized I had placed both my parents in the sea. No remnant of ashes in the ground. No DNA record that they had once lived.

In Hollywood movies, characters return to gravesides to find peace, reconciliation or comfort. I liked the idea. An enactment that hooked my wish for connection. Maybe talking to the dead somewhere can be comforting. But that was just one way, as if something material was evidence of a life once lived. Twenty years ago, I had arranged for an Alan M. Kennedy headstone to be placed in my father's family plot, just so the world would know he once was.

Would I ever have an eternal place to call home, a place where those I loved could come to find me, to talk if they ever needed to? A part of me wanted that so much. Another part offered, *maybe they won't need it.* Maybe they will carry me close to their hearts and that will be enough.

Starting to Read

2017

I WAS IN MY MID-TWENTIES when I realized it was significant that I couldn't remember the first six years of my life. That it wasn't a party gag anymore. It was cause for concern, along with why standing up for myself triggered weeks of self-doubt.

Working as a reporter in Dallas, I had come across Alcoholics Anonymous and the research showing that children of alcoholics shared certain behavior patterns. Later, when I was a graduate student at Oxford, I had begun my first talk therapy, and when Niels and I, by then married, moved to Hamburg, I started psychoanalysis. Three times a week I lay on a narrow beige couch looking out at a green garden framed by a long-needled tree laden with pinecones. At first, I focused on the details of my busy days rather than what went on in me when I was quiet. But I gradually learned. I began to trust that I could voice every kind of emotion and my therapist wouldn't punish me. I began to try out the art of disagreeing with Niels and also loving him. I began to be able to say yes to having a family.

Now, after my mother's suicide, with those diaries floating in my mind, after returning to our home in Germany following the cleaning out of her apartment, I called my analyst again, wanting to reconnect. I kept thinking of the small books lined up in the wooden chest, four tall numbers on the fore-edge identifying their year, as if they were soldiers lined up in a tomb. I remembered opening that chest after she died and slamming it down. How could I summon the courage to broach it again, like opening a crack to some unknown force? Why was I so terrified of these little books? In my imagination, their dusty clouds would swirl up and invade my lungs and my mouth and nose; my eyes would tear; I wouldn't be able to breathe. If I touched them, she would win.

Finally, in 2017 when we moved permanently back to the US, all five of us here now, I knew I had to start being serious about this story, so at least my children would understand my journey, where their grandmother ended and their mother began. Where they began. In the midst of all the logistics and organizing and resettling, my heart raced. I'd read them. I'd burn them. I'd find out she had a terminal illness. I'd find out she wasn't my mother after all. I'd find out that my father wasn't my father.

My mother had left her words behind, knowing me, knowing I'd choose to tell my story and thereby tell hers. A daughter who always wanted to know things. A dead mother who could be a star at last.

By the beginning of fall that year, fear had turned to acceptance. I had been given the chance to unlock a mystery. Whatever I would find—Black Box treasure or Pandora's Box peril—would help me understand myself better. Life is a journey. I was ready.

* * *

In October, I began to read.

The first morning I wake at six, determined to make this reading task a ritual, thereby to sustain me when it gets too hard and give the drumbeat should I become reluctant. I make coffee for Niels and head out to my little writing nook in the yard, my footsteps slowing as I approach. I can see the boxes through the window. Do I really want to take this on?

I open the first worn, red leather diary gingerly, spooked by the ink on the page, in the slanted handwriting that has been a signifier my whole life. I can see her holding the pen in her left hand, hand curved in an awkward embrace so different from my straightforward pen-between-thumb-and-third finger.

Even now, after estrangements and disagreements and having lived a half a world away, I know my mother intimately, the way an only child of a single mother knows. It is a powerful twosome, magical in some way. The knowledge of our mother is inscribed on our daughter bodies, all those many years in her presence, her tone and breathing, in the way her eyebrows arch, in watching her long hands, once smooth and slender, turn imperceptibly brown-spotted and wrinkled. We cannot see our mothers' change occurring, yet the changes become a part of us. We hear her narratives. We know what she has chosen to tell us; both about her childhood and about how her childhood influenced her mothering.

In my case, I already suspect what Jane told me about my life is not the whole story. It isn't the not telling; it's what she did not realize she was not telling. I don't know what I will find.

Her outer story to the world about her own childhood was that she had been forced to move house and school every two years as the daughter of a naval commander in the 1940s. She had been shy and over six feet tall. She had suffered in that military life, only blossoming when she got to boarding school at fourteen, where she modeled herself after Grace Kelly, and developed her plan to marry a man who could guarantee her privilege, safety, and class. I know after college in 1960, she and her best friend Mary drove a Morris Minor convertible all around Europe for six months, photos showing silk scarves protecting their hair from the wind on the roads, mid-calf skirts and old-fashioned luggage. She and Mary moved to Manhattan and worked in the Associated Press research library, where my mother met Alan Kennedy, a handsome New York reporter who she hoped someday would be a senator.

"He was everything I ever wanted," she said to me. "He shopped only at Brooks Brothers. He graduated Phi Beta Kappa from Columbia. His parents had an estate in Quogue where we could spend the summers. And he was being sent to India as a foreign correspondent."

They married in 1961 in the Lady Chapel in New York's prestigious St. Patrick's Cathedral on an icy January day before flying off to Rome and then to New Delhi, where my father had been assigned for three years. Those India years—the heat, being a *memsahib* to servants, the introduction to *darshan*, which was the inadvertent bestowal of honor and glamor by association—embedded themselves on my mother's soul, and thereby onto my soul. She was a wannabe Jackie Kennedy, wistful and yearning, and those years were deemed the best years of her life. She loved telling me that I was born the only white baby in New Delhi's Holy Family Hospital, with geckos crawling on the delivery room ceiling.

But in 1964, after three years, their India adventure came to a crashing halt. My mother had taken me to visit her parents in California for the first time and while there she had received a telegram that Alan's contract had abruptly been canceled. In shock and disarray, my father haphazardly packed up their India possessions, and they were forced to move back to the United States.

My mother spoke rarely of the reasons for this dismissal, implying in later years it was my father's procrastination tendencies and dark insecurities that endangered his career. I would later discover in my own years as a reporter that many journalists shared procrastination and hidden insecurities, as well as the abuse of gin and whisky, so those could not have been the main reasons. Perhaps his temper had made him unwelcome? Perhaps some ruinous event had occurred. In any case, we moved from a New Delhi house with five servants and a car and driver to a shabby furnished apartment in New Jersey across the river from the Manhattan skyline.

By the time Susannah was born I was afraid of his rages, much
mitigated because the servants were always around. But it was
embarrassing to have the shattered dining table chair in evidence. There were only seven of them, all Queen Anne high-
backed and upholstered in heavy fabric—quite gorgeous really. All were sold when Alan was fired and the AP only paid for
a few personal things on the return leg to New York. I missed
my record collection most. (June 30, 2003)

Their return was such a blow to her status that my mother never
spoke of those years, except to say she was forced to learn to "home-
make" on her own, imitating her memory of the Indian servants and
listening in on Jersey housewife neighbors. She took me on the train
almost daily across the river to Manhattan as she searched for an Upper
East Side address.

"You toddled along beside me, holding onto one of my fingers," she
liked to tell me.

My father eventually found a job as an editor for McGraw Hill,
and her perseverance paid off. After two years, we moved to a two-bedroom apartment in a building with an awning on East 85th St. just off
5th Avenue, around the corner from Jackie Kennedy. The world was
back in its proper order.

It is here in 1968 that my mother's daily diaries begin. I am four
years old.

At first, as I read her handwritten words, I'm both bored and irritated. Mostly, the entries are bland sketches of Upper East Side housewife days in 1968. The descriptions resonate with pre-feminist urban
America. It isn't the *Gossip Girl* and *Primates of Central Park* of today.

Up at 8:30. Daphne came to clean at 9:15 and at 11 Susannah and I went to Metropolitan Museum. Looked at Impres-
sionists and 18th Century Romantics and some Rembrandts.
Then met Helen and Lois at restaurant at noon. Talked of PS6

with Lois whose husband is on school board. Susannah and
Avery good but ate little. Home and rested, then to library
in pm. Walked home along Park Ave. Noting various lobbies.
Rockefeller says he will not run for pres. I am glad. RFK will
get my vote unless Lindsey is dark horse for GOP. Slept well.
(March 11, 1968)

She describes how the mothers, all living within a few blocks' radi-
us, exchange child-sitting:
"I brought Susannah to Patsy's and I went to the Mill's luncheon."
Or "took care of Chris while Lynn went to the obstetricians."
I knew by now from my own life that mothering is an art of trans-
lation. One doesn't give one's children to others if there is no trust. This
means that she felt she fit in. They shared the same values. While I read,
I notice I'm envious. I feel I'm walking through an old glamorous movie. I imagine husbands wearing dark suits and tipping their hats in the
elevator, bringing colleagues and friends home for dinner. Everything
is orderly and cared for. It is a perfect picture.
Suddenly, I encounter something new. Briefly, as if she dared not
go into detail, she writes:

Alan to bed drunk at 2 a.m. and punched me and said to get
out of the bed. He couldn't stand sleeping in the same room.
(April 30, 1968)

Drunk at 2 a.m. Punched me. Said to get out of bed.

I read that again and again. *Drunk at 2 a.m.* I call up later visions
of my father's face turning dark at a moment's notice. Slurred speech.
The smell of gin on his skin. *Punched me. Told me to get out of bed.* In
my mind I imagine my mother in a moment of waking; perhaps the
image comes from post-divorce years, when I was allowed to snuggle
next to her in her big bed when we had houseguests in my room, when
we were safe together.

I both want to read more and bury it back in the box. I knew my father had been violent. I had witnessed it myself in later years. But she had never spoken about the details.

I imagine her in New York, lying still, hearing him walk heavily through the door, pretending to breathe deeply so he thinks she's asleep. What kind of man punches his wife in the middle of the night and tells her to get out of bed?

It is the "get out of bed" command that stays with me. He wasn't only violent. He felt entitled to wake his wife from sleep in her very own bed. He punched her. Not slapped her. Not shoved her. I'm imagining her nightgown is rumpled, her eyes weary. He orders her out. Where did she go? The couch in the living room? To my room? Did I feel her snuggling in beside me?

Suddenly I have a sense of a twin bed, of my legs curved under a sheet and a tucked-in old-fashioned green wool blanket with a green silk border, of a barrier beside me keeping me from falling out. But I am falling out. *Thunk* onto the floor. Do I cry? Is that before safety bars? She curves around me, tries not to cry, soothed by my breathing. I am soothed by hers. I wonder at myself. Surely, I must have heard him yell? Or maybe she does cry, lying next to me, shaking while I lie in the dark, pretending to sleep, knowing I should not know any of this.

Further on in the journals, months on, she prays the neighbors don't hear the plates smashing at night or discover the bottles of gin in the trash. She describes abusive rants three or four times a week, often with violence, smashing and hitting.

A disastrous fight, knockdown drag-out brawl in which Alan hurt every bone in my body and beat me until he himself was exhausted. I am writing this the next day. I have a black eye and bruises and ache all over. (October 12, 1968)

Nauseated, I feel like I am reading about someone else's life.
"Just sit with it," Niels says, after I tell him about the discoveries.

"I'm here. Come talk to me if you need to."

Frequently she describes my father falling asleep on the living room couch and vomiting all over the rug. This is an element of degradation I can't quite get my head around. He was supposed to have been such a fastidious man, with fancy cufflinks, wool overcoats and dress hats. Can people really live such double lives? Why didn't anyone help her?

> I had to run from the apartment to escape his insane rage. I was dizzy from the blows and dressed only in my nightgown and robe. I didn't know where to go so I went up to the roof until I could get command of myself a little. Then I feared for Susannah and crept down the stairs and halls and entered the apartment silently. I heard him speaking to my father on the phone. (Travels Diary, no date)

I can feel myself inhabiting her experience. The adrenalin, the fear. I think about that nine-story building where we lived that I have walked by as an adult, the fire escape, the Manhattan rooftop, gray asphalt with its cluster of air filters and unwelcoming chimneys.

But then as I go back to read it again, I discern there is a story she is not telling. My story. I realize she left me there with him. I doubt he waited until I was sound asleep to work himself into a rage. I must have heard them fight. I must have been listening, pulling myself into a ball, holding my wooly lamb, wondering when it would be over. Did I slink into my room and hide under the covers? Did he ever threaten me?

The two-bedroom apartment she describes in New York is small. I have a vague vision of a bathroom with black and white tiles. I recall a picture of me standing next to a Christmas tree, holding a doll. My face is pale and my shoulders droop. I look immensely sad. I always found that picture arresting. I usually try to weed out unflattering pictures from my own family collections. Yet she kept that in her album.

Once I asked her about it.

"I look so sad here," I said.

The air stilled around her and there was a pause.

"Yes."

That was all she said.

Then suddenly I am remembering my mother reacting years later to my cousin Caitlin's bruised face. "It was Luke. I know it," my mother had insisted to me on the phone.

Caitlin had slipped and fallen on the steps. "It was just an accident, Jane!" Caitlin had apparently said.

But my mother had called me again the next day. "Caitlin was here. She brought pictures. She had too many pictures. Why would she do that other than to disprove the obvious?"

"Accidents do happen, Mom," I remember saying. I loved my cousin and didn't want to think she was lying. Her husband was a little withdrawn, and he certainly didn't like my mother, but he didn't *seem* violent.

My mother was insistent. She remained worked up, a storm within. Weeks later she repeated, "I just know there is something bad there."

"Mom, nobody can really know about someone else's marriage," I said. "But it seems unlikely."

"I don't respect a woman who allows her husband to beat her," my mother had insisted again.

* * *

Looking back, I see so much revealed in this conflict with my cousin. I already knew that Caitlin and her siblings had been raised by alcoholic and violent parents. I had heard some stories from Fionna as I grew older, as she explained why she never drank. I also knew that of the seven children, only one had gone on to have her own children. But it is now that I begin to put the pieces of the puzzle together. I begin to see connections to their life stories: how one became a nun, two developed schizophrenia, one became an alcoholic, two were disabled and placed in homes and only Brianna had children herself. I am beginning to question the significance of family silences, to see that my grandfather's younger brother had actually terrorized his wife and children, and that my grandfather and his brothers and sisters had known and did not intervene. That is shocking in a larger extended family that advertises itself as close and interconnected. Were they unable to? Were they simply not interested in the full picture? Their children, when I ask now, look regretful. But what were they to do? They were children. It was up to their parents to take a stand, they say.

I begin to look with different eyes at the larger family. My mother's ten years of domestic abuse had never been part of her public narrative. This meant she could not tell the story of Caitlin's bruises in the context of her own experience. This would have given her concerns authority and weight while also allowing for nuance and careful listening and perhaps reassurance. Rather, I see both women interacting in the context of a larger family culture that is inarticulate about destructivity in its many forms.

Jane's marital abuse had never had the chance to dilute, like an oil stain fading through many washes. Instead, she had stuffed the stained cloth into a corner of the cellar where it hardened and became ingrained. Even if my cousin *had* been beaten and was in denial, my mother's emotional accusation got its momentum from the repression of her own experience. It was as if she herself were being abused again. Like trying to hide a beach ball below the ocean surface, repressed experiences come shooting up eventually, uncontrolled, in any old direction. The results are harmful.

Thus, instead of doing the necessary work to understand the dynamics of a relationship with my cousin she had once loved, Jane cut Caitlin out of her life forever.

One morning, after re-reading the words in my mother's diaries, the image of me huddling in bed, the ongoing descriptions of my father's vomit and the anger and the booze, I feel the need for a break. I make tea and roll out my yoga mat, stretching muscles that have stiffened during the hours of sitting. I go to the bathroom and as I wipe myself see red on the toilet paper. I look in the toilet. Bright red in my feces.

Oh, my God. I freeze inside. *Oh my God.* Full-blown hunkered-down panic, frozen.

My heart jumps way too fast. It lasts one, two seconds. *Boom, boom, boom.*

Rational thought jostles in: "Oooooh, I ate chunky red beet soup yesterday."

But it is too late. I am in emergency mode. My heart is beating furiously, my face feels pale. I know I'm going to die.

I wash my hands, slink upstairs to Niels and collapse on the bed.

"What's wrong?"

I tell him.

He laughs. "It's the beets from yesterday, silly."

I should be comforted. I should be able to shrug off this moment.

But the diary is changing me. I am living in another world, slithering down the panic slide. All I can do is repeat a mantra all day of *It's soup, don't worry. It's soup, don't worry.* I cannot calm myself down. I fear it's cancer, something sudden eating me up from the inside, something I cannot fight or control. Something that will destroy me. I'm the little girl in her room saying a mantra. *She'll be back. She'll be back.*

This lasts all day. I can't read anymore. I try to cover it up, trying to function as a sane mother for Leah, who at fifteen is going through her own difficult transition from Germany to the United States.

The next day the beets are in the past, yet I can't rid myself of the fear. I'm still in dread, cortisol and adrenaline high.

Over the next few days, I calm down and begin to see the connection. Wow, psychosomatic reactions are no joke. How can mere words written on a page evoke such high alert?

I walk to the beach, barely noticing my neighborhood's little houses and quirky front gardens as I pass. An image comes.

I am sitting at dinner. It must have been when I was seven, before Dad moved out. There is a napkin carefully placed on my lap as I've been taught. My arms are moving, industriously cutting a steak so it makes no sound, also as I've been taught. I'm listening to my parents converse about the day, but I'm nervous. Daddy rises up, knocks his chair back with a crash, raises his voice: "What are you implying, you bitch!"

Suddenly I know with certainty that such outbursts were frequent, that they could come without warning. In my memory, my heart beats fast. I am afraid for my mother. I don't know what to do except to stay very, very still.

Here at the beach in Santa Cruz, the waves deposit their foam on the sand. I watch the state park rangers gather up the trash by the beach restrooms. I can feel my shoulders ache.

This reading is not good for me.

* * *

It becomes clear there had already been four years of violence before the diaries began, that even when she was pregnant with me, even in her idolized India my father was often abusive.

> I remember it like yesterday. How the pain of contractions caused me to wring Alan's white duck trousers as we inched along in the back seat of the Associated Press car. Lal [their driver] delivered us to Holy Family Hospital amid camels, bullock carts. I, as always, deferred to the workday, not wanting to call Alan early in the pm, not realizing labor had begun. Only a half-hour from arrival to becoming a mother at 7:30pm. The terrible disappointment of not producing a son. The worry that my daughter had no chin, would not be beautiful. The pride that she was perfect and I was a mother now. Tears and terrible headache. The tears at Alan's irrational drunken rage about something the 3rd day. The headache from saddle block. (September 18, 1992)

A drunken rage on day three of my life? I pass over the comment about my chin and her wish for a boy. This is all such new information.

Well, not new exactly. But, like hiking into a small canyon only to re-alize it leads to another canyon and another, and that the mountain ridge that looks close from the bottom is full of cliffs too steep to climb, it is hard to reconcile this picture of extreme ferocity with the man I also knew my father to be.

That father was brilliant and melancholic and deep. He paid atten-tion to me when I spoke. He knew Mandarin Chinese. He knew how to sail. He could be kind and gentle. He liked to think deeply about things.

I try to sit with these moments, to allow some semblance of my little self in that New York apartment to come in from the sides like an apparition. I try to imagine our children as me, with all that toddler energy. What had I been like?

What comes up is an image of me approaching Daddy as he sits in an armchair. He is leaden, sad, preoccupied. He has a glass with ice and brown liquid in his hand. His sleeves lie heavy on the armrests. I talk to him, sing him a little song. He turns to look at me, smiles with a nod as if he is suddenly aware he isn't alone. But not much energy comes back from him. He watches me passively. Overlaid on that moment, I remember a smile he often showed me, a kind of self-conscious smile, as if responding to a command to be happy.

I think about Niels then, how he'd laugh and grab our children's arms as they climbed up his thighs, up and up, giggling ever higher and then, whoops, a sudden heave over his shoulder to their shrieks and laughter as he dangled them by the feet behind him. Over and over, he'd do it and then if they still weren't tired, he'd add in a silly game: "*Jetzt alle mal schnell ums Haus rennen. Ich warte hier.* (Okay, everyone quick! Race around the outside of the house! I'll wait here)." The sto-ries, the goofiness, the games, songs, tickling, running. All that physical family fun I never got. I guess my father never got all that, either.

He was the youngest of four, raised by servants and older sisters. By all accounts, my grandmother Kennedy was frumpy, formidable, a drama queen and unkind. Apparently, he never knew what it meant to be parented well. By the time he was twelve, a cousin told me, Alan

was a connoisseur of his family's whiskey imports, joining my grandfather at the expansive wooden bar in their Hamptons manor home.
By twenty-two, he had gone to Princeton and left again, found dull
and immobile in his bed. Depressed? Alcohol poisoning? After that
he held a few reporter jobs for local newspapers. I know he was drafted
into the Korean War and recruited to learn Mandarin for war intelligence. And I know that, at thirty-two, a Phi Beta Kappa key on his
lapel from Columbia, he was getting married to my mother and being
sent to India as a correspondent for the Associated Press.

But Dad never told me anything about himself. I knew of no cous-
ins, no aunts and uncles. No stories of childhood. No stories of the war.
No history of Great Gatsby parties when he was a boy living on Dune
Road. Those stories I would hear only after his death.

All I had was his agitation and rage the first seven years of my life,
hidden in the cells of my muscles.

I'm guessing now that he used alcohol as an escape. That's the
worst part of this for me. Both my parents were smart and educated.
They had the means to correct their lives' trajectories, but both chose
denial. And hidden suffering.

In her diaries, my mother describes putting on make-up to go out,
going to church, and "lying in Susannah's room sleeping most of the
day." What did I do on those days? The descriptions of my father's violence are brief, with longer detailed entries on the following days describing normal life again, as if she is relieved to get back to playacting,
even to her private, written self.

It is that set-up that impales me now. Even to herself she couldn't find
the words, couldn't view herself with agency. She retreats to details as if
to a lean-to in a rainstorm. She mentions shopping with a goal in mind:
"To the A&P for groceries," going downtown to Bloomingdales "to price a
winter coat." It doesn't sound like money is short, yet I can feel her dependence on him, and her alarm. I recall with a shock that married women in
the 1960s were legally dependent on their husbands for credit and bank
accounts. She would have had to secretly stash away some cash for herself.

Her strategy seems to have been to maintain structured days for the two of us. Daytime activities like all the other families, followed by proper dinners, with meat, vegetable, and starch. Sometimes she made dessert in the afternoon. In between there were good things, like traveling with Alan to the 1969 Washington, D.C. peace march and attending a General Practitioners Banquet where my father received an award for his medical writing.

I hope I can remain strong and not let the rages and resentments I feel towards Alan bubble to the surface. For he is trying, can sometimes be wonderful to me and to Susannah and I think he needs us both and probably I need him more than I am quick to admit. I want to try to be good to and for him. (December 31, 1969)

It feels, knowing my mother, as if the thing she was least able to forgive is the could-have-been: If he had been able to balance his drinking, she could have been a senator's wife. She could have been a society hostess with a cook and a maid. She could have had a summer house in the Hamptons.

My father drank my whole life. Sometimes more, sometimes less. He drank spirits and he drank to get drunk. When I was a reporter for the *Dallas Times Herald,* my cousin Fionna took me to a meeting for adult children of alcoholics. It was the 1980s. Mainstream media was beginning to write stories about denial and addiction, and that was leading to more public conversations. I was meeting more and more people who were "on the wagon."

Yet only once, in graduate school, after I had been in therapy awhile, did I push myself to use the term alcoholic in his presence. We were having lunch in a restaurant.

"Alan, can I ask you something?" I was using his first name by now, something he had suggested after he went through *est* (Erhard Seminars Training).

He looked at me steadily with watery blue-gray eyes. "I am receptive to whatever you want to ask."

I took a deep breath. *Go ahead. Ask.* "Why have you never gotten help from AA?"

My father's jaw tensed, and his eyes narrowed. Instantly, I was on alert.

"AA is for losers," he spit out. "Misfits whining and sharing their dirty laundry. It's not for me."

My heart pounding, I did not challenge him. I did what I always did, toting up our father-daughter ledger. Which was worth more? A scary fight for personal truth or the continuation of an amiable conversation about college, politics and world order?

I rarely saw him. I nodded, "Okay," and dropped the subject.

In the diaries, my mother writes that Alan did try AA at least once when I was young.

> Alan came back white-lipped with rage at obscene and disorderly conduct on street. He drank a martini and I am plunged into despair. Guess I really put faith in his admitting to alcoholism and joining AA. Know this will lead to spiral of drunkenness. (March 16, 1968)

As I read, I am angry at the world that surrounded us. Why didn't anybody intervene? The neighbors should have talked about it, should have provided her a safe place to escape, should have helped press charges against my father. *Shoulds, shoulds.* But maybe she denied it all. Maybe the neighbors thought: "They have a right to a private life. I don't want to be a busybody." Surely, they must have known, heard through the walls. Perhaps they thought they could help more if they stayed in the background. Or perhaps they were just cowards, hiding behind, "It's none of my business."

My mother was also in those years a devout Catholic who believed deeply in heaven and prayer. She and I went to Mass every Sunday and she often related to me with great emotion, "I am so grateful for my faith." She pitied me when it became clear my college exposure to philosophy and social history was leading me away from weekly churchgoing. She felt I was losing something precious. And yes, I can still feel the comfort of kneeling next to my bed every evening and saying my prayers. It felt like safety, to know a guardian angel was out there watching over me. It is powerful to release one's worries at the end of the day and to know someone is listening. For Catholics, marriage was considered a sacrament for life, and I think my mother, for many years, did not consider she had the option of leaving my father. I think she felt trapped and betrayed when she desperately approached the priests at her parish to ask for advice.

> They were utterly disinterested and uncomprehending of my pitiful attempts to get help. "Say 10 Hail Marys, my child, and go home to your husband." (May 23, 1994)

Reading about these years is frightening. But also brings strange comfort, absolution for my lifelong terror of raised voices and violence. *Oh, this is why.*

There was that couple on a *vaporetto,* a public water bus in Venice, once when I was twenty-four. I was sitting with my boyfriend. We had just had dinner. We were on our way back across the water. I had been living in Egypt and India. I had been backpacking alone. I thought I could handle anything. The man was drunk and berating the woman and she was yelling back. They were at least thirty feet away. The night was dark. *"Vaffanculo,"* she yelled the obscenity into his face, eyes bugged, face red. I switched from hip to hip on the seat. I tried to look out the window at the other boats. My eyes returned to the two. My heart beat fast.

My boyfriend shrugged. "They are just strangers. Let them be."

But I couldn't stay calm. I was jittery, unable to follow his words. My ears stopped up. I couldn't think clearly. "Let's get off the boat!" I panicked, grabbing his hand at the next stop so I could escape, escape! Puzzled, he followed me off, his right hand reluctantly attached to my left, being pulled like a water-skier before catching the power of the tug line. We stepped fast onto the bobbing gangplank, nowhere near where we had intended to disembark.

He looked at me, his head nodded to the side quizzically. "What is going on?"

I wanted so badly back then to be the Marion Ravenwood character in Indiana Jones, the tough gal who drinks a man under the table in a rowdy bar in Nepal. I wanted to be sovereign and cold and unreachable.

Now, I was ashamed, my façade cracked.

"I don't know," was all I could say. My insides trembled. We waited for the next boat to continue our journey home. He held me close on the bench on the floating platform, the deep *brrrrr* of the engine of the next *vaporetto* approaching in the distance. In a few minutes, my heart calmer, I flirted again.

I had never had memories of my first six years. My parents were secretive. Their narratives of my early childhood felt like mere outlines. Similarly, my father never talked about his family. I didn't even know enough about family histories then to think to ask him. Now I know there are many people who live this way, never asking, never knowing, assuming the lack of detail means life was safe and supportive.

The few times I asked my mother directly, she stayed vague about my father's behavior in my early years. I'm guessing she was pleased that I did not remember. I would be spared, in her view. "He was always kind to you," she said a few times, and that seemed to be explanation enough.

While I remembered one huge fight right before their divorce when I was already seven, I had always assumed I remembered it because it was an unusual and violent fight, not that it was just one of hundreds of violent fights. I did not yet understand the connections between childhood trauma and memories. I had to decipher them through random events—like discovering a hidden object through the absence of reflected light. Now the generational connections are clear:

> I recall a cryptic calendar entry I once came upon at the boat-house. Maggie [my father's mother] was in hospital all bruised

up and injured apparently. The words that resonated were to the effect, "Jim brought me beautiful roses and apologized." Did Alan learn violence at his parents' knee? He slapped me before we were married even. (June 30, 2003)

Feeding the Pills

Early 1970s

MY GRANDMOTHER GUMMY'S WATCHBAND barely fits around my index and middle finger. I balance it gently, place it unclasped on top of my wrist as if to double-check my judgment. It is a slim leather brown band, attached to a dime-sized face with four Roman numerals marking its quadrants. It's so tiny and delicate; it is almost comical to be reminded she was 5'10", practically my height. That this actually fit around her wrist.

I found the watch this morning in the bottom of my red leather jewelry box, a present I once received for Christmas from Niels. I have mostly costume jewelry there, strings of beads Julian and Dylan brought back from their trips to Africa, peace signs and silver necklaces I picked up in California. And this watch, which I have kept there, never wearing, never throwing away, since my mother died. It reminds me of Gummy, who reminds me of being loved. But it also presents a question. Why did my mother hide so much?

Every summer from 1966 to 1969, my mother and I interrupted our New York life and flew in a TWA 707 to the golden hills and cricket grasses cradling my grandparents' California house. It felt like the flip side of my life in Manhattan, as if we time-traveled and were suddenly somewhere safe and kind. Gummy took me along to feed and brush the horses. I learned to ride, to climb trees, to swim. I gathered the apricots and figs in the orchard. I played endless rounds of Queen and Princess with my best friend Carol, who lived close by, as we waited the required hour after lunch before jumping back into the pool. I got a tan. We watched the Apollo 11 moon landing. I wonder what would have happened to me if I had not had those summers of warmth and safety.

In July 1969, my mother wrote in her diary: "Only one more week in this lovely home. Susannah said today, 'Why can't we live here forever?'"

A month later, she is back to describing the violence in New York:

> I can still see Susannah standing in the bathroom with her hands over her ears as Alan and I battled on Monday. ... She is so touchy and upset and bursts into tears over little things when she and I both know her heart is broken over her mother and father. I don't know what to do other than get away. (August 20, 1969)

When I was halfway through first grade, my father applied for and got a job in San Francisco and we moved from one side of the country to the other. For a few weeks we lived in the brown and red Pacific Heights Inn on Union Street, the same motel where Jane would later execute her suicide. Then we moved into a two-bedroom apartment with wooden floors, high ceilings and two bathrooms a short walk up the Franklin Street hill from Sherman School. For a while, life seemed calmer. I started piano lessons. I saw my much-loved Gummy every weekend. In our old photo albums, there are pictures of my father riding on their horses. There must have been some good times in between the bad.

> A peaceful and somewhat happy day ended in disaster with Alan beginning a browbeating session on me, which precip-

itated a frenzy of violence from me giving him a black eye. Susannah was in the middle of it and utterly terrified and crying pitifully. All her fine presents—a rented piano from Alan on Bank Americard which means more debt —her sleeping bag, her clothes and toys all lovingly given by devoted parents and grandparents came to nothing but a terrible end. (December 25, 1970)

According to Jane's college friend, Mary, my mother still hid the abuse from her parents. Irish Catholicism ran deep. Divorce was a sin. Until that Christmas. "She drove down to her parents' house that day, allowing them to see her with bruises for the first time," she told me recently. "This was the final straw that convinced them to help her."

In the following days my mother writes in the diaries she wants to separate, but she is afraid my father's despair at losing his family will weaken her resolve. I tell her what most children say about fighting parents: "I want you and Daddy to live together more happily."

My grandmother—interestingly, my grandfather is not mentioned—helps her rent a studio and while Alan is on a business trip, Jane moves my father's belongings out of our apartment. I don't remember those months in 1971. I don't remember the heightened suspense of her distraction while she organizes the logistics of her coup. I don't remember boxes or, after the boxes, the absence of his things. She must have walked me to school down the hill and returned home to sort and parse and make choices. Did she pause for a moment, hold a scarf to her nose and drink in the memory of him sledding with me on his back in Central Park? On that hill near the Met? The shelves must have been bare once my father's books were packed. Was she relieved? Did she take pleasure in placing the three matching blue and white Indian vases just so in the new shelf space that she had created? Did her shoulders relax? Did she breathe again? Did she pray to be forgiven when she went to church? There is no mention of anything so detailed in her diaries.

Spent the better part of the day organizing Alan's stuff and taking it to his apt. I hope Alan won't plunge into depression, as seeing all his things in his new rather than old abode shows the permanence of my decision. I do want to get it over with. It's all work and some pleasure, as I like to settle a place and make it look nice. (January 12, 1971)

I vaguely recall visiting my father in his studio apartment. I remember sadness and scruffiness, that certain rejected-dad look of a room devoid of love. No pictures on the wall, no place settings on the table. More like a transit station. My parents filed for divorce quickly after their separation, in a California no-fault decision. My father didn't contest it. There was no need for court testimony documenting the violence. I imagine Jane was relieved nobody would ever have to know. She wanted to put those years behind her and forget them.

Except, of course, psychology doesn't work that way. What you've lived always lives with you.

Extended family peered down at me with a kind, "How are you?" though it was such a new thing to be a child of divorce in 1971 that it was like asking a refugee from famine with a full refrigerator if they remembered being hungry. Did they really want to know the details? Did anybody really want to know what a child of a depressed violent alcoholic felt when the violence disappears?

I remember complaining to my mother, "They are always asking me how I am." I must have been thinking about how to respond. Nobody else in my second-grade class had divorced parents. There was some vague disquiet amongst my friends' mothers, as if they spied that first tendril of discontented fog creeping under the bridge. I tried not to cause embarrassment. I didn't want to be labeled an unbalanced child of divorce. I raised my hand often in class, I wanted to learn, and I wanted to be loved by the teacher. At some point I decided on a stiff, "It's good that my parents aren't fighting anymore," as an answer to any queries. I remember some puzzled expressions, rebuffed by my tone that, following my mother's lead, left no invitation for further questions. No nuances. No parsing out of meaning. It was done, and now, move on. It was as if a sudden patch of happiness had appeared on the ice.

* * *

My mother and I settled into a new phase. Life became peaceful. I attended an elementary school I loved. She enrolled in courses at the University of San Francisco to get her master's teaching credential and started the required student teaching.

I ran loose classes, playing James Taylor records and talking with everyone individually about grades and what they wanted out of class. They argued vehemently for higher marks when I have been extremely lenient as it is. Home to get Susannah... then to a record store on Sutter for *Jesus Christ Superstar* and Flax for a projector pen. (November 12, 1971)

She had envisioned teaching her beloved Emily Dickinson and Shakespeare to college-prep high school students when she started. But in San Francisco the only jobs available for teachers were in the new, federally funded reading programs at schools with primarily Black students in less privileged neighborhoods. So, after the divorce, my mother was hired at Pelton Junior High in Hunter's Point and then at Benjamin Franklin Junior High in the Western Addition. She was idealistic. She would be the teacher whom her students remembered.

While I did my homework, I heard her telephone one mother after the other, each evening, "Hello, Mrs. Roberts, this is Jane Kennedy, Tyrone's English teacher. I wanted you to know that Tyrone wasn't in class today. Do you think you can help him catch up with his homework?" This was a time drenched in racial politics, a time of Black Power, of *Soul Train*, of protests around desegregation and busing. Growing up the daughter of an admiral and the wife of a foreign correspondent had not prepared her for it, but she thrived in the theater of race relations, and it launched her—and me, by default—onto a trajectory away from the military- and-finance-culture of my grandparents.

Inspired by her students and the surrounding '70s San Francisco politics of equality, we picketed for the United Farm Workers, handing out leaflets in front of the Marina Safeway. "I am a 1st grade picket," my sign said. We read books together. We became a photogenic mother-daughter pair.

At least once a semester, on the weekends, we would pick up a carload of her rowdy students in our red Scout jeep and drive down to my grandparents to ride horses and swim in the pool.

> We drove Hwy 1 through Pacifica and at Half Moon Bay stopped for a picnic lunch on the beach. The girls ate off and on all day and I know enjoyed themselves to the hilt. They exclaimed, "That's a baaad house," when we drove up. Mother was her usual gracious and charming self and we rode the horses at the Webb Ranch and then went for a hike down the Christiani trail. After getting all my laundry done we loaded ourselves in the car and drove home. A good day. (January 28, 1973)

I had no words for it then, but it feels to me as I read that those three years were a kind of numb post-trauma recovery. I was grateful for peace. I took what I was given without a huge display of personality. I remember the smell of the black leather back seats of my grandfather's Jaguar and the subdued radio voices with, "You were listening to the Boston Symphony Orchestra rendition of Bach's *Concerto in C minor for Oboe and Violin*," on the way to Sunday Mass. I remember camping in Yosemite in my grandparents' motorhome, when I began to dream of being a forest ranger. Rangers seemed tough and kind. They could live in the wild on their own. I wanted that strength.

But when I was in fourth grade, shadows appeared around the edges at Gummy and my grandfather Grand's house. Long used to debilitating bouts of asthma and migraines, my grandmother at 61 was diagnosed with a recurrence of lymphoma and began chemotherapy.

As I begin reading about these months, I already know that what happened to my grandmother impacted all our lives. I am aware that as an adult I have avoided watching or reading stories that deal in illness or death. I know I instinctively avoid conversations that hint at grief or mourning, feeling panicky as a topic moves in that direction, changing the subject or leaving the room. My German friends have told me over the years that my avoidance was irritating, as if I pushed away their intimacies, built a wall between us. Indeed, maybe that is what I have been doing.

As I hold the diaries in my hands, I don't really know yet why I am so afraid. I am reluctant to continue. But I read.

Though still mostly about classroom plans and daily activities, the diaries in late 1973 begin to include other stories. One weekend in October, my mother and I went down to the house in Portola Valley and found Gummy moving slowly, and mostly sleeping. When she moved, she meandered. Apparently, she asked me over and over to go "find Muddie for me." Muddie was my great-grandmother who lived in the city. It was confusing, and eerie.

> Daddy, Susannah and I are just sitting in rather a heartbroken state as we watch Mother wander the house. ... Her primary fixation is on Muddie and she constantly asks Susannah to go and get her or search for her. This is stunning for Susannah. Her Gummy who was such a large and wonderful part of her life suddenly reduced to an irrational person... Mother began her first radiation treatment today. (October 26, 1973)

Our regular weekends in the country, still as beautiful as ever, with the horse rides and dog walks on oak trails, with the chance to play dress-up with Carol, became fraught. I began not to want to go. At the same time, my mother increasingly needed me gone. She was now a glamorous divorcée. She began to date. She worked long hours, often staying after school and into the evening. I began to know a lot of babysitters and then to be left on my own more and more.

What strikes me in Mom's writings is that Gummy's declining health takes very little of her time. The details are written out but there is no nuance, no sadness, no expression of the devastation it meant to watch her mother's health deteriorate. This absence would be notable for any daughter observing a mother's illness, but even odder because later in life Jane always proclaimed to me how much better she had gotten along with her own mother than she got along with me.

"Gummy and I had the same temperament," she often told me. "We were both superficial and liked the finer things in life." The implication was they were like two peas in a beautifully formed pod and that I was a lentil. "You are more like your father," she'd say with a sigh.

I would expect her sadness about her mother's illness to last more than a couple of sentences sandwiched between going sailing with Miklos, a nice dinner with Martin, or details of a teacher event being canceled. Weird. Was she resentful because she was finally getting a chance to live just at the time her mother was dying? I read further.

> Mother is rather pathetic to me. So self-absorbed and dependent upon Daddy. She is afraid to drive, to be left alone, go on trips. In short, is just not my real mother. (November 21, 1973)

I begin to see something familiar: Her mother ceases to be a legitimate mother when she stops being able to care for Jane.

One day I accompanied Gummy and my mother on an errand to the Stanford Shopping Center. In the Emporium's beauty salon on the second floor, they were shown many samples of wigs, all gray, but different colors and lengths.

"This one would look lovely on you," said the man who had been presenting the wigs. He had surveyed the plastic heads with their varied fittings of hair that lined a wall, picked one of them up with a whoosh and presented it to us. "Feel how soft this is. These models feel so natural because they are made of human hair."

Both women reached out to run their hands down the gray cascade of locks. They nodded as if human hair were an important factor in their decision.

I swiveled back and forth on the stool nearby. I imagined women chopping off their hair and selling it to this man. I hated this place. Gummy tugged away the wig she had worn into the store, revealing her wispy pale scalp. It didn't look bald like my grandfather's head. It looked more like patches of baby's peach fuzz with tendrils that didn't belong. The salesman spread his hands underneath the human hair wig and lowered it gently down onto my grandmother's head as if she were a queen being crowned. Gummy stared straight at herself in the mirror. She didn't turn her head side to side coquettishly, trying to get the view from all sides as most people would.

My mother said, "Oh, that's so pretty."

Later, back at my grandparents' home, a neighbor dropped by with some fresh tomatoes from the farm stand at the Webb Ranch. "Oh, you look good, Adrienne," she said. "It compliments your eyes, looks really natural. I can't even tell the difference."

Yes, you could. The new hair looked too purplish, too shiny. I wanted her to have her real gray hair back.

When I think of my grandmother then, I think of urgency and bewilderment. A lost person. Lost attention, lost love of animals. Gummy was living at home with my grandfather and uncle Steven, my mother's younger brother, then in his twenties. Steven had just ended his three-year tour as a Naval officer. Gummy and Grand had flown to travel with him in Australia and New Zealand just a few months before. He must have been expecting to alight at home, a place of safety, to breathe in before deciding what to do next. How sad for him to be seeing his mother this way. But these are just guesses. I remember no such talk. I knew my presence was meant to cheer them up. I felt guilty and selfish for not wanting to visit.

In the city one night I was woken by my mother careening around the apartment, stomping from the back bedroom along the long hall to the living room, her footsteps fast on the bare floors. I followed her.

She opened and closed the windows, unlatching them, pushing them open to the dark night, pulling them together again. Over and over.

Her white nightgown flowed around her legs.

Her eyes did not register.

I watched from the hall.

I was a silent, undetected observer of my mother's strange performance until I eventually returned to bed.

In her diaries, I find:

> Mother taken to Stanford for another brain scan. I did laundry and talked to Steven who is shaken and rather adrift right now. Mother and Daddy got home in time for lunch. She is not so deranged as before, but is rather more like Muddie, wandering, forgetful and full of things that didn't happen. I am very much opposed to her having any more radiation as she made quite clear her wish to die and not have a prolonged depressing illness. However, Daddy and especially Steven feel all must be done that doctors say. (January 29, 1974)

They moved Gummy to the Julia Sanatorium. I visited her in the nursing home only once, trailing my mother down a pale ivory hall that smelled like pee and disinfectant. Gummy was sitting up in bed and the room felt crowded. Her skin was gray and wrinkly.

My mother, tense and distraught, urged me forward. "Look, Mother, Susannah is here."

Gummy looked wild; her hair had grown in differently, like a strange wiry afro. It didn't belong on her face, so pale now. Her eyes focused on me but did not recognize me.

"What time is it?" she asked.

I froze. Was I supposed to answer?

"It's 10 past 11," someone said. "Almost lunchtime."

"Yes, what would you like for lunch?" someone else said.

Gummy looked uneasily around the room at the faces staring at her. "What time is it?" she repeated. "Please, can I leave? Please, don't leave me here. What time is it?"

Someone tried to make conversation.

She became increasingly agitated. I scanned for pinecones on the evergreen tree outside her window.

One school night during those months I was again woken by my mother's strange movements. I listened, startled, to the unknown sounds, and they did not stop. After a while, I slipped out of my twin bed and walked over the wood floors around the corner to her room. I stood at the foot of her four-poster bed. I had never seen my mother cry. I stayed there quietly.

She keened over and over: "Why won't she die? Why won't she die?!"

I stood still.

The sniffles eventually slowed.

"I'm okay," she said. "You want to sleep here with me?"

In my memory, I slipped in beside her. It was familiar. Warm. When we had guests we often shared a bed, a closeness I always cherished as if it were a gift. That night, alone just the two of us, I imagine she calmed down and eventually drifted off to sleep. I imagine I was calmed as her breathing slowed.

Her diary says I slept next to her that night, but I don't remember her ever talking to me about what happened. I think she felt if she didn't talk about it, it never happened. But such a scene did happen and seeing her in a jagged state frightened me. In the best of worlds, I would have been comforted. Instead, my presence comforted her. Through her being comforted, I could calm myself.

I began to believe that if Mommy doesn't say anything, maybe it did not happen. I learned to mistrust my own memories and intuition. I learned to view my capacity to calm my mother as the underpinning of our togetherness.

On February 12, the diary reads: "Today is Mother's birthday. She did not die. I tried so hard."

I don't know what my mother meant. Had she tried to arrange for less care so that Gummy would die a faster death? Had she tried to kill her?

On February 16, we drove down to spend the weekend at my grandfather's house. Sometimes I slept in the small twin bedroom with the antique knocker on the door, but that evening we shared the pullout bed in the den. My grandfather made a steak on the barbecue. He was good at cooking meat. My mother made some green beans and potatoes. Uncle Steven worked on the cars. I set the table as I always did for the four of us. The dinner was quiet. Nobody really had the wish for much conversation.

Around 7 pm my mother announced she would be going out and would return an hour later. It seemed odd that she would leave. The rest of us watched television. My grandfather had invented a system of turning off advertisements with what he called a "blab off." It was a push button on the end of a long cable. At commercials, he would silence the sound. He always watched Walter Cronkite deliver the news and his favorite show was *Monty Python*.

My mother returned as I was brushing my teeth for bed. She didn't talk much. I didn't ask her where she had been. She did not read to me or remind me to say my prayers. The next morning, a doctor called with news that my grandmother had died in the night.

Her diary describes what happened:

I went back to what is left of Mother. She was wearing her pretty red nightie. We talked of God. I had my pills in my purse. I fed her 20 pills, like a mama bird feeding her baby: Pill, water, pill, water. She took them as if I were a nurse doing the rounds. Nothing. No eye contact. She wasn't really there. (February 16, 1974)

As I read this, I skim over her handwriting. I don't want to linger. I don't want to reread. I register what she has written. But I keep skimming forward. Now I'm no longer paying attention to her words. Unbidden, a scene comes to mind. My grandmother was in our apartment in the city. She was ill but she was lucid. She had driven up with my grandfather to the city for a concert. They came for an early dinner beforehand. In our hall I came upon a hushed consultation between my mother and grandmother. I heard the word "Seconal." At age ten, I didn't know that was a sedative. They stopped talking when they realized I was close.

Now I force myself to slow my thoughts. Had my grandmother really told my mother to give her pills, to end her suffering? Had that scene really happened at all?

When I tell Niels and Leah that evening about what I have been reading, I tell them in a strange, cold voice. I'm not happy with my tone. It is as if I'm reciting in that voice used on an airplane to explain how to put the oxygen mask over your nose and mouth.

Leah blurts out: "What?! Nonna killed her own mother?"

My stomach tightens. *Don't overreact. Don't become hysterical.* I counter with a calming sentence. "I'm sure she thought she was doing the right thing."

Niels says, "Well, that sure adds drama to the family history, doesn't it?"

Maybe it all makes sense. Maybe it isn't a big deal after all.

I imagine how my mother felt. I see my grandmother's gray hair, her wrinkles, how her wit and big personality, her twinkly eyes began to fade and disappear. I see love. I see my mother seeing her mother suffering. I see Jane intervening to end her mother's suffering, just as she later pushed everyone else when pets or people were ill.

"Put them down. End the cruelty," she admonished so harshly. I never liked her brutal tone. Maybe now I'm understanding where that ferocity came from.

Before returning to my office to read the next day, I walk to the beach. I search out the horizon, seeing the waves crashing on the lighthouse, watching our big, beautiful dog pull on the leash to get as far away from the water as possible, like a maiden aunty in dainty heels would skirt a mud puddle. This scene always amuses me. I try to let the thoughts come up in my mind, to just let them approach, see what I find. Is it disgust? No, that's not it. I see my mother trumpeting to herself that nobody else was courageous enough to be an advocate for a gentle demise. She would have thought helping my grandmother die was a loftier, more humane goal than keeping her alive on chemotherapy and machines. For a while I walk with that possible truth.

Later, I return to my desk and that volume of the diary.

The second time I read it, I shiver. *Oh my God. My mother murdered my grandmother, my Gummy.* My stomach roils with the reality of the scene. Pill after pill, she set out to end her mother's life. She actually did it. She gathered the pills beforehand in some sort of clandestine expedition. She planned it. She executed her plan. Then she squeezed that secret down deep into her innermost heart and went on about her life. The gall takes my breath away.

Machiavellian, almost. Such a calculation. Morally and practically.

In 1974, euthanasia was illegal in California. What she had done was considered murder. Not only was she risking her own life, she was risking mine. Had she thought about what would happen if her deed were discovered? Was she acting on an obligation to her mother's wishes, risking everything for her? Or were the gathering of the pills and feeding them to her mother to spare herself the discomfort of watching her mother's decline? I think again of that fleeting mini-conversation I seem to remember between Mom and Gummy. But am I remembering it correctly? Or am I making it up?

I stretch my historical gaze out to a larger horizon, trying to calm myself down. I retreat to my academic self. I see the pills as an enactment of an ethical dilemma—one that can be debated yes or no. I begin to feel safer. My heart beats slower. My breathing quiets. It reminds me of why I always loved studying. As soon as I can absent myself from an emotional tangle and approach it as if I am asking a philosophical question, I have always felt better. There is nothing that cannot be looked at from more than one perspective.

I return to her diary:

> The next morning at 8:30, Dr. Hayes called to say that Mother had died in her sleep about 5 a.m. And so my fun and beautiful mother is in heaven and we are spared the further hell of her ravishment. We were all stupefied with relief and there were so many people to call. (February 17, 1974)

Her prose is so spare. She writes nothing of the emotional pathos behind a daughter taking her own mother's life. Instead, she seems to view herself as a good savior sparing her mother from the ravishment of a hard disease.

I talk with Niels that night. I begin to remember conversations with cousins. They know I'm reading her diaries, and a few had begun to look at me with a certain glance. They seemed to know about Mom and Gummy, too.

The next day, I read the entries about Gummy's death again. Only then does it occur to me: My mother was not the only person that mattered in this scene. My grandfather and my uncle had been Gummy's full time caregivers. My grandfather, a respected Rear Admiral and former aircraft carrier commander, had shared a lifetime with my grandmother. The doctors viewed him as her next-of-kin, not my mother. Then there was Uncle Steven. He loved Gummy, too. Maybe even more urgently, as he was younger. My mother had circumvented them both. She had not consulted them. She had simply acted.

This was long before hospice became a mainstream offering. Maybe my grandfather and my uncle had indeed not been ready to have a sober conversation with the doctors about letting Gummy die. Maybe they had wanted to hold onto hope that the doctors could offer more interventions. When a patient's family is in denial, doctors are known to keep trying. Maybe the Catholic faith of my grandfather and uncle went deeper, was purer, held them accountable for the afterlife. Intervention in death would have been a mortal sin.

Perhaps Gummy, when she was still cogent, had sworn Jane to intervene. "Don't let me suffer." Perhaps.

But what does that say about my family? Cousins corroborate: "Adrienne and Jane must have had a pact—if I get too ill, you must take my life. They were close. It rings true." But what impact does such a pact have on those who are left behind?

At the very least, there was an iciness present in my mother's actions, an iciness needed to suppress the consequences. To not grieve. To not feel. To lie to the people she loved most. To return to her father's house—Steven's house, too—after feeding the pills to her mother. To lie next to her daughter in the guest bed, breathing and waiting for the news.

In my imagination now, she tossed and turned. Maybe she wondered whether Gummy would be woken by nurses on their nightly rounds. Maybe she wondered whether Gummy would vomit up the pills. If she did, the ruse would have been exposed. Maybe she made up an alibi while she lay next to me. Maybe she wondered if her brother and father might turn her in if they found out.

> I lay in the den bed and watched the stars and marked the
> hours by the Balch table clock. Perhaps I slept. I know I did
> for I dreamed of cancer. The dawn was clear and there was
> frost on the grass. (February 17, 1974)

Her gamble paid off. The nurses did not check. The sheriffs did not come.

But it seems to me the price she paid was to cut off a part of herself. To force herself—and by association the rest of us—into lying about Gummy's death, thus severing us from a process of shared mourning. Grief is healing. She never healed.

The next morning with the doctor's absolving call, she put it all behind her and planned a funeral. Shortly thereafter, Phyllis, newly widowed herself, entered our lives and from one day to the next Gummy vanished from the family narrative. My mother, Steven and I continued to see my grandfather and Phyllis often, but my grandmother was no longer part of their stories.

I missed her. "Why doesn't anyone talk about Gummy anymore?" I once asked my mother on our way home from a visit.

I remember only a vague "I'm sure she's happy in heaven" as she drove, and then silence. I was used to such responses.

"Don't underestimate the effect of the strict faith the family shared," a cousin says now. "Their Catholicism was a particularly rigorous form of the religion, one imbued with guilt and sin and fear. Your grandmother and mother were more free-thinking."

I find this confusing. "Free-thinking" would perhaps have allowed my mother and grandmother to approve of euthanasia just as they approved of birth control. Both were forbidden by the church. But what did the silences reflect? Immediate guilt? A larger family culture of avoidance? I do see that whether it is called *Irish-Catholic stoicism* or *an intellectual preference for the rational*, there was always a wish in my family to avoid the messiness of emotions.

Avoidance doesn't erase the imprints of what happened, however. I think the deeds surrounding my grandmother's illness and death remained in my mother and therefore in all the rest of us, chipping away at intimacy and shared love.

As I prepare to read on, I can already see the tendrils wafting, the ties from her past snaking around her suicide headstone like dreadful, sticky weeds.

The Girl in the Attic

1970 and 1975

IN EARLY ELEMENTARY SCHOOL YEARS, I remember the frequent companionship of my imaginary friend Helen. She and I created names and blankets for all my plastic Breyer horses. Sweet Rosebud, with her white forelock and splayed legs eating grass for the first time. Racer, with his powerful stride and tail flying back behind him. Helen and I loved a whole herd of horses that we would take care of together. Helen lay next to me on my pillow at night and we whispered—as if I told her my thoughts. As if she were always there.

One summer afternoon four years before Gummy's death, I was at my grandparents' house in Portola Valley. It was a dry, hot California day. My hair was damp from swimming. I had just learned the back-stroke. Gummy braided my hair after lunch. She had rules. I always had to take a rest. If you swam on a full stomach, you'd get cramps. Today Gummy said I could come play in the unmown pasture since the horses were out front.

I tamped down a nest for myself in the tall yellow grass. Then I directed Helen to sit across from me—"You sit over here next to Lamb" —propping up white fluffy Lamb on the blanket and laying out the teacups. "Would you like a slice of lemon?"

Crick-crick-crick. Crickets made that sound. I squinted my eyes really tight and concentrated on looking between the blades of grass, but I couldn't see anything moving its wings.

"How many rooms should we have?" Helen and I were going to make our house bigger. Trampling more grass, leaving little hallways in between rooms. It was one of my favorite games, making houses for my animals in the grass that grew tall over my head. Sometimes my best friend Carol was here, but today Helen was my buddy.

I remember that so clearly.

Yet there is no mention of Helen in my mother's diaries. No evidence she existed. Where had she come from? Where did she go?

It wasn't until five years later, after Gummy died and my grandfather remarried, and the adults were sipping cocktails in the living room, that my step-grandmother Phyllis dropped a bombshell into the conversation.

"Why has nobody ever told me about Helen?" she asked.

That day we had been in the kitchen before dinner. Phyllis had been on a roll. "Did you know your grandparents slept in twin beds?" she asked me. "And everyone says they had such a good marriage." She *tsked* irritably.

I had never thought about twin vs. queen marriage beds before. But I sensed she was criticizing my cherished Gummy. I didn't like that.

"And did you know your grandparents had another child? That nobody ever talks about her?" This sounded really wrong. I went mute as I helped her cut the ends off the green beans.

Phyllis had snapped up my grandfather within a year of Gummy's death, transforming him from a shuffling man in mourning to a man in his sixties who laughed and planned trips around the world. She was talkative and sexy and lively. I missed my grandmother terribly; still, Phyllis was entertaining. She told me stories about life on the San Mateo County grand jury. About her Swedish mother and her years on the girls' basketball team in Philadelphia. This last I always found confusing since Phyllis was so short. Her yarns were sometimes ribald, like "my nipples were so strong, they rubbed a hole in my bra," and left my eleven-year-old self pondering what it meant to have steel nipples.

So, at cocktails, when Phyllis brought the subject up again, this time in the company of my grandfather, my mother and Uncle Steven, I wasn't completely surprised. My ears pricked up at the name Helen.

"I was rearranging the books in the den and took out some old albums," Phyllis said. "In one of them there was a picture of a child's tombstone in Arlington National Cemetery! It said: 'Helen, daughter of Capt. J.F. Quilter, USN.' Why have I never heard about her?"

Phyllis looked around the room, waiting for a response. Nobody talked. My mother swirled the olive in her drink. I slunk down to the carpet to cuddle with the dogs. If anyone, my grandfather would have to say the first words. He had been a naval aviator and ship commander. He was a benevolent force but not a man of many emotions. Phyllis was still standing, waiting.

He glanced at me, "There are painful things that are best left unspoken," he finally said into the silence.

Uncle Steven came to the rescue, changing the subject to a familiar family topic: "Did you see that GE stock rose two points yesterday? You worked for GE didn't you, Phyllis? I hope you invested in your former company."

My grandfather followed suit in a calm voice. "Yes, the new CEO, Reginald Jones, seems to be doing a good job." The conversation went on from there. No more mention of Helen. Phyllis headed into the kitchen. I could see her head shake.

Later that evening, as my mother and I drove up Highway 280 toward San Francisco, I asked her to explain what Phyllis had said.

"Helen was born when I was four. There was also a baby brother Joseph—before that—who died after a day, but I don't remember him."

The red Scout was rumbling slower along Cañada Road by the reservoir. These were the years before the eight-lane freeway was fully completed. "Helen was born healthy but contracted meningitis at a pool when she was two months old. She lay in an attic room, a vegetable with a giant head, for five years. It was ghastly."

She stayed silent, her only movements her hands gripping the smooth black steering wheel.

I slid myself horizontal on the front seat bench so that I could duck under her arms and snuggle my head onto her lap, my pre-teen body making that familiar childhood position a little cramped. Seat belts wouldn't be required until the 1980s. I lay there listening to the motor, the lights from other cars on the empty highway occasionally passing by. It felt cozy, just the two of us. *What does a giant head look like? Did she have hair?*

My mother's baby sister Helen was born in January 1943 in Washington, D.C., three years after a traumatic premature birth and then death of a boy, Joseph. I piece together a skeleton of a story from family letters and my great-grandfather's diary, all archived in my mother's papers. For example, my grandmother's loopy lovely handwriting in a letter to her brother describes Jane as having adored her baby sister. "She's crazy about Helen and has had most of her little friends in to see her."

But when Helen was two months old, she developed pneumococcal meningitis, a bacterial infection. This set in motion a back-and-forth of tragedy and gnarled response to tragedy that has imprinted itself through my mother's psyche even onto the lives of my own children born fifty years later.

When Helen took ill, my mother, by all accounts a timid and sensitive child, appears suddenly to have been left at home as her mother focused on the baby. It was wartime. There was rationing and the news was full of dread. Her father was working at the Pentagon.

> At 4 years old I felt abandoned and unloved alone in Arlington with the maid and my kitty cat as Mother remained mostly in Washington at Children's Hospital. The war was in full cry and Dad often was preoccupied and absent. (December 1, 2006)

Months of sulfur treatments at the hospital saved Helen's life but she was brought home in a tragic state of ill health—not being able to hear or communicate, with a hydrocephalic swollen head.

Any four-year-old, seeing her healthy baby sister disappear and then return home uncommunicative, with bulging eyes and a swollen head, accompanied by unfamiliar smells and sounds, would need intense comfort and attention. She would need explanations in bite-sized increments. She would need reassurance that what happened to Helen would not happen to her. "Will I wake up with a big head, too?"

Seeing the lifelong effects of those years on my mother now, I'm guessing my grandparents were not able to supply this necessary attention. Either because they were overwhelmed themselves—with rationing and wartime and now a disabled baby—or because they themselves had been raised to think that answering such emotional needs would be spoiling the child.

I try to put myself into my mother's place. Did she sit by Helen's side? Did she try to comfort her, or hold her? Did Helen have epileptic seizures; something I read is a side effect of the illness? How would young Jane, seven or eight years old, in elementary school, with the usual, "Draw us a picture of your family," and, "Write about your brothers and sisters," have incorporated such a sibling into her life? Could she have invited her "little friends" home anymore? My mother's diary words about those years, rare, were always imbued with sadness and puzzlement, as if her life had been overcome by a hurricane and nobody had explained why the trees were falling.

> The Chopin in last evening's concert has wafted all sorts of childhood memories to me: Muddie playing in the drawing room of our big formal Washington house. How talented she was and how sensitive to me, moving her bedroom up to the third floor when Helen died and I moved up there and did not want to be alone. (April 27, 1982)

Jane's grandparents moved from San Francisco to Washington to live with the family after Helen's hospitalization. I'm guessing her grandmother Muddie did her best to replace the affections and attention of parents who were preoccupied with the war and with the needy baby. But something else must have been amiss to create such a lifelong effect on my mother. Did Helen shriek? Did her diapers smell? Did they put lavender oil on her pillows? Was the door kept closed? Did they warm her bottles on the stove? All I have as a witness are my great grandfather's words from his 1947 diary:

> Was awakened by Muddie and Adrienne this morning at 6 a.m. and was told that our precious little Angel Baby Helen was taken by our Dear Lord at 4 a.m. this morning, the Dear Little one passing to Heaven direct in her sleep. Dr. Millican was called and came immediately and certified her death. ... Helen was 4 years 5 months and 8 days old. The undertaker took her remains at 7 a.m. after which Jane was awakened and told the news. (June 15, 1947)

Helen died just before my mother's ninth birthday. That means that for my mother's entire awakening childhood, learning to read, exploring friendships and the neighborhood around her, she lived in a household with an obscure, severely disabled child and her nurse.

After Helen's death, I see no evidence that my mother was held, given loving hugs to embrace the sadness of Helen's fate. I suspect they simply went on as if it were behind them, assuming that to talk about it would only prolong the sorrow. According to this philosophy, it is better to try and forget. Emotions are a misguided indulgence. This would explain Phyllis' appalled question why nobody had ever told her about Helen.

But for my mother, memories unprocessed did not vanish. They were just hidden in the body and in the recesses of the mind. We know that unconscious matter left unaccompanied, comes bubbling up unexpectedly, often showing itself in anger, in obsessive control, or in agitation. The diaries show those fateful years with Helen dominating my mother's inner life forever.

> The appalling downward spiral and painful procedures tried on that defenseless four-month-old combined with the prayers and hopes for a miracle bring me to tears. ... Dad, Mom, Muddie and Granddaddy soldiered on taking comfort in togetherness and the love they had for each other. ... Spinal meningitis, hydrocephalus, blindness, brain damage. No wonder I take such comfort in the idea of death. But with Helen, long years in a vegetative state awaited us, coloring my childhood irreversibly and irrevocably informing my old age. (March 24, 2008)

My heart goes out to timid Jane who ate too little and grew too tall and never learned to give words to her emotions. Jane grew up and had many paths open to her to soothe the rough imprints of childhood. But she did not grow out of the trauma by grieving and talking. She did not make peace with Helen's death through faith. She did not work it through in therapy. In fact, in adulthood my mother waved understanding away like the captain of a sinking ship waves away a rescue.

Adult Jane appeared strong, but she seems never to have understood the effect, not only of Helen, but the lack of emotional parenting she received. In her diaries there is no exploration of the in-between spaces. I am left to imagine parents unable to give words to grief, who preferred denial, upon which children project misshapen self-narratives to survive.

It matters because this legacy haunted my mother her whole life. It hounded her inner psyche, negating a sense of trust that she would be taken care of. It denied her the understanding that dependence and closeness could be good. But it also haunted the rest of us through her. To any pets in less-than-perfect health, she slammed out the phrase:

"Put that dog down!" Of people aging or ill she said the same. There was no space for exploring details, nor talking about different paths of treatment and their consequences.

Niels once joked, "If I break my leg, don't let her near the hospital."

It surfaced when a teenage cousin was in a car accident and lay in hospital with a traumatic brain injury. Agitated, my mother called me, chanting over and over that Clara "should be allowed to die." Her opinions were so immediate and violent, and they were coercive.

She considered those of us weak who gave space to consider details and choices. To be strong was to be like her. To my mother, there were no choices. End it now. Pull the plug. Give the pills.

Being Tall

1975

IT IS A YEAR AFTER MY GRANDMOTHER DIED. I am holding a pale blue plastic object in my hand. I press it as instructed, registering its unfamiliar smoothness against my palm. For such a grown-up object, it feels so light. I practice a few times. Pushed just right, its top rises easily, then closes again with a satisfying snap. I like the snap. I do it again.

"See how each pill is identified by a number? That's the order in which you have to take them. Every day at the same time. You can't forget."

I look up at the doctor, his kind round face watching me carefully, then back down at the 28 little pills snuggled in bubbles next to tiny, printed numbers. Every day? Was I supposed to bring them with me on sleepovers?

I am 11 years old.

My mother and I had been pilgrimaging to the UCSF pediatric endocrinology department for months now, participating in a program that would prevent me from growing to her 6 foot 2 inch height. I had just been handed my first month's ration of pills in its circular bed. And I didn't quite understand what all the fuss was about. True, I had been the tallest child in sixth grade. I was always at the end of the line, or at the back of group pictures. But I didn't mind. I came from a family of tall people. In church our entire pew was a wall of over-6 footers, male cousins and uncle coming in at 6 feet 5 inches. I was used to looking up.

In the car, on our way to the appointment, my mother had repeated her familiar litany against tallness.

"I was a giraffe, a freak," she said, her hands gripping the steering wheel of the Scout. "In Atherton, Mother got a friend to hook me up with the Social Register Cotillion. A cotillion! I was miserably wall-flowered."

I guessed this meant she had been sad. My mind pictured flowers and walls but I couldn't put that together with something that would have made my mother so upset.

"What is a cotillion?"

"It is when teenage daughters are 'presented' to society by their fathers. They dress in beautiful dresses, learn lady-like manners, and attend a dance."

I pictured big hoop dresses on Scarlett O'Hara. Wow. *What would that be like?* Swish, swish, swish. Layers of tulle like the tutus the older ballerinas wore in my long-ago ballet class. *Sigh.* I had always wanted to be one of those dancers. There was a black and white picture of my mother in a white flowy dress on the bookshelf. *Maybe that's what she was talking about.* I'd never seen those kinds of clothes in California.

My mother's hands moved down the steering wheel. "A cotillion is a horrible social ritual that you are *never* going to have to be in. Thankfully, nobody we know buys into that outdated nonsense." She paused. "Maybe Jennie might be presented, I'm not sure."

Presented? She seemed to be saying I was supposed to be happy not to be *presented,* whatever that was, but something nagged at me. Jennie was the only other girl in our San Francisco hillside building. I pictured her mother brushing her straight shiny hair each morning. Jennie seemed to have a perfect life. She had a mother and a father and a brother. Her father wore a suit to work every day. She attended private school. Their wide arching stairs were visible through the living room windows in the early morning when I walked past to get the bus to my neighborhood school. Her bedroom was lined with hand-made cabinets, everything in its place.

Now I pictured Jennie in a big hoop gown and frowned. I wanted to wear one, too.

"You don't know what it's like when all the boys are shorter than you at a dance. The story of my life. The only man I ever really felt comfortable dancing with was John Kenneth Galbraith in India." She took on a dreamy look. "He was the ambassador, and he was 6 foot 4."

I had heard that story many times before. It seemed to go with gloves and tailored silk dresses. That was India. But what was my mother like as a girl? I pictured her in a teenage hoop dress, hand on a boy's shoulder, his head at her chest. But wait, they had to dance touching? Yuk. *What was this dance thing? I* knew of *Soul Train,* the kids break-dancing on the school playground and the Hustle my friend Sharon and I practiced in her upstairs room. There was no touching in my kind of dancing.

As I watched the traffic light turn yellow and then red, I think back to Joey tapping me on the shoulder when we were leaving Social Studies yesterday. "Hey, Susannah, would you go with me to the dance next week?"

Backpacks knocked at him as students streamed out of the class-room, his fingers twisted the top buttons of his green polyester shirt while he talked. *What was he saying to me?* I'd seen the posters around school with pictures of corn and pumpkins and glitter: "Come one and all to the Harvest Corn dance 3-5 p.m." But until yesterday I had not considered those posters might concern me.

Across the street from our idling car, a couple of men holding hands stopped to kiss. I continued thinking about Joey. I had the feeling I was supposed to be excited like those guys, but all I felt was panic. I had stopped breathing when Joey asked me about the dance. *What? Dance?* Joey had run his hand through his thick black hair. He had been waiting for something. My mother said I should always be kind to boys. My heart was pounding. Without thinking, I felt my head shake left to right.

"No, sorry," I mumbled, looking down at my shoes. I picked up my books and raced into the hallway. I felt relieved and guilty at once.

My mother's words interrupted my thoughts again. "I didn't fit into any clothes, so Mother learned to sew," she said. "How awful for her."

My grandmother's face appeared in my mind, her twinkly gray-green eyes and perfectly symmetrical features. My heart ached. I missed her so much. I missed playing double solitaire with her, and mahjong. I missed all our shared horsey stuff, wielding a hoof pick just so, digging in to loosen all the dirt that had hardened under the hoof before going out on a dusty trail ride. Gummy had knitted me an aqua and red jumper with an upside-down pyramid on the front for my ninth birthday. So maybe she had once sewed my mother's clothes. It didn't really make sense though. Both my grandmother and my mother had been seen by everyone I knew as exceptional beauties, who preferred to oversee a house full of servants than spend hours over a needle and thread.

I focused back on the story my mother was telling about her height. We stopped at Fillmore and California streets waiting for the light to turn.

"Only now do I see how sad my grotesque growth must have made Mother," she continued.

Grotesque? I don't want to be grotesque.

It was true that my mother had been unusually tall for a woman of her generation. She claimed she was 6 feet 2 inches but it seemed she was even taller. Uncle Steven was 6 feet 5 inches. I know that by eighth grade she was over six feet tall. I also can see that in pictures with my father, who was 6 feet 1 inch, she always stood in a slight curtsy, leg bent to the side, to create an illusion.

In her telling, her height was a fundamental disfigurement, an archaic source of social and psychological suffering that lay at the core of everything she lacked. It was not part of her character; it *was* her character.

"When I am reincarnated, I want to come back as a tiny Vietnamese woman," she often pronounced. Her audience inevitably laughed, thinking it a joke. Jane held herself upright with impeccable posture. Surely she wouldn't want to be anyone else.

Despite how others saw her, and how she wanted to be seen, inside my mother's psyche, tallness seems to have taken on absolute putrid power. She blamed it for everything bad in her young life, as if it were an inevitable burden of character. It was something upon which she hung all her insecurities and shortcomings. Because I, her daughter, was an extension of her, I would inevitably suffer as she had suffered.

My mother's campaign for height intervention began when I was six, as soon as we moved to San Francisco from New York. "I took Susannah to her doctor's appointment. Dr. Madden is very nice but not up on the estrogen height regulatory bit," her diary notes.

In sixth grade, when it was clear that I was now the tallest in my class, she found doctors at the University of California medical school (UCSF) willing to include me in an experimental study. Estrogen was rumored to be a miracle method of stimulating early cartilage maturation through premature onset of menstruation. This would trigger the natural biological process of slowing growth.

UCSF was perched at the base of Mount Sutro in the middle of San Francisco. It was a gleaming modern building with walls of glass, full of sunlight and friendly nurses. I had to go quite often for regular taking of blood and x-rays of my wrist, which seemed to be the most easily accessible bones to document. They never made me feel afraid. Dr. Trevino, my pediatrician, was short and kindly, with a wrinkly smile that put me at ease as he evaluated the latest picture of my wrist bones and even when I was lying on the pallet, and he was lifting my underwear waistline to check for developing pubic hair. Such protocols made me uncomfortable. Who wants a strange man looking there? But I don't remember any lingering shame from those years.

My mother urged me to be quiet about the program. No need to tell anyone at school or in the family quite yet. After the first few months of evaluation, Dr. Trevino predicted I would grow to my father's height, just over six feet.

Dr. Trevino called to say Susannah's height prediction is 6 foot 1. She'll start pills in September probably. Oh, dear God, don't make her that tall. (June 26, 1975)

My mother pushed for me to be accepted into the pharmaceutical arm of the study. It was at that point that my father entered the picture.

In those years my father was unreliable, dropping in and out of my life, drinking more. Although he had regular court-ordered visitation weekends with me, he only sporadically turned up. There were many mornings of waiting for the doorbell to ring with my bag packed. I remember the hope he would come, that he was often hours late, and that he often didn't pick me up at all.

"That's your father. Get used to it," my mother would say when she saw me slumped in the living room, waiting yet again.

She complained he was often late with child support money. Most likely, he knew if he picked me up my mother would remind him of the missing checks. Maybe it was a choice between being berated by my mother or seeing his daughter. Or maybe he was just busy with himself. He was planning on getting married to Harriet. He had work.

That year he forgot my 12th birthday entirely, calling a few days later with a slow voice. "Susannah, I am ashamed I didn't call you on your birthday. You know I love you."

"Yes, Daddy," I sighed. "I know."

I knew he wanted me to see him as a good father. I tried. But the occasional attention he provided was not the same as the solid love of a showing-up father. Sure, he cared for me when he thought about me. He was a warm-hearted man. But I have watched Niels fathering our three children. I have seen what good fathering looks like. It takes time and energy. It is a lifelong commitment. *Real love is actually showing up, Dad.*

When my father did pick me up, we did special things like trips to the Steinhart Aquarium and sailing lessons on Lake Merritt in Oakland. It was on one of those weekends that I felt an opening to talk.

"How was your school week?" he asked.

"It was okay. I went to Lori's house on Tuesday. I'm so jealous because she has a baby kitten. Oh my God, it was so cute, Daddy. It was tiny and had tiger-colored stripes. I wish Mom would let me have a kitten."

"Which friend is Lori?"

"She's really nice. She's Japanese and she lives in one of those old houses on Pine Street with a million steps leading up to the front door."

We were unpacking groceries and he was getting ready to make dinner.

"It was a good place for me to go after school because it is close to UCSF," I said. "I could just take the bus from there."

"UCSF?" My father turned back from the refrigerator.

"Yeah, it was just a quick appointment this time."

"What do you mean?" He leaned against the counter. "Do you go there often?" His voice became clear.

I sensed I was creating some trouble. But I also sensed a need to tell him.

"Yeah, every couple of weeks. I need to go for an x-ray, and they take my blood."

Now he was staring at me.

"Why? What are they doing?"

"It is something about being tall. Mommy doesn't want me to grow tall, so they gave me some pills to take."

As a parent, I think how my own insides would have been in five-alarm fire mode hearing this from my child. "I'm going to call your mother," he said, going into the bedroom. *Uh-oh.* I waited on the couch, my feet swishing back and forth, neck scrunched down and my shoulders high. A familiar posture. I listened to his angry voice through the wall. Some words like "experimental therapy," and "how dare you" wafted through.

When he returned, he sat down carefully beside me and took my hands. "Susannah, look at me."

I forced myself to look away from the carpet and into his eyes. "Your mother and I don't agree about these pills. I want you to talk about it with someone. I don't want you to feel you are being coerced into something that you don't want."

My mother's diary notes the other side of the conversation:

Alan called and made the expected federal case out of estrogen therapy, which was to start today.
(September 3, 1975)

Once he got wind of the estrogen plans, my father appeared more often in my life for a while. The UCSF program was my mother's doing, but it brought me my parents again. I remember enjoying it when my father was involved. Not only because he was my father but because he became more solid, more decisive than he usually was around my mother. As a medical journalist, he was an expert in medical research. Here he could be a father with a cause to fight.

> We met Alan and drove over to Berkeley to talk with child psychologist Dr. Pierce. The upshot seems to be no estrogen therapy. I am very bitter and resentful that Alan has effectively decreed this although who can tell. Susannah does not seem very interested one way or the other. (September 25, 1975)

My memory of that appointment places me in a leather chair, hands hooked under my thighs, on the door side of a carved wooden desk. The frizzy-haired psychologist tried hard to get me to engage with him.

"You know I just talked a little while with your parents. They told me they are divorced. How do you feel about that?"

"It's fine. It's better now that they aren't fighting." My rote answer. Somewhere inside I knew what he was waiting to hear. My hopes that Daddy would stop drinking and come back home. That Mommy would be happy. I didn't have the words to tell him of my heartbreak. What can a child say of divorce? It marks you for life.

On the way home across the Bay Bridge, I'm guessing my parents must have talked in the car. But maybe not. My mother may well have fumed silently. She was good at that. All I know is that according to the diaries, a month later my father changed his mind. The experiment was on again.

> Took cable car downtown to have lunch with Alan. He agreed to start Susannah on estrogen. I am immensely relieved, but hope the delay is not too great. (October 27, 1975)

At the beginning of November 1975, I started on a prescription for Premarin, a conjugated estrogen used nowadays primarily to treat postmenopausal symptoms. It was supposed to accelerate puberty, which in turn accelerates closing of the growth centers of bones.

> This day Susannah got the prescription ... I pray that it works and that she has no contraindications. I rushed to Marina to pick her up at 11:15, rushed to UC hospital. She had a blood test and then I put her on a bus back to school. ... I barely made it to my class. Not your most relaxing of lunch hours. (November 6, 1975)

I began to take my "pill," the round plastic container resembling the other kind in my mother's medicine cabinet. Every day. Twenty-one days of hormones, seven days of placebo. I couldn't tell anyone. When I spent the night at Sue's house, I kept the container tucked deep down under my clothes. I worried about remembering the pill at the right time.

On December 30, I got my first period.

"Mommy, my period is starting," I remember saying when I spied some blood in my panties. The nurses had prepared me for what to expect. My mother had some pads stored in the bathroom. She showed me how to attach them to the belt. I felt kind of grown up.

Junior high was not easy for me socially. There was bullying and racial violence. Like everyone else before the widespread marketing of adhesive pads, I wore enormous sanitary napkins fastened with an elastic belt around my hips to keep the pad in place. Since I was afraid of going to the bathroom at my bleak, cavernous school, I was always worried whether it would last all day. In my memory seventh grade is full of a lingering smell of dried blood, mine and other girls' passing close by my desk.

Then, at the end of March, my mother abruptly changed her mind.

> Today was a momentous one because Susannah discontinued the use of estrogen. I have been frightened by the reports of

cancer as a result of Premarin. I pray she will not grow over 5 foot 10 inches but will have to rely on prayers rather than medicines. We had a long talk with Dr. Trevino who is pleased with this decision. (March 12, 1976)

I was relieved to get off the pills. Immediately I had no more monthly bleedings. I no longer had to worry about leaking at school. I didn't have to worry about keeping a secret from my friends, and not spending the night at anyone's house during my period. I hated answering all those clinic check-up questions, getting my wrist x-rayed for bone growth, and being checked on for breast development and puberty. Otherwise, as with many experiences in life with my mother, there was no emotional follow-up that I can remember. I was expected to put it behind me and forget about it. I'm guessing from her diary entry that Dr. Trevino himself was not sure I belonged in the study. Perhaps my mother's emotional investment in the experiment troubled him. My height prediction was not so dire after all.

I actually stopped growing at 5 feet 11 inches. Was this because the first progesterone-triggered period indeed began the process of slowing my bone growth, or would I have been this height no matter what? Niels is 6 feet 1 inch. Our boys are 6 feet 5 inches and Leah is 5 feet 11 inches like me. I don't share my mother's belief in tallness as a defect. Being tall is a good thing in our family. It allows us to see over crowds and walk confidently down the street.

I am sympathetic to my mother's disfigurement narrative only to the extent that it must have been difficult in her generation to grow so tall. She did stand out. It was never an option for her to blend into the background. But like all narratives, it can be weaponized. That is where I see its significance for me. By blaming her height for her lack of inner peace, she never had to search for another way to understand herself. Like the boy who never moves out of the mailroom can blame the shape of his ears instead of a lack of ambition.

The experience with the doctors solidified my blind trust in my mother. She was always sure that what she advised was right. I always believed her, wanting it to be true. She never shared her doubts. One day she simply announced I should throw away the pills, and I did.

Except that for the next decades this medical experiment episode bobbed around in my subconscious as a shadow object. Whenever I heard rumors connecting early estrogen and infertility or breast cancer, I worried I might be more vulnerable for having prematurely forced a change to my natural biological timeline. When gynecologists later urged me to use the Pill as birth control, I was reluctant, worrying it might add onto something already triggered in my system. When I caved to their insistence, it was with a reluctant, "Okay, I'll try it this time." But twice, when I was eighteen and when I was twenty-two, mood swings and weight gain forced me to stop estrogen contraceptives after only four months. It seemed not to suit my system.

As I read the diaries now, I can replace some of those shadowed worries with fact. I've now lived the decades that back then I imagined. I was only on the progesterone for five months, which is reassuring. It was likely not long enough to cause long-term effects. My natural menstruation started on my own timeline when I was thirteen and a half and has gone on long into my fifties with no problems. I have had three easy pregnancies and natural births. But I wonder whether my aversion to pharmaceuticals and my turn toward alternative medicine flows in part from those years. Something left me panicked by medical tests and interventions. I don't trust the mainstream medical system to work on my behalf.

A Day on the Bay

1977

THE BACKDROP TO SAN FRANCISCO IS THE BAY, with its blues
or grays, the weighted-down Chinese freighters plowing under the
bridges, the iconic *dooooop* foghorn from Alcatraz. It brings wind
and sea lions and crabs.

Fishermen earn their success by knowing what is under the water—
the currents and the poisons. But in my mother's world, the ones who
like to think they owned the Bay were those who sailed upon it. The
captains with their sloops and their yawls, their slips in Sausalito or in
China Basin or, finest of all, in the St. Francis Yacht Club, nestled for
almost a hundred years along the northern San Francisco waterfront.

After the divorce, my mother was entranced by those sailors. She
often beckoned me to that yacht club's proximity. To walk nearby, to
sunbathe on the Marina Green, to encourage me to get a job as an "Ex-
plainer" at the old Exploratorium, housed in the cavernous Palace of
Fine Arts across the street. Again and again on the weekends she led
me past the boats, sometimes as a prelude to hiking across the Bridge,
mostly to just hang out on the grass and people-watch. Frisbee tossers,
guitar players, and runners stretching.

As I read the diary entries in 1977, I wonder about this focus of hers. Was she unconsciously inoculating me, a homeopathic walk-by, so frequent exposure would ensure the moneyed class would brand itself onto my brain? If not her, then me?

In April 1977, she met a handsome divorced man named Royce Covington. Royce took her sailing, and then to dinner at the coveted yacht club.

"I felt at long last like I was not looking in anymore," she writes.

On Opening Day on the Bay that year, an April day known for its boat parade to mark the beginning of the sailing season, she was invited to accompany Royce and his "happy-go-lucky" daughters on his 36-foot sailboat. Either I was not invited, or it was my father's visitation weekend. But I, aged thirteen, wanted to go out on the Bay, too. My father had grown up sailing on the Long Island Sound and the Atlantic. Later he would own a sloop and teach sailing in Key West. But in 1977 he was politically radical, involved in civil rights, and known more for his frayed "Save the Whales" T-shirt than for his once-natural Brooks Brothers suits.

His self-image was all off kilter. He thought himself a lifetime boatsman, but the only sailboat he could afford that year was a kind of lowest-budget portable catamaran. Perhaps he bought it in a moment of make-believe—this time he would manage to get his life back on track.

My father had remarried when I was twelve, in a Golden Gate Park ceremony with a justice of the peace. Harriet was a wiry 50-something science writer. She was friendly enough to me, but when she laughed between cigarette draws, she coughed, and she had squishy puffy bags under her eyes that made her look old. They moved from charming, tasteful apartment to charming, tasteful apartment—always located around Coit Tower. Neighbors sometimes called the police. Supposedly my father once split open Harriet's head. Evictions came for disturbing the peace "with their drunken brawls," a diary entry of Mom's mentions.

I was ambivalent about spending time with my father. When he was sober, he was a scholarly, engaging conversation partner who followed the news and had been all over the world. But, at 50, his face

looked gray and baggy, the lines of virility still there but bloated, a little like an old famous actor. His skin had taken on that bitter drinker
smell. His knees were too pink, his beer belly too evident. I never saw
him do a day of cardio in his life.

He often promised something to me and then forgot. I was used
to it. He embarrassed me, but my mother gloated too strongly, and I
felt protective of him.

This day, upset that he had been spending so little time with me, I
requested we try out his new Go Boat, the low-budget catamaran. He
grudgingly arranged to put it on top of the beat-up green Volvo and
drive with me over to a marina in Sausalito. I guess he wanted to show
off with something that he remembered being second nature to him,
once practiced to his core. He wanted to make his daughter proud.

The afternoon started off fine. It was cold and gray, and never
warmed up, a typical April on the water. The breeze was strong and
exhilarating as we zipped over the whitecaps. There were so many boats
out, skippers eager to start the sailing season with a good adventure. I
remember wondering if I would see my mother out there, though I was
sulky because I knew Royce and didn't like him and his oh-so-perfect
daughters. I spent most of the first hours perched in my white Irish
sweater and yellow sailing jacket on the canvas platform strung over
the pontoons, shivering, but also thrilled. It felt good to be sharing the
outdoors with my dad.

The little boat had been heeling hard, part of the fun. Then I heard,
"Move to the starboard!" My father was yelling. I threw myself to the
right on the platform to be a counterweight to the wind. But we heeled
too far. Suddenly, I was in the water. The cold made me draw quick
breaths; my wool sweater was quickly sodden. My feet were slipping
out of my beloved leather deck shoes with their non-marking soles.
Gone. *Mommy will be mad.* I clung to an upturned hull. I could see my
father's dark hair bobbing a few feet away, his mustache above water
level, his puffy drinking face calling at me to hang on to the hull. I
remember feeling heavy with wet clothes. Waves whacked against my

ear. He wasn't there anymore. It was just me and the Bay. Suddenly his face reappeared. He grasped the sheet to lever the hull over against the current. The boat was upright again. Did he pull me onto the canvas? Did I haul myself up? All I remember is that it was freezing, and we were soaked. The wind had shifted, and it was slow going. I wanted to be home. We barely spoke. We hunched silently on the canvas, looking toward Sausalito in the afternoon gray. It was taking forever. I was shaking. Probably so was he.

Then we heard a posh voice call, "Shall we give you a tow?" It was Royce's sloop, coming on the opposite tack, slowing down and pulling around, with my mother on it and the two friendly daughters and other ladies in hats. Humiliation filled me. I watched my father's face. I could see his impulse to reject their offer of a tow. He would make his own way home, thank you. I saw Daddy take in my sodden clothes and the chilly wind.

"Yes," he nodded. "Thank you."

My mother tossed him the end of a yellow towline, which he tied around our mast. Royce ignited his motor, and our little mini boat caught the momentum and started west behind them.

Whenever I think of that day, I flash on my mother standing at the bow under her voluminous straw hat, pulling in the line and waving goodbye. All her 6 foot 2 inch length clad in a blue and white bikini; showing off tufty blond pubic curls on top of long, tanned legs, waving to us. That image can't be right. April in San Francisco is too cold. Yet it sticks, drawn from a catalog of summer sails. I hated her showing off.

My mother wrote in her diary:

A long and adventurous day on the Bay. We sailed all around Angel Island and eventually tied up with the wonderful 57-foot-deep racing ketch, *Lightning,* owned by the Karrs. We had our chicken and quiche and wine and coffee and cookies... About 3:30 we headed back to the St. Francis Yacht Club for a Mariachi party on the deck. On the way we ran into Alan and Susannah in the Go-Boat. They had overturned and were righted again but freezing. We towed them a short while. (April 24, 1977)

Did she offer to take me on board with Royce? I suspect no, awful as that feels now that I am a mother and imagine coming upon my child sodden and cold. I'm guessing she both wanted her stylish afternoon to continue uninterrupted, and wanted to ensure I received a message about my father's caretaking limits. Even if she had offered, I don't know whether I would have accepted. I already knew the patterns of power between them. I would probably have chosen loyalty to my father's failed attempt to do something good for me.

On the catamaran, I turned stalwartly toward shore as we neared Sausalito. We made it back. We tugged the boat out of the water; packed it on the car, drove back to my father's apartment, heat blasting over our feet. I remember finding Harriet transfixed to a television movie, sniveling loudly, her eyes bloodshot, her nose snotty. She barely noticed us. I had a shower to get warm.

I don't remember ever talking to my mother about that day and she never asked. Just as with my grandmother Gummy's death, I suspect I vied for myself. It would take years for me to learn that there was another way, that some parents make a point of reviewing the good and bad of a day with their children, that there are explicit dinnertime games or the telling of the day's "roses" and "thorns."

At bedtime, my mother always called to me, "Don't forget to say your prayers." Maybe this call embodied the same intention. But the child at the table is accompanied while the child in prayer is alone. Certainly, I tried to ensure my children never witnessed a drama or had an argument or a heartbreak without me circling back to inquire if they were okay. They were never supposed to worry that I didn't acknowledge them.

Riptides

2017

I'm halfway through reading the diaries and I've decided to keep a record of the memories and reactions that are surfacing. I'm on my way to a writing group in the Santa Cruz mountains that will hopefully help me make sense of it all. I pull right, off the empty street, into the Rotten Robbie gas station. *Hmm, $3.19 a gallon. What would it have been at Costco? I should have gone there. No, fill it up, you'll only worry, being up in Bonny Doon with just that little bit in the tank. I'm late, maybe I should just fill up $10 worth.*

Credit card in, I pump the gas.

My head feels full of stories and scenarios, a little dazed, full of my dead mother's words that I have been reading all weekend, still shocked by how much it drains me to identify with her when she is kind, how capable I am of feeling her feelings and forgetting about myself.

Five minutes later, I wait to make a left turn back onto what is normally the busy four-lane Mission Street. *No traffic. Nice. Is it always like this on a Sunday morning?* I start across, intending to turn into the far lanes. Halfway out I look to the left, register a green car speeding directly toward me. It would crash right into my driver's side door. No swerving necessary. Just straight in. I stay there, paralyzed, watching it come closer.

Move! Now! Somewhere words materialize. My foot presses hard on the gas pedal. I zoom safely across into the empty lanes, even before the Prius has to brake. My heart is pounding. That was just a millisecond. I had felt frozen, as if I had been ready to welcome a disaster, as if I were a bystander to something I had no control over. *What the hell?* I pull to the side of the street.

Instantly, my mind brings me back to Manresa Beach. I'm standing rooted to the sand, watching Leah's ten-year-old little head bob farther and farther out to sea. Just a second before, I had been calmly indicating she must swim to the side of the riptide, gesturing, *move right, move right,* arms beginning to windmill to mime she must swim, swim! Then, suddenly, she is only a little blond head, getting lost in the waves. I just stand there. I am disconnected from myself. I had just seen the lifeguard pull a swimmer from exactly this riptide, which had prompted my mimed instructions to her. I can see his red trunks in my peripheral vision, reaching for his red rubber rescue tube, running into the surf. I somehow know he is going to save her. But why don't I move? Why didn't I do something myself? Was I just going to stand there while my daughter drowned?

I'm scared by these two encounters. I tell myself it's okay, somewhere I had known the lifeguard was there. Just as I knew I would move the car to avoid the crash just now. But it's like those times we drive and then realize we are twenty miles farther along and don't remember getting there. What is really going on with me? In the face of danger, why do I feel I am reverting to something archaic? As if I should just curl up into a ball and put my hands over my ears. If I just wait it will be over.

It isn't until I begin to come upon research on the effects of trauma on memory that I can piece these interactions together. Much like finally understanding how that scene of domestic violence on the *vaporetto* triggered a panic, I see the daze created by years and years of exposure to my mother's words and actions short-circuiting my adult self.

Busing

1975

BY THE TIME I GOT TO JUNIOR HIGH SCHOOL, our family reality had changed—my grandfather had married Phyllis; my grandmother Gummy was no longer part of our conversations. My father was ready to remarry. My mother was dating, and I was being primed for the progesterone pills. All that brought its own complexity. But those years were, foremost, dominated by the experiences my mother and I had in urban schools. Almost like being caught in no-man's land between two countries at war, it colored our futures. As a teacher to inner city Black students and then to waves of refugee Asian students, she learned to advocate for social justice and moved farther away from the world of her parents. I learned to be street smart and I learned to sidestep.

Tap, tap, on my shoulder in class. "Hey, gimme your pencil."

Oh god, leave me alone. Please don't bother me.

Poke. "Hey bitch, gimme your pencil!"

She was sitting on a bench behind me. Her friends had pencils. Rubber soles squeaked as shoes changed position on the waxed floor. There were snickers. I felt queasy. She was wearing a green polyester shirt and had her hair in cornrows. She looked older than the others in our seventh-grade gym class.

We were gathered in the cafeteria filling out a human health worksheet. I had seen her causing trouble the first week. I concentrated doubly hard on the words on the paper in front of me. Poke, even harder this time. In my timidity, I finally decided to rely on the teacher to settle this.

"Mr. Johnson, Jolanda keeps poking me."

Mr. Johnson looked up, but all he saw was Jolanda staring out the window. Jolanda scared me. I knew she didn't really want my pencil.

"Imma catch you after class, stupid bitch!" she sniped at me. I felt my shoulders constrict.

I had already figured out never to go to the bathroom in my new school. Marina Junior High in San Francisco was an impressive building. Its stone neoclassical facade and tall ceilings both dwarfed and intimidated its students. I had been looking forward to leaving elementary school. Finally, an end to those boring sixth grade fraction repetitions and smeary textbooks with simplified illustrations. But Marina was like many American schools built in the 1930s, a bit neglected and too expansive to oversee properly. To this day, when I approach a school bathroom, I tense. I am ready to find high-ceilinged gray walls, a row of grimy windows way at the top, hazy smoke-filled air, and a bunch of tough Black girls lounging on the sinks by the mirror. To the White girl frozen in the doorway, they say: "What you lookin' at?"

And the 12-year-old me is backing hastily into the hall. *Never mind.* I won't need the bathroom ever again.

At lunch recess, after that fraught gym class and then algebra, I sought a bench in the schoolyard flush against the building. I perched on the smooth wooden slats and looked around for a teacher on yard duty, my red checked lunchbox open on my lap. I secretly surveyed the four-acre asphalt playground in front of me. The mass of kids all seemed to be screaming and playing tag. Maybe they were having fun. I didn't see anyone I knew. I unrolled the top of my lunch's wax paper bag. A butter and honey sandwich. *Yuk.* My least favorite. At least there were raisins, too. And a chocolate chip cookie. I looked up. Jolanda and four other girls had gathered around in a semi-circle.

"Bitch, you gonna get up here and fight me?"

I sat perfectly still. "No."

Maybe she would go away if I didn't respond.

"Punk, you think you better than me?" She waited.

Where is a teacher? "No."

What had my mother always said? Pretend to be tougher than you are.

"Leave me alone."

Her friends grabbed me. I held onto the lunchbox for a second. Then red checks fell with a metal jangle to the ground. Whack. She punched me in the back.

"Go away!" I turned and wrestled myself out of their arms, felt my fist strike something of hers, felt my wrist collapse too weakly.

Jolanda laughed. The tension left her friends' bodies, they started walking away, jostling each other, having a good time. I was shaking. I slunk from classroom to classroom for the rest of the day; terrified I'd run into her again.

I walked home on the route I knew I'd find only safe people going in and out of their apartments, my backpack dragging on my shoulders as the hills got steeper. I watched television and put the chicken potpie into the oven for dinner. When my mother finally returned home after her staff meeting, I told her what had happened.

"Well, what an obnoxious girl!" she said. "I'm glad nothing more happened to you."

I couldn't imagine going back to school the next day. "I don't want to go to school tomorrow."

"Just shine her on," she said. "They're just acting tough."

My stomach hurt that night.

The next morning, I took the 41 Union bus to school, telling myself to relax, knowing I would not run into Jolanda as I rode the public bus. She came with the yellow school buses from across the city. I didn't run into her at school. In fact, I never saw her at school again. But a few days later, one of her friends hassled me. School was becoming a frightening place. My mother wrote:

I do feel bad and wonder if I should put her in a private school. She likes the teachers however. We'll ride along for six weeks. After dinner studied Italian and then did exercises and listened to calm music. Got some summer photos back. (September 10, 1975)

For my mother, who wrote a book called *Lanky Honky Bitch* about being a White teacher in San Francisco public schools, I think teaching was a vehicle to escape her own inhibitions. A classroom offered a stage upon which to act and inspire. She loved literature. She thought it fun to require her students to learn vocabulary words like "dolt" and "pusillanimous." But it was also real. The potential was there to make a true difference. She wrote:

> Guiltily I insisted on class spelling tests and vocabulary lists for homework, with stand-up oral spelling bees for review. This "outmoded methodology" was administratively frowned upon and I tried to assuage my feelings with the realization that a test at the beginning of class was a good attendance and attention getter. Scores improved as did enthusiasm for the ritual as the months passed and the necessity for doing some studying at home sank in. … "Number your papers from one to ten," "No name, no credit," … was a regular litany, but it seemed both to energize and soothe the youngsters who often felt visceral discomfort at the word "test" and who had to be convinced that they could succeed if they studied beforehand." (*Lanky Honky Bitch*, pg. 59).

Her diaries describe the struggles of those first years, but her public persona was pure confidence. To an entranced audience of family or friends at dinner parties she would often relate her classroom adventures.

"You should have seen what I did today," she started one time. "The class was in chaos. Ezekiel came in late. Some brother or other had lit one of his braids on fire."

My mother pushed her chair back from the dinner table, ready to leap up to enact the scene.

"Students jumped up around him," she continued. "Oooo, that be baaad," students yelled."

My mother rose up. "Chaos. What was I supposed to do to get back control of the classroom? I yelled 'Quiet!' but nobody listened."

She took in the entranced audience around the table. "So, I climbed up onto the teacher's desk, all 6 foot 2 of me, I grabbed onto the biggest dictionary I had. I held it up over my head. I let it fall. *Blamm.* I got everyone's attention." She hooted with pride.

Everyone laughed at the idea of this proper white lady climbing up on the desk. I wished I could be so entertaining.

My mother also began to have a secret affair with a charismatic Black administrator around this time. "Tell him 'She is on her way to Abu Dhabi,'" she'd instruct me brightly when the phone rang, motioning I should pick up the handle.

"Good evening. May I speak with Jane?" a Barry White voice would say smoothly into my ear. My heart would sink.

"No, she isn't home right now. She is on her way to Abu Dhabi," I obediently recited.

I hated being forced into such a farce and didn't understand the theatrics. How could he believe she would leave me while she flitted off around the world? I surmised she was avoiding this man's calls because he was bothering her. Now, as I read about her affair in the diaries, I'm sure the instructions were code words for their secret weekend rendezvous. Perhaps Abu Dhabi was a certain hotel. Sometimes she changed it to Palm Springs. Sometimes to Paris. It was all so preposterous.

Both my parents, who had been educated in private schools, were firm believers in public education. My father was inspired by his work with the Zone II Council, a citizens group ensuring San Francisco adhered to federal desegregation policy. I overheard his heartfelt arguments on the importance of busing and rezoning. "The only way to enact lasting change was to bring children of different racial neighborhoods together," he would say.

I wanted to do the right thing. The busing experiment in San Francisco meant Black and White students were transported in yellow school buses across the city in certain grades. In third grade I had been bused to a predominantly Black school. In 7th and 8th grade, Black kids were bused to the junior high in my area. While elementary school desegregation worked well, the reality of race relations on the street in junior high and high school was precarious.

I never walked without being vigilant, ready to cross to the other side of the street if it looked like trouble was ahead. I remember each bus ride being a calculation, drivers regularly stopping the bus because a fight had broken out among the teen passengers. I already knew a White girl should never, *ever* sit in the back of the bus. Often, I preferred to walk home, my heavy backpack bouncing as I counted the steps up the hill, one to 100 and then back to one. Fear and anger at school filled all the in-between places. The prevailing rage amongst students meant any "Yo Mama" could result in a fight. Class was constantly interrupted by a lightning strike tearing of hair and earrings, or a discipline referral banging on doors on his way to the principal's office. I trod carefully and often hid in the library.

But I loved my teachers. I had a few friends, and one best friend, Lori. She was a misfit too, a stocky Japanese-American girl who would eventually become a rock drummer and an artist. We kept each other company walking up Fillmore Street before getting on buses crowded with students chatting in Cantonese. My 41 Union bus passed through Chinatown, and I was always grateful for the crowds of Asian students, long black hair often smelling like another kind of cooking oil. They wouldn't attack me. They wouldn't touch me where I didn't want to be touched. Even though I was taller than all the girls, I felt I could hide with them in the front of the bus until my stop came.

At home, I was what was called a latchkey child. Too old for babysitters but not old enough to babysit others, I was often alone while my mother attended faculty meetings and project groups. I watched afternoon television: *The $100,000 Pyramid, Hollywood*

Squares, I Dream of Jeannie. I did my homework and put myself to bed. I read grownup books like *All the President's Men.*

And Holocaust literature.

Those cattle cars, those children.

Reading about that dreadful sorrow, much worse than my own, always seemed to ease the tightness between my ribs.

First Kisses

Late 1970s

SNUGGLING IN MY TWIN BED AT NIGHT with the light off and the door, as always, left open a crack, my family of plastic Breyer horses watching from the shelf, I heard James and my mother smooching and kissing goodnight. *Yuk. Ewwww.* I was grossed out, at age ten, and also uneasy, as if I were privy to something unseemly, and a little curious. Why *did* she murmur and kiss so loudly right outside my bedroom door? Is that what kissing sounds like? I had no memories of the sounds of love between my mother and father, and television at that time showed only chaste pecks on the cheek. I had no idea about any of that man-woman stuff. All I felt was uncomfortable. So, for a long time I just put the whole subject out of my mind. Kissing became something vaguely powerful and threatening, like the rumble of thunder in the distance. I had no interest in junior high school Valentines. No party games, no Spin the Bottle. I remember eighth grade friends in a circle on the fields adjacent to the Marina, flirting by searching for a bottle. Long before any bottle could be found, I had left, stomach clenched, for the hilly walk home, my heavy bags of books a comforting totem of the safe haven of reading. No dating, no boys. I avoided it all.

Until Noah—who was tall and high cheek-boned and had just moved back to San Francisco after years in Israel.

I can't remember the details of my first real kiss. It was hurried, after he brought me home from the Harvest Ball at the Hyatt Regency my sophomore year in high school. In my vision are Noah's lips unannounced, heading down toward my mouth and my lips miraculously staying still so that I actually felt the touch of his skin on mine. Less than a second, and so unspectacular. So different from those screen first kisses my daughter now learns from—drawn-out Hollywood seconds full of longing and perfect arcs and just the right amount of anticipation. Wow, those kisses make me want to be fifteen again like nothing else can.

But I do remember vividly my first languorous slow dance in the basement hangout room of Noah's family's Richmond District townhouse. We had finished celebrating a Friday night Shabbat meal. His mother, with her thick curly red hair and vivacious personality, had welcomed me warmly to the candlelit table. Noah's younger sister and brother had been there, too. Even more than the brief delight of lips on lips I had now experienced a few times, it was that evening of being welcomed into a family entirely different from my own and their foreignness that started me down a path so different from my mother's.

Jane and I would never learn to share the girly closeness of whispered women's wisdom, nor were we ever able to find a vocabulary to talk about the unexpectedness I'd encountered peeking into the world of Noah's family. My life would lead toward questioning my culture and curiosity about other places, but she never wanted to share such discoveries with me.

Up until that Shabbat evening, Noah and I had shared bus rides and phone calls and the daily gossip of high school students, all relatively mundane and expected. I *liked* him. But that evening the *like* opened into something more curious and powerful, altering the boy I had known. The formally set table and a light-hearted hush in the room showed this was an event repeated so often it had never occurred to the participants to be self-conscious or shy in its sharing. I was a guest in something secretive and magical. I had no such rituals in my twosome house of Sunday Mass and silver place settings. Noah's mother solemnly struck the match to light each candle, waving her hands toward her face, covering her eyes. The strange-sounding Hebrew words, *"Baruch atah Adonai..."* were sung in a foreign rhythm, and the *"Shabbat Shalom"* each child knew to respond in turn was spoken clearly and honorably. It was as if this boy I was getting to know at school was suddenly transformed into someone with unexpected and desirable layers. There was a surprise here, a depth to him.

After dinner, Noah had simply announced we would be going downstairs for a while. He had put Lynyrd Skynyrd's "Free Bird" on the turntable. He pulled me to him, and we slow-danced and kissed forever, my first exploration of tongues and clothed heartbeats. It was the kind of encounter I'm always wishing for my own children, slow and melting and really rather innocent. On the way home on the bus across the city, we sat close together just behind the back door, and every time he touched my hand a lightning bolt went through my body. If I let myself stay awhile with that memory of him, I can conjure up the way his cheek blushed slightly as he laughed and inclined his head in what I now recognize was hidden lust. His fingers played with mine. I registered that my underwear was moist between my legs. Back then I did not know of all these things, but it wasn't unpleasant or weird. It was pleasurable. And I was in love.

My mother's diary does mention the two of us, but while Noah was becoming the center of my emotional life, she was focusing on the happenings of the outer world. Diane Feinstein became mayor of San Francisco. Before that, Harvey Milk had been assassinated. Teachers would go on strike in the fall of 1979 and she would be laid off and rehired as a substitute without benefits. Her uncle Ed had had a stroke, a demise of an already violent man, which would tear apart the cousins my mother had come to rely on as close relatives. She was just forty-one, but she sounds to my ears thirty years older.

> Another solitary and boring Saturday. Re: my non-existent so-
> cial life, I have consciously disengaged from those I know and
> do not enjoy. So, for boredom with people I have received bore-
> dom without people. ... Susannah is in a snit over Noah. She
> will alienate him with her possessiveness. (February 17, 1979)

I most certainly did not come home and tell her about slow dancing or Shabbat. My mother told me nothing about her inner life, and
I was figuring out that restraint was better than sharing when it came
to emotions. For a while she seemed to like Noah, but she was not at-
tuned to the world that was opening up in my soul.

In February, she wrote:

> I am really paying some dues with Susannah lately. She is not
> studying, is willful and defiant in a nice quiet sort of way. ie...
> "Come home right after the game" brings a phone call at 5:50
> asking to eat at Noah's. "Write to Sarah," no letter. "Study," —
> she's asleep on the couch. "Get to bed at 10 o'clock," and she
> starts to wash her hair at 9:45. (February 13, 1979)

That February and March my grades started to slip. My school days
were consumed with seeing Noah, sharing a few moments, walking to class
together, arranging to attend his basketball games. Every sign of distance
from him was a worry that became an inner catastrophe for me. I couldn't
concentrate on any schoolwork. From A's, I began to slip to B's and C's.

At the end of March, after four months, Noah told me he wanted
to "see other girls."

School became torture. Mom was amazed at my sadness, expecting me to shrug his rejection off like light snowflakes from my shoulders. "He needs to see other people. He's a young man," she told me
repeatedly. Her diaries give no clue that she understood what the loss
of this boy might mean for a girl from a broken home who had suddenly learned to love.

I spent weeks retreating at night to the living room so that my mother wouldn't hear me crying. Finally, she suggested I go visit my father in Washington D.C. for Easter break while she visited cousins in Virginia. We flew together to the East Coast and it was a big adventure for me to travel by train to Washington alone.

In Washington, Daddy picked me up at the station and drove me back to the pretty townhouse where he was living with Harriet. He was still working for McGraw Hill and she was a science writer for the Smithsonian. While I was unpacking in their basement guest room waiting for dinnertime, I surveyed all their books. I wondered what he had planned for the week. He had told me on the phone that the new Air and Space Museum was really interesting. Suddenly my ears picked up a sharp crash overhead. I stopped breathing, poised like one of those statue games as a child. I must have known that sound. My braid fell to the side. I waited. One, two, three seconds passed. Okay. *Relax! It was nothing.* I reached into my suitcase to take out my toothbrush to put near the bathroom sink. Then I heard Harriet's voice, a muffled yelling. I couldn't make out her words, but they were loud and angry. Another crash. She was throwing plates. My father's lower, irate voice followed. Then more plates.

I sat on the edge of the bed. My mind felt like it was stuck in gelatin. I surveyed the room. The red wool carpet, the white pillow on the bed. I couldn't move. More fighting upstairs. It didn't sound like it would stop. *Didn't they remember I was here?* The voices continued. I stayed on the bed for what felt like an hour. Then I walked over to the door, put my hand on the handle, and turned the knob. Crash. Another plate. I closed the door quickly. I could feel my insides shaking. *This isn't fair!* A few more minutes went by. Muffled voices upstairs.

Then, as I sat there waiting, something changed. *Hold on, I'm a teenager now.* In an instant my lungs opened up. My shoulders released. I was still afraid but there was something new. I was also angry.

I'll run away. I pictured him coming downstairs and calling my name. "Susannah?" A knock on the door. No answer. Guilty, he'd open the door and find me gone. Harriet would be sorry for causing this. Shame on them. I eyed the sliding window of my basement room. *I'll sneak out!* Heart beating wildly, I put my clothes back into my suitcase and slid the window open. Now that I had finally come up with the plan, I didn't want them to interrupt me before I left. I clambered out and hustled around the back corner of the townhouse.

A few blocks away, I found a pay phone and called my mother's first cousin Jenny. She lived in Arlington, which wasn't that far away. She was the kind of mother who would drop everything for a hurting child. I knew my mother had told her I would be in D.C.

"Jenny, this is Susannah," I said. My voice must have sounded small. "My father and Harriet are fighting and I don't want to be here anymore."

"Where are you?" she asked without any preamble.

I looked around for the street signs. "I'm on the corner of Woodley Road and Wisconsin."

"Do you feel safe where you are?"

It was late afternoon, it was a residential neighborhood and there were people walking their dogs. "Yes, I guess so."

"Wait there. I'll be there as soon as I can," she said.

Jenny and Greg took me in without question or drama. They just set another place at their table, made me a cozy bed on their porch, and said I was welcome to stay as long as I wanted. I'm guessing Jenny must have called my mother, who called my father. In the evening she came onto the porch.

"Honey," Jenny said. "Your dad is on the phone. He would like to talk to you."

Reluctantly, I followed her back to the telephone by the piano.

"Hello," I said quietly.

My father's deep voice spoke slowly. "I'm sorry this happened, Susannah."

"Yeah."

"I'd like for you to come back."

I remember holding the phone. I remember feeling pulled back toward him, thinking I shouldn't make a scene. I should just return and not be a burden. *Don't be so dramatic. It wasn't so bad after all.*

I remember saying, "I want to stay here."

And feeling strong. I was old enough to choose.

In Front of the Camera

1980

"OH, YES, HON, NOW LOOK INTO THE CAMERA. Look up at me like you want to fuck me right here. Great. Now look at me like I'm your bad dog that just peed on the floor."

It was another Saturday photo shoot. I had started modeling my junior year in high school, somewhat reluctantly, urged along by my mother. We had always relished reading *People* magazine together, and she loved the idea of a daughter who models. I liked the idea of it, too. The reality was different. It was a job that involved taking the bus on the weekends to some unspectacular location like a boring suite of offices on Pine Street, sitting for an hour while make-up was applied by a professional stylist then strutting around in front of a man and his camera—it was never a woman—for an hour or two. After Noah broke up with me the previous year, I had a few desultory dates, mostly with boys my mother's friends set up for me, or from then-all-boy-school St. Ignatius dances that I was jostled into attending.

"Just go, you'll have fun," my mother would say. *Ugh.* The boys annoyed me, and I'm sure I annoyed them.

What had really been happening was I had begun to develop a double life: the real me versus the one getting attention out there in the world. This new double identity was full of strange challenges, like how to pretend to be someone confident while quaking inside, or how to flirt warmly while keeping distance. It was an identity change by attrition, animated by DNA that grew me tall and fair, powered by a troublesome wish to make my mother happy.

The summer I was sixteen, my mother turned forty-two. She was single but having a secret affair with James, an older, married man. She was struggling on a teacher's income yet yearned to oversee a staff of domestic servants. Summers became her getaway. The dollar was strong and our travel guides were *Europe on $10 a Day*. I was her accomplice. We had already been to Venice four times starting when I was nine, the summer my grandmother's cancer had returned. That year, I had shared my European adventures with two plastic horses, heads sticking out of each side of my purse as if they were peering out of a stall. They had been my friends.

I had taken happily to the task of reading the city guides as we picnicked on baguettes and salami in London and Paris and Rome, deciding which museums or new churches my mother and I would visit that day. In every new church, we lit a candle and made a wish, a game that meant I saw a lot of churches, and we uttered a lot of prayers.

"If I were to die now please note. Jane Quilter Kennedy hated being so terribly tall and she hated being not rich and famous," her diary reads from January that year. I'm guessing her prayers revolved around wealth and fame. By then, mine were prayers for boys and grades.

In those summers, she and I became a comfortable traveling team. The days leading up to the trips were always full of her worries and plans, last-minute packing and fretting. But we would eventually settle into a companionable twosome. I had her attention finally, and she could relax. Her spirit was hindered by private anxiety, which I felt but did not understand. She turned to her love of Italy and took comfort from "the only sure thing a teacher's life gives me, a long summer off." She always seemed happiest in Italy.

The first big change that led to my double life in high school was my hair. Though I had been blond all my childhood, my teen hair had started to turn darker—like my father's, more evidence for her that I was closer to his alcoholism and failure. When I was thirteen, on a stopover in Paris, which sounds nicer than it was on our low budget, my mother pulled a package of hair dye and peroxide out of her suitcase. "You don't want to let your hair go dark, believe me," she said to convince me. I wanted to be beautiful like she was, so although it felt wrong, I dutifully put my head over our hotel room sink with its hot and cold separate jets and allowed her to apply the dye. The next day we ran into one of her friends.

"Oh, you dyed your hair!" her friend said on the street corner.

"No!" I yelped. "I just shampooed it." I knew she knew I was lying, but I looked her steadily in the eye.

The hair dye was just the beginning.

The second part of my change was a result of cross country and track, which on the surface was promoted by my new best friend Mela nie, an avid runner, but in my heart was a tactic to rekindle former boy-friend Noah's interest. Noah was an athlete; he would be on the team. The most recent summer in Italy had swelled my confidence. Boys and men had started to pay attention to me. It was now not just my long-legged blond mother with an accompanying child who got the calls of "*bella*," but it was the two of us, looking almost like sisters that caused a commotion wherever we went. "*Siete sorelle?*" they would ask. My mother would feign a blush, "No, she is my daughter," and would laugh in delight as one much shorter delightful Italian man or another would hold his hands to his heart and fall backward in theatrical love.

I figured my Italian experience would somehow have changed me and that Noah would notice. *Noah will watch me sweep through the finish line strides ahead of everyone. He'll walk over and say he misses me.*

My first race in Golden Gate Park that September started off with a circle around the track before heading off onto a three-mile dirt path course. Full of adrenalin, I kept up with the pack around the oval, but found myself breathing hard and woozy by the last corner.

"Put your hands above your head," Coach Thomas yelled.

My legs already wobbling, I stopped. *Woah, shit, what's happening?*

"Hands above your head," he yelled, coming toward me.

We were practically alone now, as all the other runners were gone. "Keep going, walk fast, you'll get your oxygen levels back. You don't have to run the whole way. Just do your best."

Well, this wasn't going to catch Noah's eye, that was clear. But with the coach's help, my concentration narrowed from everything going on around me, including whether Noah was watching (he wasn't), to an inner place, to slowing my breathing, to putting one foot in front of the other. The beginning of learning to value inner strength. Just keep going. Just finish the course. And somehow, I did. Noah's family moved to Beverly Hills, but I continued to train. I dreamed of running into him in a state meet. I dreamed of a new seduction.

A byproduct of this track fantasy was a changed body. My mother's favorite phrase reverberated still: "Susannah Banana, you are like a calf and I am like a foal."

Photos show that though I was slender all through this period, once I started track and modeling, I became unusually skinny. I was barely eating—half a grapefruit and orange juice in the morning, perhaps a sandwich or cookie for lunch on the back lawn, and then workouts every day after school. By the time I walked the half-mile up Eucalyptus Drive to the Muni stop to head back to the other side of the city to be home around 7 p.m., I often felt I would faint on the tram. I wasn't a strong runner, whether due to genetics or my unbalanced nutrition. Did my mother worry?

There is nothing in her diaries about this, just annoyance that I was not studying enough. "She spends too much time at track. I don't see her studying much. She is so tired her light is off before 10."

Junior year, within a few months of "getting my portfolio together," which meant paying for pictures or finding a young photographer with whom to exchange modeling for photos, I had an agent, a flamboyant tall Black man whose office was in a semi-abandoned building south of Market. This in itself felt grownup, as South of Market then was a seedy part of town, a place I never would have gone as a White high school student. Leon was funny, and for the most part watched out for me. A minor in the modeling business has precautions in place. I wasn't allowed on shoots alone unless Leon knew the photographer. I wasn't allowed to work late hours. I wasn't allowed to do anything full- or semi-nude. I was paid more than $100/hour when I had paid work, and that was a heady amount for a teenager in 1980. When cousin Trevor—a gay New Yorker, teller of scandalous bathhouse tales—visited, he and my mother would coach me in how to become The Star, to learn to use men rather than let myself be used by them.

"I can just see you towering over them," Trevor hooted.

"The client will say you need to do a summer of runway work for him and then he'll take you on as a cover model," sang my mother. "And you'll snap your fingers and look him in the eye and say, 'This girl is no bimbo. Show me the money first.'"

They would be off on a rollicking riff that perfectly reflected my mother and Trevor's love of the stage but had little to do with me.

One time another model and her mother came over for tea.

"Margot and I found the best nail person," her mother said. "Margot, come here, show Susannah your nails."

With enviable delight, Margot held out her slender hands.

"Look how her beds are perfectly oval," her mother continued. "She got called for a go-see for a lotion company next week."

Margot seemed very proud and swished her straight brown hair. "Let me see yours."

My fingers would never be that tiny. I couldn't muster the interest. I felt I should. So, I tried. I held out my hands. I never even wore nail polish.

"You have wider beds than I do, but your hands are very pretty," Margot said. "Do you prefer square nails or rounded ones?"

We somehow managed an afternoon tea together, but I knew I would never be a hand model.

Instead, I was mastering the language of camera love. It was the precursor to the selfie smile: *Happiness* projected through every pore. Pre-smart phone, not everyone could do that special kind of smiling, just as not everyone can walk the high-heeled runway strut. Despite endless pacing with a book upon my head and my hips jutting side to side, I never felt graceful in high heels. But I had a good smile.

* * *

In June 1980, at the end of my junior year, my mother and I prepared to leave for Italy again. The dollar was high against the Italian lira. She rented out our apartment for three months, betting that a summer in Venice would ease her unhappiness and give her strength for a new school year. I was almost six feet tall, had long blonde hair and was very thin. I had just been on a go-see to Esprit, a hot fashion brand at the time, and been hired for their prestigious catalog, which meant a week-long trip to Mexico in the fall and dancing on the sand for Oliviero Toscani, a *Vogue* photographer. The pictures from that audition show me high jumping around in various positions; arms splayed playfully, every visible rib like a starving zebra evident under my tube top. Their parting words to me after the go-see were, "Don't eat too much pasta!"

I was looking forward to my other life, time with my mother away from her fraught San Francisco persona, time to wander Italian streets, to watch people. A part of me was still the little twelve-year-old who calmed her mommy's nerves by anticipating which terminal we needed in the airport, who read aloud to her for hours from *Watership Down*, who slept in the neighboring twin bed during loud midnight *temporali* thunder and lay patiently in the sun for eight hours a day until her attention awoke to me again.

But this would turn out to be a different summer, one which turned the tables on our mother-daughter balance.

By then, we knew Venice better than regular tourists. We felt almost like we lived there. We knew how to walk our favorite paths to San Marco, which *vaporetto* to take to the Lido, and which restaurants were both inexpensive and delicious. Last summer, after a couple of weeks of surveying the scene at the crowded public beach, my mother had begun to tire of the stands with cheap Limonata and curious bands of youths who crowded around: "*Che bella, quanto sei alta? Giochi a pallacanestro?*"—"How tall are you? Do you play basketball?"

She had discovered that a 6 foot 2 inch model-thin blonde and her beautiful now-blonde daughter could meander onto the lush green grounds of the two Lido luxury hotels without anyone batting an eye. She had begun to tutor me in pretending to be a fancy hotel guest.

"Look like you belong and you do belong." We had taken to our lounges as if we lived there. "Walk straight in, don't fidget, head proud, look like you know where you are going."

I hated it. I spent most of my days on these excursions fretting each time a white-uniformed staff member approached. I was sure we'd be evicted. It never happened. Nobody seemed to care. Her gamble worked.

After a while, she figured out the guests in these beach resorts traveled back and forth to Venice via sleek mahogany private taxi, and that they did this by presenting a special guest pass. So she invested in a room for a night in the old-world Europa & Regina hotel, and sure enough we received white passes with gold CIGA Hotel lettering that conferred our privileged guest status for a day.

From that first boat ride to the Lido, I was enraptured.

The movie-star beautiful driver extended his hand to me, guiding me onto the rolling boat. Our hands and eyes zinged, as every such encounter zings with Italian men adept at complimenting a woman for being a woman in whatever shape and form. I relaxed on the U-shaped cushioned bench in the back along with the other guests, next to my mother, hair down and blowing in the breeze, round '70s sunglasses shielding our eyes. I felt so glamorous, so gorgeous. I was sniffing at the air of the rich and I liked everything about it. I loved racing past the public *vaporetti* across the huge lagoon. Until then, the slow public boats heading to the beach had chugged along with a welcome churn and groan. Now we left them far behind.

Our arrival on the beach island Lido this time was along a hidden landscaped canal passage, to dock next to a wooden pier with a blue awning and liveried doormen. *"Buon giorno, Signorina,"* they said. Then we walked through the vast high-ceilinged, marble lobby to appear at a pool with perfectly manicured dark green lawns, cushioned lounges, and stacks of fluffy towels. It was a type of heaven.

The next day, we checked out of the Europa & Regina and carried our bags over to the other side of the Grand Canal to our modest pensione. There was no air conditioning, bathrooms were down the hall, and shared. But it was vine-covered and charming, old world and beautiful. It was our familiar Venetian home away from home. And now we had our CIGA cards. Very carefully we altered the pen-written dates to show we were CIGA guests, not for that one Europa & Regina night, but for a whole month. Each day, we walked over to the CIGA hotel, through the lobby doors, onto the waiting taxi pier, as if we were returning from a shopping spree, to board the *motoscafo* directly to the beach. I was afraid of being turned away, that somebody would find us out. But I made do. And learned to pretend.

One particular Venetian restaurant had become a favorite of ours. Tucked off a *calle* near the Rialto, its many dining rooms attracted locals and tourists in the know. It was a hive of activity. It was a world of chaos and formality, 12-foot white walls hung with a mishmash of paintings. No guest was rushed; tables were awarded for the evening.

Three years before, on a visit to the restaurant, a young man in a waiter's starched coat had kept appearing in a corner of our dining room. He was standing still and observing me. He was handsome but didn't look like a playboy. I blushed. A few days later, we ate there again. There he had been, shy and regal. His very hesitancy seemed flirtatious. As the evening went on, our waiter began to make a fuss, exaggerating his pouring of the water and my mother's wine, and as we laughed, he extended the game. He began to play the matchmaker between us. The young man blushed. I blushed. It was so much fun.

Part of the enjoyment for me is to see Susannah blossoming into a boy-crazy flirt and see how many admiring stares and smiles she gets. (August 18, 1977)

It was a new experience for me, shy as I was.

Two summers later in 1979, we were back in Venice, but the restaurant was *Chiuso per ferie* (closed for vacation). So, we ate somewhere else and strolled to San Marco. My mother splurged on a special drink at Grancaffè Quadri, one of the old-world cafes on the square, small round tables splayed around an orchestral stage. Two twenty-something men walked by and tried to catch our eyes. Something about their audacity and fun and intelligence caused my mother to flirt back. I was mortified. She invited them to sit down. They spoke good English. One seemed interested in my mother and the other in me. It turned out the cutest one of them played the guitar and insisted on coming to serenade us at the pensione the next evening. My mother agreed. What was she thinking?

Indeed, they arrived the next evening after dinner, to find us sitting in the garden under the grape arbor. Carlo sang beautiful Brazilian jazz and classical, words and melodies. The water lapped against the stone steps, the *putt-putt* of small motorboats and the occasional slap of an oar was the percussion. Carlo invited us to his family's small apartment in Mestre, and in the next few weeks, because my mother spoke Italian, our families became conduits to our romance. We were invited out on a boat trip with a cousin. We were invited to their cabana on the section of the Lido crowded with families. Our days began to fall together, and the evenings, when finally, Carlo and I were left alone, meant strolls along the Zattere, an ice-cream cone at Gelateria Nico, scouting out a wide concrete bench for an endless kiss infused with the enticing smell of summer, garlic, cologne and his cigarettes. I loved the deliciousness of the moonlight and the water, the feeling of being welcomed into a family, of being cherished and included.

This junior year summer, however, everything changed. Though Carlo expected to start where we had left off and I had been looking forward to seeing him, I also could not resist visiting the restaurant to find the handsome waiter. And there he was. The blushing and glances began again.

It turned out the young man in the waiter's coat was the owner's son. Ah. The other waiters played Cupid, he brought me a red rose and made it be known we were not to pay for dinner. When we left, he met us at the door.

"Will you be on the Lido tomorrow? *Ci vediamo là?*"

It turned out that his family rented a cabana at the very five-star Excelsior hotel that my mother and I had been sneaking into. So Paolo and I began to meet on Wednesdays, and through his friends I was brought into another kind of Venice. Owning a prominent restaurant meant Paolo was learning to rise at four in the morning to barter at the market for the best catch of the day, then create the menu. His future meant accepting a life of few days off, of financial responsibility for an extended family of restaurant staff, and deep roots with friends known since childhood. It meant protecting his Venetian identity, raising his children in Venice. It was honorable and very different from the "you can become anyone you want" culture of American teenagers.

My mother, meanwhile, was studying Italian every morning and getting closer to Carlo's family. Their genuine warmth and friendship, which grew into long exchanges of letters and regular visits, filled the increasing gaps between Carlo and me. Though he rarely came to the Lido anymore, the families maintained an opening, allowing us to navigate the hurts and years later become true friends. I wasn't yet at a point in life to value Carlo's struggles with his military father and was drawn to the liveliness of his family's Venetian cabana life, the card games, the tanned skin, the bikinis on grandmothers, the gossip and the naturalness of the generations all together. For my mother, this was the closest she had ever come to real Italy. For me, it was a cultural balm, too, but I was intoxicated with an attention I wasn't used to getting.

* * *

The Excelsior pool, for example, was another world entirely, a world of foreign hotel guests where the Italians in the beach cabanas never trod. Zami was a wealthy Maronite Christian from Beirut visiting with his family. He had thick hair with loose blow-dried curls, wore designer loafers and a family ring on his index finger. He strolled rather than walked, had a twinkle in his eye, and could banter with his mother and sisters in French, English and Arabic.

> Susannah is out again with yet another handsome young man. This time a wealthy Lebanese who, I believe, will stay for another week. ... I write a lot about Susannah and her conquests because I live vicariously, being completely eclipsed this trip by her youth and beauty. It is tough. She has broken Carlo's heart I guess. But who can blame her for wanting to partake of this fabulous social whirl. I hope she keeps her head. (July 25, 1980)

Zami asked me to go for a walk on the beach one day, and then to join his family for dinner. He was fascinating to me, gorgeous, multicultural, and obviously a catch, but somehow the watchful eye of both our families made me bolder, and him more circumspect. We began to meet for walks in the evenings after dinner. Holding hands, casual brushing of hip against hip as bridges led to covered passages which led to hidden squares with perfect places to lean into each other and kiss. He was a master of the caress. He loved Venice as much as I did. He told me stories about Maronites and Beirut and family feuds and honor and the rich juxtaposition of Arab and European cultures. I was hooked. When I admitted one night on a walk that yes, I was still a virgin, he paused in his stride and laughed.

"Oh, my," he said. He shook his head. "Well, there is no way I'm going to be the first."

I was hurt. Not that I would have slept with him, but I wanted him to consider it.

"The first has to be special," he said.

And so began the rest of the summer of a tightrope stretched between Carlo's cabana, walks to the Excelsior hotel pier where I'd meet Paolo and his friends on his Wednesday day off, and other evenings with Zami. It didn't work very well for anyone but me.

It has been accomplished. We have departed. My heart is almost physically in pain. It was hot. Zami called, Susannah wrote to Paolo. ... We packed and bid goodbye, Michele took photos, Motorscafo came and for L18,000 deposited us at Ferrovia. The 4-hour train ride was horrid, hot, crowded, but on time. I sat in a stupor and thought about past months. I had wanted a romance, in fact no one even looked my way, save to gasp at my height. I was completely relegated to mother of a beautiful daughter. (August 21, 1980)

When I look back, it feels significant that it was a summer of juggling curiosity while also navigating deep unspoken maternal envy. It had been heady male attention, a tightrope of flirtation at a time when I was just beginning to imagine a life different from my mother's and with no father to provide a balance. No wonder I never really trusted female friendships. When I read the diaries, I am thrown back into the thrill of those Venetian evenings, the gentleness of being courted in such a romantic city. I remember being torn between following my mother's rules, "Be back at 10," or for a disco with Paolo, "Be back at 1," and the seductions of a sophisticated Arab elite world radically different from my high school reality. I found all three men fascinating. In fact, most of my interior and intellectual growth as a young person would continue to take place in the company of interesting men. I wonder now if my curiosity and perhaps a bit of recklessness was inevitable.

Pretending

1981

WE WERE ON MARK'S PARENTS' BED, a giant grown-up expanse of matching green paisley bedspread and pillows, in a proper Tudor house in San Francisco. It was my senior year in high school.

"What if they come home?" I had asked a few minutes before.

I was cautious about being interrupted by his parents, but Mark had a magnetic draw on me: his lips, those lashes, those cheekbones. I let myself be led up the stairs.

"They aren't here. They won't know," he whispered.

It was the afternoon, after school, and we had come back to his grand two-story house to hang out. After getting a soda and cookies—wow, a house where the mom stocked the refrigerator with snacks—Mark and I moved next door into his bedroom and onto the bed. Familiar notes of synthesizer and guitar filled the room from the stereo, then came Roger Daltry's raw voice about waking up in a Soho doorway. The Who posters covered every inch of the high wall. Mark wanted to be a drummer. He always talked a lot about The Who. I always listened. At some point we were both on the twin bed body on body, lips delicious and full.

"Let's go upstairs," he whispered, for some reason wanting to move to his parents' bed.

When we were upstairs, and my blouse was unbuttoned, and the quilt was crumpled to the side, he asked shyly "Do you want to see It?" I knew what he meant, and I knew enough about boys' psyches to know I shouldn't say no. I remember in my uncomfortable glance something purplish and alive that was playing peek-a-boo inside his gaping jeans. I was apprehensive. Mark was good to me. I wasn't afraid. Yet I didn't want to see more. I summoned an admiring, "Oh, wow," and pulled him back down to me with a kiss. Soon after that I announced it was time to go home and left for the bus stop.

I had never seen a real live penis. Television and movies were not full of the Mature Audience references to masturbation and dildos now on Netflix. Sex was still magical and unknown. Despite Italy. Despite modeling. But there was something else, too. My make-out forays with Mark were my first adventures into skin-on-skin intimacy. I knew to go slowly. What I didn't know was that I had someone else being part of it along with me. Sometimes it was an inner voice: *She's going to know. Don't, don't, don't. She said not to. I shouldn't. I won't*—and sometimes actually coming in and disrupting us.

> I woke at 1:30am and found Susannah and Mark who had come in at 11:30 in the living room with lights off—very disillusioning and upsetting. (November 8, 1980)

Mark, with his thick eyelashes and chiseled features, had flirted with me at the beginning of senior year. He was outgoing and given to hysterical bursts of laughter and theatrical sneers like a playful rock star. He was funny and not afraid of making a fool of himself. After my delicious summer in Italy, he had possessed an extraverted charm that was so much more intriguing than the, "Hey, baby, want a ride?" I would get when walking to an American bus stop or the, "What radio station do you listen to?" conversation starters from other high school students.

He was also a Pitter, one of the elite amongst Lowell High School's student gathering places. "Pitters" were made up of trumpet players, future novelists, and Haight Ashbury thrift-store shoppers. I never felt mature enough for their so-confident chic. But my mother's constant mantra since returning from Italy that summer, "Marry rich and you will be able to live in a style to which you are accustomed," had begun to assume weight in my psyche, the way background hypnosis penetrates a sleeping patient. She wanted me to have a sophisticated life. The Pitters represented a type of glamor not travel and languages and fancy hotel boats, but bongs and shrooms and "What is your sexual fantasy" confidences. They were miles ahead of my innocence.

My curfews were strict. There was no flexibility. But that wasn't so bad.

Susannah had a 2 1/2 hour booking with Macy's. She incurred my anger by not getting home until 5:45 and then leaving the kitchen in a shambles after dinner, which I had cooked for her and Mark and Miklos. Her thoughtlessness really infuriates me, especially because I feel rotten tonight. She is ecstatic over social life and bookings. My happiness comes if she gets an A. (October 31, 1980)

Mark urged me to rebel. "Who does she think she is? She needs a man herself and then she'll relax."

When I was young, my mother kept her sexual encounters outside my life. "I never wanted you to have 'uncles' at the breakfast table," she'd occasionally say. But, by high school, I was already years into her secret bond, her "never tell anyone" about the men who called her, especially James.

Mark scoffed, "Come on, I'm sure she's been with a man since your father. It can't be that she's been alone all this time."

I lied, as I had always lied to everyone, cousins, neighbors, friends, bald-faced lies that she required of me. I was completely loyal. But I had also been plagued for years by nightmares. Often they were of house fires. Mom would die and leave me. I woke with heart beating, waiting until the walls became familiar again, the sound of the fountain outside my room comforting my loneliness. It was always just the two of us. Outside of her presence was only emptiness.

I fought for later curfews and more freedoms.

"You have no idea how good a daughter I am. So many other kids drink and party and have sex and dye their hair purple and stay out all night," I yelled one night.

"You have no idea how good a mother I am," she lobbed back. "So many other mothers drink and party and have sex and stay out all night."

Wow. She had me there. I was grateful she didn't do those things.

"Geez, Mom, okay. But still, you aren't being fair."

"I may not be fair, but I'm right," she tossed back. "You know what I say, nothing will come of giving the milk away for free."

"Mom, I'm not sleeping with Mark. I just want to be able to go to the party this weekend."

My mother's face drew in on itself. I could tell she didn't believe me that Mark and I were not sleeping together.

"How am I supposed to believe anything you tell me?" she said, shaking her head in a quick side to side as if she were affirming some inner dialogue. "Look at your grades last semester! If you aren't sleeping with him, then what are you doing with your life? Wasting it away for a silly boy."

"Mom! You don't even believe me?"

"You're right. I don't. Your father always looked at me with that same expression. Trying to get me to believe him."

Sometimes our fights ended up with me feeling so infuriated that my only recourse was to storm out of the room and slam my bedroom door. Especially when she repeated I was just like my father or that I wouldn't amount to anything because I was lazy.

* * *

She became obsessed with my college applications. In her diary she wrote:

I am afraid to come home to the mail for fear of the other thin letters which I cannot reasonably expect will be thick. God, I am aching with the defeat and disappointment of it all. Never realized before how parents suffer on behalf of children. I just feel so grim that this destines Susannah for less of a life, like mine, for God's sake. (April 5, 1981)

In fact, I had applied to eight Eastern colleges and one safety school in California. Fitting to my non-straight-A grades, I was only offered a spot at the safety school. I was disappointed and a bit ashamed. But not really. I must have somehow already sensed that my mother's choreography of life was built on control over me, and though I truly enjoyed thinking and learning, I was drawn in more deeply by the emotional power of the boys I loved and what their contrasting worlds might offer. Looking back now, I see that this didn't matter at all. The self-destructiveness of high school grades was my kind of teenage rebellion. Detours make life interesting, as long as they are matched by a little luck and, at some point, common sense.

One Saturday evening, Mark and I parked my mother's Scout in the garage on the street below after having driven to the movies. We then climbed the L-shaped red wooden stairs up the back of the building, our breath coming heavier as we neared the top.

"Do you think I can come in for a little while?" He leaned against the side of the door as I searched for my keys in the backpack.

"I dunno. Maybe she'll already be watching TV in her room."

He tickled me and we raced through the co-op hallway and out the other side onto the courtyard. I dropped the keys with a loud jangle. Laughing, we approached the brown oak entrance to the apartment.

They must have heard us just at that moment, for when my key turned, the loud clack of the door lock followed by the familiar door-opening creak, I was surprised by a bumping and scrambling from my mother's bedroom. "Come back in ten minutes," she commanded me from the back. Startled, I stopped.

"Did you hear me!" she said, the question transformed into an order.

I retreated outside, closing the front door.

Turning, I saw Mark's wide eyes and could see he was about to burst out in hysterical laughter. "She has a man there." He grinned from ear to ear. "She has a man there!"

"Come on, let's go back downstairs." I felt no glee. I was mortified. What was going on? Why would she tell us to leave? What was happening?

Mark couldn't contain his amusement. "Oh my God, Her Majesty has to get off her high horse."

After ten minutes, counting slowly to allow plenty of time, I led the way back upstairs. Once again, I opened the front door. "Mom?"

"I'm going to bed. Mark should go home," she called from her room. The apartment was quiet. My insides were keyed up with adrenalin. I turned to Mark, who had followed me into the hallway.

"You'd better go home."

He rolled his eyes. "Yeah, okay. But I'll call you," and he lowered his voice to a stage whisper, "to find out the details tomorrow." His eyebrows wagged as he backed out the door. I closed and locked the door behind him, the squeaky clunk of the bolt echoing extra loudly.

Brushing my teeth in the bathroom that I shared with Mom, I heard her television through the closed door. When she watched television, her bedroom door was always open.

The next morning, it was as if a thick silent membrane existed between us. Questions percolated in me and then disintegrated. My stomach tensed and relaxed. Her proclamations of the last years circled in my head. *Too young. I don't want to hear about it.* No uncles at the table. *I am fine by myself. I don't need a man. No sex before marriage. Not in my house.* She was always so clear and so sure of what she counseled.

Looking back now, I see that evening as a watershed. I see that a pattern began to germinate, in which I knowingly denied what I knew to be true. During the following weeks, Mark would start to gloat about my mother's double standard, to school friends and even just with me. He expected me to delight with him in the discovery of my overly strict mother's secret sex life. But instead, I defended her silence.

"You have to keep quiet! It's her business. Don't tell anyone." I shut down conversations, ignoring puzzled looks, abandoning any teenage prerogative to be critical and rebellious. Instead, following her lead, I trod a precarious trail—witnessing a truth and fiercely guarding an untruth. I had actually interrupted her with a lover yet went on as if such a thing could never happen. Instead of conceding she had been discovered, she pretended it hadn't occurred. It shielded both of us, much as she had been "shielded" by her parents from the facts of her baby sister. *Don't tell and it won't be true.*

For many years following this night, I allowed no one to criticize my mother in my presence. I became the symbiotic guardian of her honor. I would actually feel pain at any hint of irony. No, she *really really* has no men, I insisted to my cousins at every family event, even as I memorized the latest fib I was to tell her lovers. "My mother isn't home right now. May I take a message?"

"Yes, she *is* fabulous and independent and thriving alone," I always agreed with her friends, even as they themselves stumbled through relationships and failed post-divorce dating rituals. My mother was in an envied super category of the 1970s, a charismatic career woman and single mom who needed no one.

"Oh, my God, I just *love* your mother," one of her friends told me when we found each other together in line in Safeway. "I hang on her every word!"

On its more private levels, this symbiosis between my mother and me fostered a blurring of distinctions between my intuition and others' narratives. Especially when it came to women. In professional situations, I grew to never trust anyone. Healthy skepticism may have helped me avoid career paths that would not have been good for me, like saying yes to working as a lobbyist for a dubious consulting firm rather than going to grad school. But in private, I usually swallowed others' statements of facts over my own intuition. This led to weaker friendships and, in the long run, to a lack of a voice. Forthright, mature women scared me even though I wanted to be like them. I see now that I often chose women friends who opted for silence on uncomfortable topics, which allowed me to collude with their denial. This was familiar to me.

I remember when my close friend Sophia's marriage was floundering. We spoke almost every day when our children were small, either in person or on the phone. We had long and easy conversations about child development and the world of early mothering we shared. Her narrative to the outside world, and probably even to herself, was one of a solid home life with a happy marriage. When I began to sense she was unhappy, it felt like an intrusion to ask her about it. It wasn't my business to be nosy even though we were close friends and I cared about her.

Then she began to mention frequent fevers when her husband came home at night. After the fifth time in a month, I dared to ask her if maybe her fevers had something to do with her husband, who I had observed could be cold and dismissive.

"No, of course not," she insisted each time. "Everything is fine. I just have a virus."

I did not challenge her. I thought I was being a good friend. But is being a good friend colluding with denial or challenging it? A year later, Sophia and her husband separated. Our friendship became more strained as she struggled with life as a single mother and I continued on solidly married to Niels. It felt like competition and envy entered our conversations in new ways that we might have been better able to navigate if our friendship had included the difficult topics from the beginning.

Back in high school, Mark had been the first boyfriend to genuinely and without prevarication criticize my mother in my presence. He represented something powerful that I hadn't yet been ready to address. My American female friends invariably adored Mom. She was so independent, so elegant and outspoken. Even in the years when my mother was the most hurtful to me as a young mother myself, it felt like they always kind of suspected I had done something to provoke her. Before her suicide set the record straight, to others it seemed that I must have been the one at fault if she didn't want to speak with me anymore.

"It's called compartmentalizing, Susannah," Mom would boast often to me. It was her strategy for suppressing unpleasantness. Her diaries in my senior year describe her passive-aggressive love affair with James. She waited for his wife to travel, was miserable when he did not call her, and yet refused to allow him to consider leaving his wife.

"Had he divorced Pamela and asked me to be his wife, the honor quotient would have been destroyed and that is so much a part of my loving him," her diary shows.

Toward the world, Mom held up the facade of a proudly independent woman who needed no man to feel strong. As I had had no evidence to the contrary, unlikely as it seems to me today, I had assumed that this meant she had no sex. Her dominant narrative was very much "a woman does not need a man." Feminism to my mother seems to have meant a woman's right to determine her own path, not so much bra burning as investing wisely and building financial security. She promoted herself as a happy single woman.

Time and again I would ask her, and others would ask her, "Jane, don't you want to get married again?"

Time and again she uttered a snort and a strong, "Never again."

She could have explained that for a formerly battered wife, a new marriage is frightening. She could have said she wanted to be in love, to have a life partner to share with, but was having trouble finding someone. Her diaries, in fact, show this part of her.

> I want someone of substance, unattached who would love me and make me his honored wife. That is what I want for the rest of my life. Love, security and companionship. Is that so much to ask, dear God? Meantime all the world's a stage. I put on a happy and confident face. (November 9, 1981)

But the world saw only that she seemed content in her hillside apartment, living according to her own rhythms, with a job and a nose for investments. Her diary and I were witnesses to the other.

You've Changed

2018

IT IS EVENING AS I READ THE DIARIES. I'm getting to the years when I am about to leave home. Niels is cooking, content in his chopping and sautéing.

"I relax while I cook," he always says, and after all these years I do believe him.

Hearing the onions and mushrooms sizzling, my stomach still constricts a tiny bit. Guilt. *I'm a bad wife.* Ridiculous. I remember the hours I pay the bills, take care of the taxes. I remember those three hours on Friday puzzling through the software problem after Niels impatiently shoved the computer away with, "I can't do this."

You just have a husband who likes to cook. That's okay, I tell myself. *A separate but equal allocation of household tasks.*

"Dinner is ready," he says. "Can you call Leah?"

I am pulled back to this day's reality. Sunk into my dead mother's descriptions of her life during my senior year in high school, it is almost as if I have to extract myself like a heron in muddy waters, legs straining up out of the sludge. Guilt and criticism. It's been a hard day's reading.

I don't say much at dinner.

"Well, this is fun," fifteen-year-old Leah says. I let the pause extend.

Niels doesn't say anything. He always has less of a need to fill empty space.

"I'm reading about my senior year in high school," I offer.

I can see them both focus, as if they are interested but wary. If they had been horses, they would have swiveled their ears in my direction.

"It is really hard to read," I tell them. "She is so sad. *And* she is so critical of me."

> Such a row with Susannah last night. She was fully dressed and sound asleep on my bed. Refused to brush her teeth, just useless, feckless and so like Alan that it confounds my peace of mind for her future. She was not drunk, of course, but the self-indulgence is just the same. ... She took the bus across town to a "pit" party. I do not know her friends now. (March 28, 1981)

After I leave home, my mother will blame herself and her lack of a man for her unhappiness. But in her diaries during my senior year, she often blames me. I was a student at Lowell, which at that time was the top-rated public school in the country. I had a mix of grades and fairly good SATs. I excelled in some classes, like Ideologies and Italian and History. I was on the track and cross-country teams and had a part in the *Brigadoon* musical. All this with an hour's public bus commute each way.

But my mother was right. I lost track of something in high school.

> I am down and depressed again because Susannah got a final C in English. She deserves anything she gets as she has not studied at all. ... I feel so betrayed. I guess I wanted her to be so much smarter than I am, one of those golden girls whose brain power just shines no matter what. (June 8, 1981)

Up until tenth grade, classrooms and Socratic questions and the pursuit of knowledge had always been joyful, maybe a bit of a quiet escape from the rest of my life. At Lowell, I had good teachers. But there were many other distractions: modeling, long bus rides every day, waitressing at a café, and now glamorous summers in Europe which seemed impossible to share with my American friends. So, I just split those summers off. Through the high school years, I worked at many jobs, and I was charming at family dinner parties. I did not have sex, even with Mark, and until a few months before graduation I didn't experiment with drugs. However, I was scattered and very busy, and somehow found myself unable to come home at 6 or 7 p.m. and then study successfully for the three hours every night that I should have been studying. So I did not get accepted at any of the East Coast colleges I wanted.

As I read the weekly, and sometimes daily, descriptions of her disappointments: my grades, my procrastination on college applications, my worries about the workload, I observe her descriptions of me turn bleaker and darker. I feel myself, the reader, turn inward, self-critical, melding my mother's words with those that sometimes trip out of Niels in our quarrels.

"I can't stand these piles everywhere," Niels has said, observing the hallway with its incoming mail and discarded kid's shoes and dog leashes not returned to their proper place.

"You always make yourself available!" he has lamented as I answer a last-minute email while he waits in his overcoat by the door at precisely the time he said he would. "We're going to be late."

So that by the end of the day today, I feel I haven't changed at all in thirty years.

It is with that mood that I come to the dinner table.

My recollection of those last months living at home is of a time in which my mother barely spoke with me, was always laden with something. As if her disappointment was so strong that she really couldn't bear to engage with me. She smiled hollowly, was busy with herself and withdrew when we were together. I felt I could never reach her anymore. Those were sad months for me, even as the diaries document that I had a very active social life (which I don't really remember much) and babysat and worked in a restaurant more hours in the week than I remember working. I was sad my mother was withdrawing, my mother who had been the center of my life and my love and my being. Yet she seemed to know nothing of my feelings, and there was no one to mediate.

> Another trauma today when I came home. Susannah was here in tears. Mark had sex with Lina Saturday night. He is destroyed and Susannah is hurt and furious. But she pulled herself together and we kept the 4:00 appointment at Model Management. The lady welcomed her, told her to cut her hair and lose 2 inches around the hips. ... When we came home at 5:30, Mark was sitting on the step looking like a sick animal. They talked for an hour. After dinner Larry, Henry and Dick came over and we talked about memo for KQED programming. I would have gone to a movie with Susannah if I had been free. (February 17, 1981)

Was Mark's fling an inevitable consequence of my reluctance to have sex with him? I know he was remorseful and wanted me to forgive him. My mother's words, "A boy who behaves like that will give you nothing but heartache," echoed in my mind, but I said no to sex for another reason. I simply wasn't ready.

This was a phase when I felt I was constantly hurting my mother—there was so much pain passing between us. Even my high-school graduation was a disappointment to her:

> Graduation at the Cow Palace, so huge as to dwarf all humanness and all emotion. Sound and color remained. Just as well, for the emotion I feel as my beloved daughter graduates is disappointment. The shock of her college rejections is constantly with me, like a bad and completely unplanned bad dream. But in addition to that is my disappointment in her intellectual effort, her ambition, her choice of friends, even her gaining of weight and the non-success in the modeling field. I wanted so much to be the mother of a star to

gratify my parental ego and that is useless and wrong. So I
am disappointed in myself. (June 10, 1981)

My grad night trip was to Disneyland. I remember that night as
being a taste of grown-up Italian eroticism, that thrilling approach and
distance to a Desired Man, rather than a boy. Ethan had been the type
of young man who learns early to replicate a handsome father. He had
flirted with me since tenth grade, gently pulling my hair as he sat behind
me in Algebra II, and then learning how to move just that bit closer in
the hallway as we talked so his shoulder brushed mine. I hadn't ever
said yes to his overtures. But he was witty, smart, and he wanted me,
and I will never forget the thrill of agreeing to stand in line with him
for the Matterhorn ride, and then that delicious leaning back against
him as we were pulled up and up to the top, praying it would never
end. My back pressed against his chest and I felt his erection—which
I didn't even then name as an erection—taking its place between us.
The thrill of screaming together down the roller coaster with him. Me!
Who had been voted both prettiest and shyest in my class of 700.

We never even kissed that night, but I remained enthralled with
those moments of erotic potential when I returned to the city. I wanted to share with my mother the wonderful evening of freedom and
relief at ending high school, even though our sparse language would
have excluded any details. I was learning to live, and I was experiment-
ing with boundaries, but that wasn't the kind of messy path she valued.

Susannah came back, had a superb time. I still don't feel much like
talking with her, am so resentful she deprived me of being proud
of my child on high school graduation day. (June 11, 1981)

Then there was the secret melodrama of my mother's relationship
with James, none of which she shared with me. I knew he was around in
the wings, but she was so adamant about the importance of chastity, of
the strength of women without a man, so reluctant to talk specifics about

him, that I settled on assuming nothing was there. Reading the diaries now, I am surprised by her sensuality, how much sex she did have on sailboats and in forests, and how unashamed she was. I am also wondering if she thought about me reading these words someday. Did she aim to show me her hidden side? Did it even matter to her in her seventies?

> We left the car and hiked way up Indian Head Trail, far above civilization and people until we found what James called a bower. There we had our wine and cheese lunch and abandoned ourselves to our wild delight at being alone, together naked under the dappled shade of a live oak tree. (July 1, 1979)

It answers one of the riddles of my early college years, which was how I could be so open to sex having been raised by a mother resembling a refined Professor McGonagall, where sex was only meant for marriage. Mom had never talked to me about her lovers, except to say self-consciously that when my father wasn't drunk, he was "interested and gentle." It was my grandfather and Phyllis who had had the *Joy of Sex* with its pencil drawings in their library, as I discovered in college.

My mother pledges in her 1980 entries that she will leave James on June 30, 1981. It will be the end of her time as a mother with a child at home. Both lover and daughter would be gone at the same time, one fell swoop to begin a new life. She says she likes such symbolism.

> I shall never forget these hot, clear days, windows open and feet bare and my child and my love coming to the end of their daily part in my life. What will take their place? What will fill the void? (June 22, 1981)

On June 23 and 24, she writes of special lovemaking with James, how close they feel, how much they love each other. Then, on June 30, he comes over to our apartment with Champagne for lunch and she announces she will break off the relationship with him. She writes she would like him to leave his wife, but if he left his wife, he wouldn't be the kind of man she could love. She seems to leave him no choice. She writes that James is desperately sad.

> After he left, it was strangely comforting to hear the oblivious self-surrounded chatters and giggles from Susannah's room where Linda and Melanie were helping her pack. I drank a glass of Champagne that was left over from lunch, sat in the dining window alcove and concentrated on breathing deeply and fighting back tears. Oh, God, why couldn't I have had an unflawed, sane husband to find when the husband-finding time was ripe? I am so afraid of the lonely years. (June 30, 1981)

All this was going on a few feet away from me. I felt her disturbance, but she let me assume all her inner turmoil was her "bad" daughter's doing.

As I read, my view of the situation shifts. I suspect there was more to the James break-up. I suspect she was terrified in a little-girl-after-Helen way that with her daughter gone, there would be no more excuses to keep James at bay. He would leave his wife and she would be given the opportunity for a full relationship with him. I think she needed his wife to remain his wife. It is a cruel choreography directed to herself and also James. It makes me wonder what kind of a partner she was for my father. Perhaps within the complex mess of his addictions and what the alcohol did to their daily lives, there was also something else. Perhaps his greater capacity for reflection triggered her to stand ever more rigid, which sparked in him a need to lash out more frequently.

* * *

Back at the dining room table, Niels and Leah both almost flinch. I have read them a few of her diary passages. It looks as if they are angry and are holding themselves back from lashing out.

"Mom, sorry, but your mother was awful and mean and I don't

want to hear anything else." Leah slides her feet up on the chair across from her under the table. She looks petulant and vulnerable.

Well, if I brought it up, I might as well dive in and share what I'm going through.

"We know all the bad stuff. Yes," I said. "But she was there. For all her faults, she was also a documentarian of my life. She observed. Not everything she observed is warped. I can see things she says about me then that are still present in the conflicts we sometimes have."

I gestured to Niels. "You know what I mean. My tendency to leave piles where I work, our fights sometimes about our styles of working. You are so disciplined. I wait for creative moods to come and go. These are things that still seem to be part of my character, thirty years later. I can't just disregard her observations because she was the source."

Leah slumps in her chair.

Niels rolls his shoulder, his mouth tightening. "You're right, her perceptions are sometimes—often even—accurate. But what she does with them is distorted. Her observations give no room. She didn't know how your life would end up but she judges you so harshly. It makes me angry to see how much influence she still has on you." He rubs the back of his neck.

"Mom, you don't see it, but you have changed a lot since you have been reading the diaries." Leah looks over at me. She seems afraid of hurting me.

"Have I?"

"Yes." Her eyes fill with tears. She looks suddenly so vulnerable. "I hate her. I admire what you are doing, but I hate her. I'm not going to listen to anything good about her. You are reading about how you were when you were my age, and you are reacting to me as if I am you. You are stricter now, like she was. You are snotty to me about social media. You read about your boyfriend and you think it is the same when I have a boyfriend."

Niels watches quietly. I can feel him wrapping his warmth around us both, his love expanding to support us, supple and sure. It feels safe. Leah and I have always been close. I've tried so very hard to be a good mirror to her. She loves me *and* she has to become her own woman. Here we are, Niels and I, connected. She and I connected. Niels and she connected. I breathe in suddenly. It is so clear. I never had this. A counterbalance at the dinner table. Someone who loves and sees, and disagrees, and can still carry the three of us together.

Later, after I load the dishwasher, and after Leah washes the pots and wipes the table, she seems distracted and down.

"Do you really think I've changed?" I ask, pulling a dining-room chair back, slightly lifting it so it won't catch on the thick Indian carpet.

"Yes, you don't see it. But I do." She's angry but sits reluctantly next to me. "I could never do something like this. If you killed yourself and left me your diaries, I would burn them."

Jesus, Leah can really call out the truth. I am in awe of this fierceness and also a little disconcerted. All I can think to do is reach over and put my hand on her forearm. "I won't do that. I would never ..."

She smiles a bit. Maybe she is relieved to hear again my reassurance I won't kill myself and that she won't ever actually have to burn my words.

But I'm scared. Am I lying to her? Deep in my heart, I'm scared that maybe I *will* end up like my mother. She was forty-something when she started to write about her loneliness so clearly, when even to herself she has no one else to blame. Now I am fifty. I've been unhappy at times. I have been lonely. Are these diaries my mother left me a blueprint of my future? Is Leah right? Is my friend Becca right? Should I have burned them?

"Be done with her, Susannah," Becca had said when she heard I was starting on the reading journey. "Go on with your life."

I shake my head as I did then, too. The only way through is through. Had Mom burned them, I would never have known about Helen, about my grandmother, about the violence. Ignorance is not bliss when it comes to trauma. It just reroutes the family problems onto the next generation.

I have six months left before fall, the deadline I gave myself to finish reading the journals. I have to be a grown-up now. I have to work this through. I have had enough years of therapy. Leah is so much more articulate than I was at her age. I must have done something right.

Leaving Home

1981

MY BODY MEMORY OF LEAVING HOME was of pulling my shoulders back and facing forward with a smile. I wasn't afraid. I was excited. But I was also sad and felt rejected. I was a bird being pushed out of the nest a little too young. Mom seemed to desperately want me gone.

> Let me count the reasons for my melancholy. Susannah was rejected from every Eastern school to which she applied, I must break with James in less than two months, I have no job or paycheck come June 30, no one rented this place, I am so lonely. I wonder how I will feel a year from today. (May 4, 1981)

The last months living at home had been ones in which my mother barely spoke with me more than to arrange for our busy schedules. Her diary indicates her usual plans for the summer to rent out our apartment and thereby finance a summer of travel were not working out. Every summer she was laid off by the school district and rehired in the fall, which meant no tenure and no pay during the summer months. Our regular evening dinners were strained, and often didn't take place at all because of meetings and work. I felt I could never reach her. She felt I was distant, too. In her diaries, Mom worried a lot about whether they "did right by me" on my public-school education. She didn't wonder about my father or our flawed relationship or her secret love life. She assumed simply that had I gone to private school, I might have been a better student and made her prouder.

Later, when I experienced that crazy maelstrom of pride and down-to-the-bottom-of-the-ocean ache of my own children going off to college, I wondered why she had wanted me to leave so badly. Had I been such a difficult child for her that she couldn't wait for me to be out of the house? This is hard to believe, since I had come home every night, I had applied to college and completed my final exams. I had worked as a barista making money at the Cannery on Fisherman's Wharf, and I had been charming at her dinner parties. Julian hadn't always been easy in his last year of high school. He had been angry, and sullen and kept to himself more than I wanted. Sometimes I dreamed of not having to navigate his seventeen-year-old moods. But when he actually left for college, proud as I was, I was also bereft. I walked into his room and my heart squeezed tight. I missed him so much. Was that at all possible for my mother? She doesn't say so in her diary.

After I leave, her diaries reveal an expansion of her preoccupation with specific dates. It had always been there. Now it becomes more obvious.

For example, every November 22 she holds a riveting lecture about JFK to her students, writing about how much pleasure it gave her to remind them of the Kennedy years, the glamor, the innocence, and the death.

Every year on her wedding anniversary, January 12, despite despising my father for a violent marriage, she writes, "This was my second happiest day."

Every year on my birthday, she writes, "This was the happiest day of my life."

Every December 31, she writes a year-in-review, keeping a list on the diaries' inside covers of the relevant names at the time, like the cast of that year's production.

I know that she strategized for years about when to end her affair with

James, finally choosing a date to coincide with my graduation, the idea of being left alone all at once, no daughter, no lover, giving her a clean slate.

I was to go off to college at the University of California, Santa Barbara on the very day I turned eighteen, so that she could always recount that doubly momentous birthday.

She planned her retirement from teaching for the momentous year 2000.

And, of course, later she would pick age 75 "because it was three-quarters of a century old" as a good age for dying and a Sunday three-quarters of the way through that year to book the motel and order the helium.

This is now the fourth month of reading my mother's diaries, day after day, week after week. It has begun to take its toll. I slip too easily into those days, almost like I'm forgetting who I have become as an adult. I'm still vulnerable to believing her vision of me, to that time when truth was what she told me about myself.

When I'm in college at UC Berkeley, having transferred there in my junior year, she writes in her diary:

> Yesterday was tiring. I hope I am able to hide how empty I am emotionally, but sometimes I sense Susannah intuits and I don't want her to. She asked "Don't you want to know me?" I said, "No." (March 7, 1983)

I remember that conversation. We were sitting in my ground floor studio apartment in a house in north Berkeley. She was doing some needlepoint and we were waiting for a rain burst to pass so we could walk onto campus. It was cozy and the space heater was rumbling. I had wanted to tell her of a recent heartbreak. I had wanted to tell her about all that I was learning, the sleeping out on the steps of Sproul Hall to protest apartheid, the philosophy professor questioning American journalism's notions of objectivity, my Latin American class on Marxism and political orthodoxy. I was so full of thoughts and questions.

It was like venturing out onto the high dive, testing the bounce.

I yearned for her solidarity. As it had really always been, in order to jump into a full life, I wanted her by my side.

So when she said she didn't want to know me, I recall exactly how that felt. I sensed it that weekend morning after she announced her suicide plans. I can feel it now again, how I paused on the threshold of our nearness, drawn to her, a few seconds of barely felt weighing of the wisdom to risk, the decision to go ahead anyway, to tell her of my heart. Then the dull hearing of her response and the backlash. I become the mouse who blames herself for having become hungry enough to venture through the crack, knowing the cat was waiting. *That's perfectly fine, Mom. You don't have to care about me. That's fine.*

Where was my outrage, my anger? I know I have those emotions. I know I expressed them to her. But in those special moments that hint at hope of connection, I am a little girl again, tricked into reaching out, allowing myself to be vulnerable.

She always said life was hard. "It's not what happens in life but how you cope with it," she'd say. But I didn't want life to be so hard. Every Sunday growing up, she took me to church. Sometimes to the conservative Saints Peter and Paul, where we would genuflect automatically in rites centuries old and an anonymous priest wreathed in incense would hold forth in a droning voice. Sometimes we went to the hippie Saint Anne's in Palo Alto where Father Olivier preached sermons about real life, where children were invited to cram together on the carpeted altar, where master guitarists lifted our spirits in joyful '70s peace songs. The atmosphere there was radiant, even when the priest preached about sadness. I liked that fullness. That we had "one sweet life," that it held promise and love and laughter despite the sorrows.

When I was ten, for my birthday I had wanted more than anything a set of the Encyclopedia Britannica. That long row of heavy uniform books, like a whole library in my own bedroom, as if all that the world knew and had ever known was available to me. I could answer every question. I could know everything. It was a feeling that I loved.

When a gray-haired professor, old and knowledgeable, told the

500 freshmen in one of my first college classes at UC Santa Barbara, "You know, the more I study and learn, the more I realize I know nothing," it was as if I had been offered an escape hatch from a twisted twosome. My mother's guidelines were old-world and all encompassing, and she was always right about everything.

"Marry money," she'd repeat to me. "Then you'll have security and can do whatever you want."

This professor was granting me entrance to a world where it was legitimate to question. I began to turn my attention to the things she did not want to know. Philosophy, political texts, history, hermeneutics, quantitative analysis to predict political behavior. I was thrilled to find everything could be deconstructed. Down to the interpretations of brain sparks into sounds into words into language. Everyone I met I asked what they did and was interested in the reply. Astrophysics. Embryology. Animal testing in cages. How can I condemn it before I get to see it in action? Electron microscopes. Languages: Italian, French, Spanish, Arabic. Computer programming: Pascal, on-off-on, analogue, var-begin, loops, hours searching for the one wrong letter that blocked the syntax of my instruction.

My loves matched my curiosity. I fell in love with smart and interesting young men, sometimes deeply, sometimes not, through my college and early twenties. Writers, thinkers, poets. Chilean politics, revolution, Marxism. Mateo was all about anger and resolve, changing the corrupt system. With him, I dreamt of righteous bombings and fighting capitalism. Then, in Rome, Gino was all about how to enjoy a good meal, negotiate social expectations, and presentation of self. Later, when I transferred to Berkeley, there was Collis and the worlds of Hunter S. Thompson and gonzo journalism, theories of fascism, stream of consciousness, and eventually it was the fun of Liam, dancing weekends in San Francisco at south of Market music clubs.

* * *

"You always talk about eyes meeting across the room. That seems totally unrealistic for my age." Dylan, nineteen, is describing life as a college freshman in 2017. He's critical of me.

"You should see them all," Dylan says. "Before class the other day we were all waiting in the hall. The professor was late. Everyone was looking down at their phones. Not one person looked around at anyone else. I was watching."

Have I been talking nonsense all these years? Maybe my promises *are* fairy tales. Maybe Niels and I raising our children in Germany has seduced me into telling stories about a world of *my* twenty-something life that truly no longer exists. This is the age of Chatbots and Tik-Tok and Zoom meetings. Am I so out of touch that I've been spinning yarns for my children all these years?

No, the best part of my younger life was falling in love with men.

I return to my office and survey the seventeen piles of letters I've just spent the past two days sorting. Wafer thin airmail letters, cards, succulent hefts of yellow legal paper. My intrepid, haphazard diary—the letters read, placed back into their envelopes, sometimes with "answered" and the date on the back and stored in an old shoebox. Rome, Berkeley, Aleppo, Cairo, New Delhi, Dallas. If the boxes hadn't been marked, the addresses on the envelopes would clearly identify my life locations in my twenties.

Rereading one man's letters, it is as if I am once again twenty, and can picture his lips, the luscious dip between his neck and his collarbone, the particular hue of his skin, the sensual gathering of hair around his navel. I am almost there, can almost smell him, remember the shape of him on my tongue. I want to spend more time here, in the space remembered. The letters tell the story of our loves and our desires. They are emotions put into words, inked on paper, matching the extravagant cogency of that particular time in life.

If I am not careful, I can fall in love with this young man all over again. I feel the same way again as I take up the next sorted stack, different handwriting, new setting, each love slightly worn or bruised by the existence of the one before. But precious precisely for that ripening. My mother was right. I spent a lot of time and energy on the men in my life. They were mostly good men. Men of words. Reflective. Smart. Challenging. There were *I love yous.* There was heartbreak. Everything was felt deeply. But I wonder if I was also so interested in men because I hadn't yet freed myself of my mother's influence and my father's absence. Through my loves, I could learn about myself in a way I had not been equipped to do alone.

At Berkeley, I encouraged my mother to come sit in on a favorite class. I was sure she would love it, too. She came unannounced on a day when class was suddenly canceled. She stood in the rain for twenty minutes outside the wrong lecture hall. When she finally arrived at the right one, nobody was there. She had been inconvenienced. Maybe she felt like she'd been purposely duped.

She wrote on the empty blackboard: "Susannah Kennedy, your mother is now canceling your tuition because your professors don't show up to class."

The professor for the next class period found it. He happened to know me. "Susannah, I thought you should know that your mother wrote on the board in my class. She didn't seem too happy."

"What!?" I replied. Famous, yet again, for my mother's doings. I was mortified. And guilty. Full of "I should haves." I should have intuited that she would come that day. I should have waited. I was sorry for her wet feet. It was somehow my fault, disgraced in my one chance to share my life with her.

She never came to a lecture again. One misadventure and you're out.

She termed my reflections in those years "self-indulgence." She always viewed my wish to know things as indolent, misguided.

"You're just like your father. He was brilliant sometimes. But he couldn't get out of his own way," she would say.

If I, too, tended toward academics and inquiry, then it was predestined that I would also fall into melancholia and failure. She was throwing me a life preserver by advising discipline, compartmentalization, and avoidance of emotions. "Papa may have and Mama may have, but God bless the child who has his own," was her often-repeated mantra from the song by Billie Holiday.

I must work rather than study.

As a result, I never considered graduate school. I never considered applying for internships with professors or grants to do summer research. I worked in the main campus cafeteria cutting vegetables. Then I applied for a job as a copyeditor at the *Daily Cal*, the Berkeley student-run newspaper. This seemed like an easier way to make money. Plus, it added to my resume. I did not know what I wanted to do after graduation, but I knew I'd better come up with some ambitious plans.

My mother had been editor in chief of her all-female college paper, the *Mills Stream*. She was enthusiastic and deemed I would be garnering marketable skills for after graduation. But her idea of marketable skills didn't match with mine. The *Daily Cal* was the threshold to multiple cultures and ways of being, and again I was questioning and curious as opposed to her discipline and limits. I liked reporting perhaps in the same way shy people like acting. They can slip into a vessel that allows them to be bold. I wanted to witness rather than tear down. I loved my *Daily Californian* press credentials for the 1984 Democratic National Convention, loved being a part of the pomp and balloons and passionate speeches. But I was interested in complexity, in the certainty there was always one more lens through which to gain insight.

The *Daily Cal* was complicated for other reasons, too. One day I found out that Paul, the student editor in chief, had the hots for me.

"I'm tired of fantasizing about her; would it be all right if I asked her out?" he asked a male colleague who was known to be my friend.

Corvin assured me he had replied, "No, it would *not* be all right." But now I knew.

I could feel that Paul's attraction to me gave me one step up in our editorial transactions, that there was some sort of power here which made me uncomfortable. When I asked my mother what to do, she responded: "A frail male ego and a beautiful woman demand collaboration. Shine it on, honey." I listened to her advice and didn't call him out. But it complicated my days. I worried when a date with one star reporter almost ended in a kiss. Would he gossip? Then, when I became involved with another reporter, I wanted to keep it quiet so Paul wouldn't find out. Now, though it all seems like a harmless world in miniature, I see from today's vantage point that these were the beginning #MeToo power relations of corporate culture.

I was running and swimming daily. I was fit and my hair was long. I was also smoking cigarettes, something I had dabbled with since my sophomore year in Rome. Smoking went well with the atmosphere of banter, drinking, buddy jokes. I liked being one of the boys. But now that I think back on it, there were a lot of knowing looks exchanged as Paul and his fellow reporters cajoled me into a surprise late-night porno showing on Shattuck Avenue. Cigarettes and pornos. There was ever more I could not tell my mother.

The summer I was managing editor, I often called her for advice. I worried I had taken on a managerial position above my competence, that The Peter Principle was lurking. Her counter interpretations were always feminist.

"You're the only woman. Of course, it is tough."

In the end, I resigned over a conflict about a midnight deadline. Truthfully, I was relieved. I felt cornered and overwhelmed. I'd really only taken the job because having my name on the masthead appeared successful. The guys were surprised by my resignation, but I suspect that what hurt them the most was the loss of me to look at every day. I would never learn to harness office politics effectively. To be tough, you should really know who you are.

I tried to communicate all of these new experiences to my mother in the two years we lived close by each other, she in San Francisco and I in Berkeley. Though she was no longer my confessor or my mentor, I continued to act as if she were, tangling myself in contradictions. I'm surprised now when I read how young I sound:

> I love Mommy *so* much. I don't ever want her to know. I am a good, sweet person still. If only at 45, I would look as young and beautiful as she. (My diary, Sept. 20, 1983)

Partly as a result of this confusing dance with my mother, I began to inhabit two personas, like an actress slipping out of her gown to nip to the supermarket in sweats and sunglasses. It is tempting to say one persona was a façade and one was real, but that's not really true. The world of men was messy and earthy and challenging. I had no solid father to give me a guiding light. I trusted no women. I trusted men. Looking at it now, it feels that I spent an enormous amount of time being indecisive and playful, letting myself be carried and seduced, re-acting and rejecting.

One weekend, my mother offered tickets to attend an Asilomar conference on nuclear disarmament with my grandfather, who was getting a lot of press for his opposition to Reagan's nuclear politics. I was thrilled to be there, listening to all these powerful people, actual decision-makers.

At breakfast we sat at a table with Linus Pauling, Vitamin C guru, Nobel chemist and Peace Prize winner. I was right next to him. I was thrilled, star-struck. So close to fame. He was old and gentle. His wife made all his breakfast decisions for him, as if he were a little boy. Later, I would notice that about other famous, genius men. Their wives usually ran their lives. The world exists largely inside their thoughts. Why is brilliance so admired, I wonder, if it means an inability to order one's own toast?

One weekend in college my father called to say he wanted to see me again. The last time had not gone so well—I had run away from his house in Washington, D.C. But by now he had discovered *est*; most of his messages were pushing me to take the Training, a two-weekend inspirational workshop popular in the 1970s and early 1980s. His pressure was tiresome. His language was very particular.

In communication with you: I took notice that I had not been. Thus, a birthday missed and a graduation not attended— big losses for me. I see that you have a vision of the possibility that the quality of life will be enhanced by your being. That is a reward for me; I am happy to be your father. (Letter, August 24, 1985)

He said he had been looking forward to our weekend visit. We met at a restaurant. I was irritable. After a while, I remember saying: "Daddy, I don't want to listen to you talking about *est* anymore if you never deal with your drinking problem."

The world seemed to pause.

"You bitch," he sputtered. His eyes narrowed. "You're becoming just like your mother."

Without even thinking it through, I pushed back my chair, heart beating against my chest, and walked out. Adrenalin shot through me, blanking out my thoughts. *Just get away. Get out of here.* I remember shaking for hours afterward. Doubting myself. Angry with him. Worrying. God, was he right? Was I becoming like her? Making him feel bad? Probably I did remind him of my mother. Probably I was being judgmental.

Now I see that each of my parents' deepest insult was still to say I am just like the other one. They were still caught in each other's web, still unable to differentiate their own responsibilities for the failed relationship, still in some way loving each other. Almost like two mountains remaining so close together that the only way water can flow between them is via a steep gorge and dangerous rapids.

Traveling Alone

1985

As a Berkeley political science major, with Zami's Beirut stories still in my ear, I enrolled in a Middle East studies course. The professor turned out to be a dynamic and humorous storyteller. His dissections of diplomacy and current events were always interspersed with vivid, personal anecdotes about daily street life in the Arab world. With irreverence and compassion and real-life experience, he tried to teach his classes of Berkeley undergrads something about another world that was more than treaties and colonial borders drawn in the sand.

To him, Arab life was about modesty and honor, about family and kinship and history. It was colorful and full of life. I took every course he taught. I tried to get all my friends interested in his classes. One day, an earnest young man in the back of the classroom put up his hand, asking a complicated question, trying to create logical sense out of illogical Maronite and Palestinian negotiations.

Professor Sadowski interrupted, exasperated at the young man's cerebral tone. "Look, you've got to understand this. They are all completely nuts." He laughed with such joy and such awareness of his student's inability to comprehend how *nuts* could be a good thing that I knew in that moment the Arab world was the place for me.

I started studying Arabic. I wrote an honors thesis deconstructing U.S. media coverage of Egypt's President Sadat. I took and passed the foreign service exam.

One afternoon I got up the courage to knock on Professor Sadowski's plain office door, pretending I was just passing by. He was bundled in scarves and disclosed he was exhausted from taking care of his one-year-old son. *Surprise.* Professors never openly admitted to a private life. He must have been feeling especially fatherly that day, for he asked what my plans were after graduation. I blushed. I wasn't really sure. I felt tongue-tied. Here the great man was asking me a personal question.

"Well, I want to work in something international. I'm going to travel for a while after graduation." I wanted to visit the places I had been studying.

He was silent. He sat back in his chair, in my memory his two silver teeth making him look like the Jaws character from James Bond. The chair creaked pleasingly. He seemed to really consider this moment, head slightly askew. "Have you ever considered anthropology? I think it would suit you. It is more about the study of real people, which you seem to enjoy."

I was taken aback. I had been hoping he would recommend me for some sort of program in political science.

"No, not really," I mumbled.

Inside I scoffed, mindful of what I had been spinning to all my mother's friends for the past six months. I was going to be working for the *New York Times,* or for the State Department. I pictured suits and negotiations in my future. I was not going to be some hippie, out living with a tribe with no running water.

He was right, though. I should have listened to him. It would have saved me some detours along the way.

The fall after graduating from Berkeley, with a diploma decorated with a blue Honors ribbon, I left my sexy, non-committed boyfriend Liam, took the $3,652 left over from my education money and my grandfather's offer to buy me a ticket to finally see my birthplace, and started toward India, timeframe vaguely one year. Along with my backpack, its exterior frame and pockets carrying medicines, sleeping bag, and winter and summer clothes, I also carried a small manual typewriter. The letters tap-tapped out on that machine I now have in front of me, in my writing nook, in Santa Cruz.

Traveling was hard. It was slow. And sometimes aggravating. But I was free of expectations. Just being was enough. Just buying a ticket for the next town. Just watching the street life pass by, observing the family lives of those who adopted me along the way. Just that filled the day.

Building upon my academic interest in the Arab world, I traveled for four months through Turkey, Syria, and Jordan before crossing the Allenby bridge to Israel for six weeks. I rented cars and took buses alone and sometimes I traveled with other Western backpackers who pretended to act like my husband in public for a few days. In Syria, I was welcomed into the family of my Berkeley Arabic tutor and had the opportunity to live in Aleppo and then with their cousins in Damascus. Not only was I learning more Arabic, but also I was navigating new streets and social rules. The challenges became figuring out how to dance in the Arab style at women's parties, when to ask about Assad's politics, when to best leave it alone, how to flirt by the slightest touch of a handshake, how to navigate the secret police's interest in my host families. I always dressed carefully and respectfully and took pages of notes on everything I saw. These were my beginning forays into fieldwork. I lived often in the moment, and I met mostly kind people.

My mother and Uncle Steven met me in Jerusalem for Christmas.

What joy to hug my wandering daughter again and to see she looks and feels fine. ... Also useful is the realization that she'd be bored stiff with a 9-5 type job or grad school at this stage in her life. She seeks life in the scary lane, friendships with shadowy PLO types and living here and there out of a backpack, often in places where an American female, young, pretty, solo, has never been seen before. So far so good.... (Jane's letter to Trevor, December 1985)

In late winter 1985, I traveled back to Jordan, and eventually by overnight ship around the southern tip of the Sinai Peninsula to Suez, and then to Cairo, where I was able to obtain residency papers as a freelance journalist. In Egypt, I lived with a group of Polish students, and then on my own, and then shared an apartment with a British woman, Sally. I studied Arabic, wrote articles, and made my money editing reports and academic submissions. It was a gigantic adventure.

> I arrived home to find the *bawab* presenting me with an electricity bill and the faucets dry of water. AGAIN. And again they apparently apologized on the television to my area because a pipe burst. ... So I sat on my bed and looked out, surprised, at a dense fog enveloping the tall buildings around me. Quickly, the grayish mass descended, transparent yet like a veil. The wind blew harder, and dark night came quickly. I ran around closing all the outer roll-down shutters and the glass windows though they do little against this *khamsin*, everyone says. Lamps on the street glow eerily in the dust. The wind shrieks outside. I can hear the trees beating with the gusts. The windows rattle. Inside I suffocate. It must be 90 degrees. No air. No water.. .. A friend came over with big 20-liter cans of water.... It is exciting to me. I've never seen a dust storm. (Letter to my mother, April 14, 1986)

It surprised me, always, in the Arab world, how sophisticated and cultured and warm so many of my Arab acquaintances were. I shouldn't have been surprised. But like an image arising during a darkroom development process, I only became aware of how American I was by going elsewhere. As a woman, I rented an apartment and drove around Cairo in taxis alone without worry. Even as a poor freelancer, I was invited along to five-star hotel discos and the duty-free market with the Johnnie Walker Black Label and Marlboro imports. This "elite class" protection made it safe for me but also felt uncomfortable as it gave me unearned privileges.

In Syria, I had been a foreign guest, a curiosity perhaps, but a counterpart. In crowded Egypt, with a large section of the population living in poverty, I was automatically a rich foreigner, the expatriate I had never wanted to be. The more I ventured into local, as opposed to foreign friendships, the more fascinated I became. Always careful to cover my blonde hair with a plain scarf in poorer neighborhoods to not stand out, I sought out contradictions. I was almost never afraid.

My mother complained that I did not write letters home often enough. But as I read in her diaries, she also profited from my travels. To her, it was glamorous.

> I assess my motherly contentment about her even being there, precious as she is to me and much as I miss her. Do I want her fulfillment or my own? The ability to be more interesting myself via my daughter's adventures and supposed successes. Even to the point of accepting her violent death I face that and am horrified to answer yes. (April 7, 1986)

Her words make sense to me when I put myself into the shoes of the Jane and Susannah of those years. We were both complicit in a certain grandiosity. I wasn't just traveling where few Westerners went at the time, but I was a twenty-something, blonde woman traveling alone in a world that was seen from home as alien and misogynistic. There was a pumped-up glamor involved in my travels, like that of a war correspondent reporting from the front lines. For me, I loved the image of "danger be damned" even though I was actually quite cautious. For my mother, she loved the story of My Daughter Alone in the Middle East. Her words, if I died *she* might be even more interesting, fit to my mother's perverse honesty. In her world, which was still my world then, a glamorous death outperformed the reality of mourning and grief.

As my journey wore on, however, inevitably I was influenced by the cultures I was observing and the interactions with people I was meeting. I was learning that how I had grown up was not the best model for a happy life. Though I wasn't religious anymore, in Egypt, God was every-where. Every conversation in Arabic included Allah's name, in greeting, in joking, in planning to meet for coffee later that afternoon, "God will-ing." In the 1980s, it didn't matter so much which religion one had there, but having a religion was expected. My liberal American pride about ag-nosticism and adventure was met with puzzlement and pity.

"Where is your family?" I was asked all the time.

"My father lives in Washington, D.C. and my mother in San Francisco."

"Ah, you mean they are divorced? Oh, that is so sad." They said this with such compassion.

"What about brothers and sisters?"

"I'm an only child."

Now the faces got even sadder. "You poor girl. You must go home to your mother. She misses you."

It irritated me to be talked to like this. What did they know? I was a traveling journalist. I was on my own. "No, I like being here."

There was then always a pause, and some sort of rise of the chin, as if they didn't believe me. "Your family. Roots. That is what tells you who you are," they would say.

I began to want that, but I didn't yet know how to create it.

* * *

After two years in Egypt and three months backpacking in India, during which I met German Niels, who would eventually become my husband, I returned to California, aged twenty-four. I had begun han-kering for orderly traffic and Safeway supermarkets. I wasn't writing as diligently as I could have. It was time to go home. I applied to 100 news-papers all across the United States. It seemed to be the obvious path.

In September I was hired as a reporter for the *Dallas Times Herald,* making $1,200 a month. In Texas—a middle-of-the-U.S. redneck-y place I'd never been and had never wanted to go. But it was a salary. I felt rich. And now I was settled.

A great sense of accomplishment and joy seizes me. Susannah has graduated with honors from Berkeley, traveled the world on her own and now has a good and well-paying job. I have no man in my life. The latter constant must remain constant. (December 31, 1987)

Those years in Dallas were challenging in a new way. Traveling alone, I had been responsible only for myself. Figuring out where to buy tampons could become my most compelling daily task, and when I found them, my day was fulfilled. I didn't have to prove anything to anyone. But in Dallas I was called upon to be part of a newspaper team, to enter a work community, and one where morale was slipping because the hollowing out of American journalism by cable and talk radio had already begun.

For someone like me, used to an intense twosome growing up, and unschooled in the humor and tactics needed to negotiate group dynamics, the newsroom was a deep challenge.

I loved riding in an ambulance helicopter, rushing out to the airport after a crash, interviewing a little boy with cerebral palsy, and scrubbing in to observe his spinal operation. I loved to learn. But I didn't thrive as a staff reporter. Despite all my travels, I felt vulnerable and insecure, retorts to office gibes coming to my mind only much later when I replayed the day. I could never really take part in office banter. There was also a male-chauvinist edge to the place. The women who did well were snappy and immune.

I took to bonding with other reporters through drinking after work; cigarettes counteracting what I always worried were my too-gentle looks. I'm tougher than you think, was my subtle message to the world. I flash now to a John Prine concert, learning to appreciate country music, tasting whiskeys, my Zippo lighter, being adopted as "Hey, Irish" by a veteran cowboy reporter with a black beard and a wry sense of humor.

Was newsroom life going to end up a healthy one for me? It wasn't that I really thought I was the same as my father, that his alcoholism would duplicate itself in me. That was my mother's prophecy. But I did see it was nerve-racking to sit in story conferences and pitch an idea. I wanted to be tough like the sassy Texan police reporter, a Dolly Parton-type who flirted effortlessly with cops and jail staff on the phone, warm-hearted and fearless. Instead, I was a too-soft Yankee with an interest in foreign cultures. I didn't love the cold calls to grieving parents for comments after a shooting, the street interviews after an accident, the sleuthing on the trail of a story. I would need to toughen up, and I could tell that would mean more whiskeys and fewer insights.

And always there was Niels, my challenging, funny, unafraid, blue-eyed, German love whom I had met in India. The first telling of our stories, our beginning affair, was part of a slow-paced life, toes in the sand on a travelers' beach in southern Goa. It was set against a backdrop of music by the Doors and shrimp-fried rice in beach shacks. We had arranged to meet again in Kerala, India, and six months later, he had borrowed money from his uncle to visit me in the U.S., where he had never been. After he finished medical school, he obtained an internship in internal medicine in Madison, Wisconsin. For four months we were geographically closer, he in Wisconsin and I in Dallas. Each airport meeting, I'd spy his worn leather coat up ahead, his high forehead and slightly asymmetrical face, and I'd be wrapped in his arms and the heady smell of cigarettes and his skin, and I was in love all over again.

I'd never liked or been attracted to anything German, whether nude beaches, or stocky men in white socks and sandals, Oktoberfests, or the pop hit *99 Luftballons*. But that wasn't his Germany. His Germany was Wim Wenders' *Himmel über Berlin*, clubs playing Patti Smith and The Clash, working class idioms, irony, and male friends who found me too polite. It was like a fundamental bad-boy challenge to everything I'd grown up with.

"Ask the questions of life," he'd say. "Don't be afraid to be alone."

* * *

On my first visit to Germany, I knew I'd learn a lot more about him. It was Easter and I had two weeks off from the newspaper. I had flown directly from Dallas.

"Hey, come sit here with me in the kitchen, put your feet up," Niels said, moving one of the kitchen chairs around in his little flat so I could extend my legs after the long flight. I Ie took a bottle of red wine from the rack. "I'll cook and you tell me about life in the newsroom. You have vacation now!"

He poured the liquid into two small Italian glasses.

"*Prost, willkommen in Deutschland.*" He reached over to look me in the eyes and clink my glass with a warm smile.

This was going to be a fun two weeks, I thought. I didn't even know about the music clubs until dawn, the Broetchen breakfasts and the Sunday walks along the river.

"After dinner, if you feel up to it, we can go out and I'll show you Reeperbahn life."

He had often regaled me in his fluent English with tales of life in Hamburg's famous avant-garde district where he lived. On our drive in from the airport, I had glimpsed only unkempt arrangements of blocks, some older wooden buildings and many neon-adorned come-hither marquees of big-busted women with bulky gatekeepers standing out front. There were hardened faces walking the streets.

For now, this all seemed exciting and delicious. I wrapped my arms around him. "No jet lag yet!" And we kissed that first kiss of getting to know each other again.

Later, as Niels chopped and stirred in the kitchen, I observed the street life two floors below.

"What does *Astra Brauerei* mean?" I pointed to a large brick building across the street.

"Astra is a beer company," he said in his resonant voice, his consonants more Scandinavian than typically German. "Do you say 'brewery'? Sometimes it gets noisy when they transport the bottles early in the morning. My hospital is just on the other side, see?"

He indicated a red brick building peeking out across the industrial courtyard. "I have the world's best commute."

There were more people out now in the evening. Cars patrolled the cobblestoned street for parking places. My eyes were drawn to the row of women in the tiny skirts and thigh-high boots at the end of the block. It looked like they were staking out a meter of sidewalk each. Almost all were smoking. Almost all were young and beautiful.

"Hey, I'm assuming those women are prostitutes across the street, right? Do men really—," I stopped talking as a dark-coiffed woman approached a hunched man walking in a gray windbreaker. There was some sort of negotiation. The man walked on.

"Where do they go, if they get a client?"

"They have rooms all around, usually near their section of the street."

"Is that all just—legal?"

Niels shrugged. "Sure. It is all regulated. They pay taxes. They have shifts and sometimes they have children. They come into the hospital as patients. They are just normal people with a job," he said matter-of-factly.

I watched a little longer but there were no more encounters on the street. Is that really a job a woman would choose?

Niels was becoming an expert on crazy people, specializing in psychiatry. Once, on a home visit, still common in medicine at that time, he had discovered a six-foot column of tomato sandwiches in the back of a patient's closet.

Niels drove a motorcycle, and he told stories about delousing homeless drunks at the clinic.

Nothing that scared me scared him.

After a couple of years more in Dallas, I applied to graduate school to continue studying the Arab world, and while I waited to hear whether I had been accepted, I moved to Hamburg.

Jane's 50th

1988

A DVD OF A SURPRISE PARTY for my mother's 50th birthday is among
my mother's papers. My cousins organized the gathering in 1988. I was
still a reporter in Dallas. The party took place at my great aunt Susie's Southern California house. In the film, we see that the door was
draped with a black wreath. The birthday cake writing, below a row of
black roses, spells "Regrets Only," and the date June 29, 1988. Guests
are all wearing black sleeve garters.

Twenty or so first cousins are gathered, along with Susie's neighbors, and friends who had known my mother for the many years she
had been a regular houseguest. The dress code seems to have been pre-
scribed black and white, and someone off camera chides my mother for
her green and pink billowy silk outfit in the way someone chides a cha-
meleon. Hilarity and laughter fill all the rooms. My mother hugs and
greets each of her East Coast cousins, genuinely surprised and thrilled
that they have traveled so far.

I am nowhere to be seen. *Why am I not there?*

The first time I watched the film, my children and Niels in the
room, I cringed. I fast-forwarded. Forward. Forward. It was hard to
watch her, her life-of-the-party acting, her beauty and her posturing.

I wanted to be a filter for my children. The funeral-tinged party, the diaries. It was too much of a harbinger of the future we had recently experienced. I just wanted the video to be over.

This second watching, though, I have slowed it all down. I am alone here at my desk. I am determined to take more in. I watch as Cousin Trevor introduces the speeches with the somber notes of Chopin's Funeral March on the grand piano.

They all knew. They always knew. And everyone laughed on.

The year she turned fifty had been a memorable one for my mother. She had won a lawsuit against the San Francisco Unified School District, in which, largely due to her own research and efforts, the district was convicted of an unlawful policy of laying off teachers and then re-hiring them as long-term substitutes without seniority and benefits. She was compensated for all those summers she had had to rent out her apartment to afford to travel, and she was awarded back pay for the lack of tenure.

"I fought City Hall. In the Middle Ages they would have burned me at the stake," she writes.

She was enormously proud of her efforts, but for some reason her struggles had not permeated into the lore of the extended family. I understand now that she had not received enough of a spotlight from the greater family for fighting the system, both as an inner-city schoolteacher and as a member of the rebellious slate of the KQED public television station board of directors. I think it was partly because her splashy politics did not overlap smoothly with more conventional interests of the greater family.

But I wonder, too, if it was just the fate of any woman in a family dominated by very male traditions of military history and finance. She provoked laughter for her provocative comments, but maybe the laughter was a way of subverting her voice. Maybe that is why she craved fame so much. "I still feel ineffably disappointed re outcome of lawsuit and lack of ability to get the story told in *Newsweek*," she wrote in her diary after her birthday celebration.

Indeed, the lawsuit certainly wasn't the centerpiece of her party. Speeches instead turned out to be more like a roast—a treasure hunt for my mother's "missing diary."

As I watch, this detail dumbfounds me. My heart beats faster.

I hadn't made it up.

Her diaries were her totem even back then.

"There once was a girl named Jane for whom diary writing was no pain," Aunt Susie reads. "Alas, one diary is lost in some nook. She will find it again, by hook or by crook. And here is your first clue."

In the film, my mother's eyes flash quickly around the room though she smiles brightly. She seems genuinely unsure whether this is real or not. A teensy bit vulnerable.

"I never did a treasure hunt before," she says, taking the microphone from Susie. "Especially not for my diary. *Nobody read the diary!*"

She says it like a statement, though it is really a question. She looks stern, like she is trying for her schoolteacher mode. "Reading a diary is despicable," she says.

She looks ready to lecture the room.

"Jane, would you stop worrying and get the next clue," interrupts Aunt Susie. Susie knows it is all just a practical joke that will eventually lead to a fake "journal."

Watching the footage, I enjoy observing my great-aunts and my grandfather, my uncle and cousins, their postures and voices so familiar. It's magical, the way their idiosyncrasies are captured on camera, Elizabeth's chortle and Susie's cigarettes. There they are. Their voices. Their movements. It's almost like a time machine.

Trevor, a professional satirist, presents Mom's fifty years of life in a made-up diary to uproarious laughter from the audience.

It *is* funny.

Trevor calls it "La Contessa, the Jane Papers, Take 2" and sets up the premise: A private investigator has discovered that Jane affords her grand style of trips abroad on a schoolteacher's salary because she is secretly married to a short Mafioso who lives in Sicily.

"Old money, but Jane has been heard to say she'd prefer it was new," Trevor jests. "The women of the household have been seen to cross themselves and spit as she approaches."

Everyone in the audience is in hysterics.

As I watch, Trevor expertly edits my mother's life into a comedic stage play with just a perfect hint of pathos and mystery.

"But Jane's main project was rearing the ideal daughter and getting her out of the house." Up comes a slide of me looking grown-up and elegant at my grandfather's wedding anniversary party a few years before. "Susannah has inherited her mother's wanderlust but not her belief that a man's most attractive quality is his ability to make money and spend it on her," Trevor deadpans.

There is great laughter in the background.

"Here is a photo of Susannah begging money from her mother, who pretends not to see her." Trevor shows a travel shot of me under a huge backpack, my arm extended toward my mother who looks annoyed somewhere past the camera.

I can laugh at the truly funny moments now. It doesn't hurt as much as it used to. My relationship to my large Irish family has always been filtered through the prism of my mother's overlarge personality. When they got together, and they got together often, there was great hilarity and poking fun. My mother blossomed under this attention. It was her milieu. It allowed her to feel loved.

At the end of her birthday weekend, she writes:

> Told by the generous talent of Quilters, [my life] didn't sound half bad. (July 1, 1988)

> I guess the best part was the knowledge so many did so much for me. I am unused to [that]. My solitary independent and self-contained life is of my own choosing but this week has been a true ego trip and beauty part. (July 3, 1988)

This is a mixed message for me. The family always celebrated her and saw in her someone to celebrate. I was envious of the laughter and love. Yet I couldn't help but take their mutual jubilation with a grain of salt. It was confusing.

At the very end of the hour-long home movie, the main party is now over, and the crowd has assembled the following day at nearby Cousin Richard's canyon house. The four youngest cousin children, excluded from the first night, now make an appearance, singing cute, "Jane sailed away on a sunny summer day" songs and acting out, "Jane in Italy" skits.

Suddenly I see myself.

Look, I was there after all.

I replay the scene in which I appear, with 1980s fluffy hair and beige Dallas office wear. I am holding a full Champagne glass high near my face, as if for protection, smiling politely in response to cousins' anecdotes. I don't seem to be saying much.

After the skits, my mother is called upon to give a speech. She challenges everyone in the room to recite "one thing" they would change in their lives right now.

She goes first. "I can say instantly. The one thing I would change. I would be small. I would not be tall." She snaps her fingers.

Cousin Melina says: "I would have taken far more risks."

Aunt Fran says: "I probably wish I had been able to tell more people how much they meant to me in their lives."

My grandfather says, "I don't want to be smug. I wouldn't change a thing. I don't think there is a more fortunate person in this house."

My mother eventually points to me, standing over in the kitchen. Her challenge catches me out.

"Uh," I see myself murmur, "mine's too personal." I know I am thinking of my job and Niels and where I belonged in the world. Those topics were weighing heavily on my psyche in those years.

I wanted to decline this truth-or-dare game.

As I watch my twenty-four-year-old self, I am rattled. Why

couldn't I just make up something cute and pithy? "*All the world's a stage*," right? That's what she always said.

But in Mom's presence, I chose the stage wings over stage center, where I knew my light would appear dim in her reflection.

Oxford

1990

I took the chance to study at Oxford for a master's and then doctorate for two reasons. One, the old buildings were gorgeous. I was giddy that I had been given the chance to study in those ancient libraries and walk those famous streets. Two, it was close enough to Niels in Hamburg to allow us to continue our long-distance relationship. We could see each other during my term vacations and sometimes on weekends.

I loved studying the Arab world at Oxford. Students were given room to explore whatever interested them, without the influence of politics. I did not have to engage at every seminar with the topic of Israel as would have been the case in the U.S. Oxford was quiet. It was understated. The tutorial teaching system meant weekly one-on-one meetings with a professor, combined with seminars, papers and research on one's own. Graduate students wrote a weekly ten-page essay arguing through a particular hypothesis, and read it aloud in tutorial, delving into finer points in discussion.

I was free. No more interviewing victims of accidents for headline material in a daily newspaper. Finally, I could study deeply. I could tap into experienced minds and think about life's big questions. Within the first term I switched my degree from Middle East studies—

emphasizing texts and published documents—to social anthropology, the study of people as they live and engage with the world. I had found my place. It had taken detours of travel and working, but eventually I found myself in the field my Berkeley professor had predicted.

While traveling, I had experienced the confusion of culture clashes firsthand, how an answer to a question about arranged marriage depended entirely on the person asking and the audience listening to the answer. In New York, arranged marriage sounded cruel. In New Delhi it was wise. "For all your talk of love marriages, look at what happens in your culture," I heard many times in different tones. "So many divorces. So many sad alone people with all those children suffering." I couldn't argue with that description.

Truth in Egypt was not the same as truth in California, or truth in New Delhi. I was finally acquiring the tools to see social fabric as something that can be deconstructed, layer after layer. I could study how gifts in a functioning social network can be seen as both satisfying the giver and implying obligation to the recipient. Or how Arab headscarves are donned as submission to a rough father, or, contrarily, as the proud regalia of a feminist. Both could be true.

Even as a child, I'd had a love for peering behind the social façade. One of my favorite things had been to entertain my mother after a party with my insights into what had been going on under the surface, how Jinny's hand had lain a little too close to Leslie's husband Rick's knee on the couch, how cousin Janine's laugh had sounded fake, how neighbor Mrs. Jones had changed the subject a little too quickly when she was asked about her son's new job.

What people hide is more interesting than what they show.

San Francisco in the 1970s had been a liberal and questioning place. Conversations everywhere—on the radio, at dinner parties, on the buses—held snippets of possibility for me. Werner Erhard's *est*, Woody Allen's twenty years on the couch, everyone's talk therapies, body therapies, Rolfing, talking to plants, Alice Waters' salads. Though my mother's inner world had remained narrow, the outer world in which we moved had been full of variety, craziness, and challenge. I absorbed that, too. Why live if one didn't live an authentic life, asking the deep questions, open to curiosity?

So at Oxford, in the midst of studying to deconstruct cultures, I sought out a therapist. Twice a week, I rode my bicycle to a quaint house on a little Oxford street to talk to a white-haired lady who helped me start the journey to understand where my mother left off and I began.

"Never say anything bad about my mother," I had sworn in bitter tones to Niels in our first conversations in Goa three years before. "I can criticize her, but nobody else can." That had been my incantation since the days of my boyfriend Mark in high school.

I remember how Niels raised an eyebrow. "Are you kidding me?" he said.

"No. Really," I sent right back. Conviction made my voice louder even than Jim Morrison's voice on the stereo above our heads.

I could see Niels' eyes cloud slightly, a private, "*Uh-oh. What am I getting myself into*," as the waiter approached with our dinner.

We still laugh about it, he more fully and I more ruefully, when certain topics about what it means to be human come up.

"We are all alone on this Earth," Niels loves to say.

"Humans need connection," I retort.

"True, but first they need to know who they are," he says.

Indeed, the prying apart of the particulars between Jane and me has been my stickiest life challenge. Niels and I still don't agree on certain philosophical points, such as whether humans are innately destructive and whether my inclination towards the good is ingenuous or accurate. Our back-and-forths have made life full and have helped us parent our children better than we were parented.

In Oxford in the 1990s, though I had traveled and worked and drank and smoked and wrote, I was still thinking of myself as my mother's protector. Even more ingrained, I couldn't rid myself of the core feeling I was living my life wrong. That whatever made me different from her was a defect.

For example, my mother was a master of the memorable scene. "Your mother is such a hoot," a friend of hers once confided to me. "Can you believe she took a turn at the pole dance at our party? And she was great!"

Mom liked to do outrageous things and then tell the story about it later. Once she was arrested for protesting a slow-down at the Orange County airport. She stepped up onto the baggage carousel and refused to leave until security put her in handcuffs and led her away. She wrote regular letters to the editor outlining San Francisco school district corruption or in support of Occupy Wall Street. When she discovered female staff at her snooty all-women fitness club did not receive maternity leave, she organized a formal protest to management and eventually withdrew her membership. All these events became stories to tell to a gathered audience, something I could never manage. As soon as an audience gave me their attention, my brain scrambled. I forgot words. I blushed.

They say therapy is the peeling of an onion, a slow approach to understanding one's core. For me it was more of a Rosetta Stone, a way to decipher the world of emotions, of complex human interchange and trust that couldn't be viewed from only one angle. It gave me a vocabulary for What Was, to help me with What Would Be.

But the lessons came in fits and starts.

One day, when I heard the gaggle of extroverted students in St. Antony's junior common room joking about an upcoming slave-for-the-day auction, I realized I was envious. Oxford was famous not only for its studies. It was also famous for its silliness and social life. I wanted to be part of the "in" crowd, too. Maybe this was my chance to be free of my motherly inner critic. I signed up and joked with my friends that it would be fun.

The evening arrived. The bar area was crowded. Everyone was in a good mood, ready for the weekend. One by one, women and men got up onto the little stage and the auctioneer rattled off their names "Okay, who wants Rob here to be their slave for the day? All your wishes will come true for a starting bid of five pounds. Dishes cleaned. Carried up and down the stairs."

Everyone hooted and hollered. "What else ya gonna do, Rob!?"
Angelina won for forty pounds.

Eventually, my turn came. I stepped up on the stage. The auction-eer was a slightly nerdy goof, but also someone with whom I'd had smart conversations. He looked uncomfortable when he saw me. He tried for the same sale. But the room grew quiet.

Nobody bid. There was a pause.

"Oh, come on folks, who wants Susannah to be your slave for a day?"

I straightened my shoulders. I tried for an ironic smile, as if the awkward silence didn't matter.

Alistair, an upper-class British guy who lived a room over from me, finally called out: "Yeah, I'll bid five pounds."

Everyone clapped with relief. "Sold to Alistair."

My cheeks burned.

I stepped off the stage carefully, nodding lightheartedly at Alistair in the crowd, and escaped into the group of students with whom I nor-mally hung out. They were over in the far corner having a beer.

"Um, what were you doing?" someone asked.

"What?" I responded, "I was just having some fun."

"You don't belong there," someone else said.

A sharp breath expanded in my lungs.

Alistair approached. *Oh shit.*

"Hey, ready for our day?" I said, still unconsciously mimicking the light-hearted provocative tone my mother had mastered.

"Yeah, er, I felt sorry for you up there," he mumbled. "Don't worry, you don't have to do anything."

My ears clogged up, and the room's rumble and laughter moved very far away.

Then suddenly I saw what they all saw. I was mature and serious, in graduate school, a former reporter. I wasn't in kindergarten.

I still had to learn to know who I was and who I was not.

* * *

"Mom?" I was visiting my mother in San Francisco the summer after my first year at Oxford. I had been sitting quietly on the soft living-room couch, pretending to read but actually waiting for a time when she might be open to a conversation. "I have a feeling you will hate what I have to ask, but I'm going to ask it anyway." I could feel my heartbeat in my throat.

My mother was sitting on a short three-legged red stool picking off mealy bugs from the philodendron in the sunroom a few feet away.

"What is it?" Her fingers reached for the next dark green leaf, turned it over, looking for the telltale white insect.

"You know I started therapy a few months ago."

"Yes." She dipped a Q-tip in the rubbing alcohol and dabbed at the leaf's underside. Nothing changed, but her demeanor felt tense. Or was I just imagining it?

I sat up straighter, let out a breath. "You know I don't remember much from my childhood, right?" She nodded slightly. "I have some questions my therapist suggested I ask you."

A flinch skittered over her cheek, whether out of irritation or out of somewhere painful. "Well, go ahead and ask." She dabbed at another leaf.

I unfolded the list that had been sticking out of my jeans pocket. The list I'd written on the airplane and had been carrying around for days. I took a deep breath.

"Did Alan ever give you a black eye or bruises?" When I had written out the question, I had opted to use my father's first name. It had seemed more adult, as if by putting him in the third person, like any man anywhere, I would automatically feel less vulnerable. It didn't feel natural, though. I still wanted to call him Daddy.

Seconds passed. My mother turned on her stool, forearm on her thigh. She looked directly at me. "Yes, he did. There were black eyes, split lips and bruises." She turned back to the leaves.

"Really," I responded. It was a question, but it came out in a low pitch, as if corroborating someone else's suspicions.

I had only one vivid memory from my life with my parents together, a fight when I was seven, after we had moved from Manhattan to San Francisco. They were punching each other, my father standing over her in the wing chair, both faces twisted with rage. Yelling. My father's pipe falling to the floor. Tobacco spilling out. My memory lingers on that pile of leaves, as if in slow motion, a little heap on the short wool rug. Then, my mother running out of the apartment. Where is she going? *Mommy*. I am crying, too, somehow, curling myself into a ball around my soft lamb under the covers, my heart beating hard, *go to sleep, go to sleep, you'll be fine, you'll be fine.*

Had I expected that fight to be their only one?

Which was better? Many fights, which meant I really had childhood amnesia? *There really was something wrong with me.* Or just the one fight, which meant I could trust my memory?

At that moment, though, in her living room, I said nothing and stayed stiff on the couch cushions. My mother continued with her leaves. She didn't elaborate.

No words formed in my brain. I glanced at my sheet. Just go to the next question. Stay on track here.

"Did you have a good sex life?" I wanted to curl my shoulders in. My voice cracked. This was none of my business. But it was a question that had no answer in my catalog of stories about my life. I had no memory of my parents ever being loving in their seven years together with me, no kisses or hugs or laughter. But they had shared one bed, so that must mean something. And I am able to love as an adult. So that means something. The thought of my parents together mostly evokes a dark unease. A weekend noon glimpse of a long lump in bed in a darkened room. Daddy hung over.

"Yes. I was enraptured by him at first." She put down her Q-tip package. "Sex is the most automatic of appetites under those circumstances." I held my breath. She took up her shears and started to clip brown leaves off the plant. "He was always kind when he wasn't drinking."

"Did he ever force sex on you?" I looked down at my list, feeling ridiculous. But come on, I was supposed to find this out.

"No." Her tone was normal, sure.

I relaxed. *Whew*. I had never really suspected he had raped her. That didn't fit with what I knew of my father. I noticed in myself an inkling of disappointment, too. Sexual violence would have made a good tale when I got back to England. *Tragic. A raped mother*. Hah. I shook my head at this perverse wish. As if my real story wasn't enough.

This was a weird exercise.

I glanced down at my list. "Did you usually send me to bed before a fight? Did I ever ask you about your fights?"

"You went to bed about 7:30 after a bath and a story. This usually coincided with your father's third or fourth drink. Fights were regular and loud," she said in a monotone. A fire engine's siren suddenly appeared in the distance. "I imagine they frightened you as they did me. I don't recall you saying anything about them." Her tone was clipped and business-like, as if she were a witness on the stand.

The siren stopped suddenly. Was there a fire nearby? She didn't seem to hear it. "My defense was to deny, deny, deny while planning my exit to California. You were always a model child, loving, bright."

She abruptly stood up and walked over to test the moistness of the dirt in her orchid pots. "Our neighbors in New York knew, but never talked about it. We played the serene parents. When your father appeared with you and me, he played that part best of all."

Her eyes looked sad, as if she had been caught out doing something bad. It was an admission of the falsehoods, the secrecy.

I hurried to the next question, sensing impatience. *She's not going to put up with this much longer*. "Did you hide things from me? I'm growing up, I'd like to know."

"I did hide things. I don't go for the mother-child confidante idea."

The church bells from Saints Peter and Paul began ringing, announcing Mass down the hill in North Beach.

"Susannah," she said. She looked directly at me for the second time. "I am not pleased about having to go back to a time in my life where I felt out of control of daily events, where I had little self-respect and virtually no sustained happiness. You and your father are manipulating me." *Gulp.* I recognized her turn in tone. She had had enough.

"Why are you bringing up Daddy?" I grimaced. *What did he have to do with these questions?*

"He called me recently, spurred by your new therapy ideas. He seemed interested in talking." She scoffed. "I don't want to have anything to do with him ever again."

She gathered up two orchids in their pots and carried them to the kitchen for their ritual root bath.

I remained sitting on the couch.

I had reason not to remember my childhood and understood better why I might have suppressed memories. But why had the neighbors chosen silence? Why had nobody stood up for the little girl?

Our Wedding

1991

MARIA, MY MAID OF HONOR, finally appeared in the worn wooden foyer where I was standing, fidgeting. I caught the movement of her arm and her laugh as she ended her conversation with someone unseen around the corner. A momentary hope flashed through my mind. Maybe it was my mother after all. But Maria smiled widely at me, no hint of a surprise in the offing. My friends Sophia and Emma, standing next to me, had been keeping me company while we waited for the chapel to fill, for Niels's parents to set up their music notes and ease the kinks out of the organ, for friends from Poland to make it to Oxford from the coastal ferry. It was 4:10 p.m., twenty minutes before the ceremony was to begin.

I allowed myself to take a deep breath. There had been some drama between Maria and me over the past weeks. Maria was Italian and beguiling, an elegant third to what had become my Three Graces friend group at the college. But Sophia, blonde and athletic, was the one who had been my sounding board when I had discovered my hand-made tailored wedding suit was a frumpy disaster, and then, panicking, rummaged through my travel treasures for a thick silk Syrian men's cloak, turning it into a last-minute wedding gown. And Emma, soon to become my sister-in-law, had been cool-headedly by my side all morning, fending off my father's queries. I had been ambivalent about inviting him. But here he was, with his companion Patty for company, his new too-big false teeth and an ill-fitting suit.

Maria now eyed the ribboned texture of my blue and white silk kaftan and my barely made-up face. "Come with me," she said, grabbing my hand and leading us all into the women's bathroom down the hall.

"I need a brush," Maria said. Emma pulled one from her purse.

Expertly, Maria's hands gathered the thick hair up off my face and braided it into a French twist. Sophia pulled out her bobby pins, her blush and concealer. I watched in the mirror as the three women worked. Their authority irked me, but I felt myself go still. I was grateful. A few minutes of feeling I was a part of a world of women, something bigger than myself, and I could just be a bride.

Underneath it all, I was on edge. Our decision to marry had been a leap into the unknown. Nobody we knew got married anymore.

My mother had announced she was not going to be there.

Throughout my two years working in Dallas, my relationship with her had deteriorated. She had loved that I was a reporter and especially that I was earning money. I wasn't so sure I was suited to the job. I could keep up good appearances from afar but in my mother's presence my personality faded away. I hid my cigarettes. I showed only the parts of myself that met her approval. Any doubts I voiced about life as a reporter prompted warnings from her; I was becoming my father, wallowing in complaint rather than building a life.

My decision to leave Dallas and spend eight months in Germany testing out day-to-day living with Niels, no matter how well planned out, was something she could not grasp. The more I loved him, the more she scoffed. When it became clear I was leaving my temporary Hamburg English teaching job for academic Oxford, her hopes for me seemed dashed entirely.

What a way to face one's 30s deep in debt in $ when she may be living in a Deutsche Mark economy. Why didn't she save more while in Dallas? Would Niels even be paid an excellent salary? Will he marry her and support her? Oh lord, all those genes predisposed to alcohol. (May 17, 1989)

Our relationship became a tug of war about guilt and loyalty, my mother sometimes offering me a hand and financial support, sometimes slamming down her inner gate, walling me off from her warmth. I hated being involved in this on-again, off-again conversation that increasingly focused on money rather than career interests and inner health and happiness. Sometimes I pulled myself loose. I got student loans and part-time jobs, applied for scholarships. By my third year, though, I needed her help. So I played polite for the sake of the support that might come.

Niels flew in from his Hamburg medical fellowship for a long weekend visit to Oxford in 1990, and we were joyfully laughing and goofing off in my large attic dorm room with its narrow twin bed when he suggested suddenly we could get married. I stopped everything to think and then said yes. It was crazy and exhilarating. We were giddy and terrified. Marriage just wasn't what our twenty-something friends were doing in the 1990s. Affairs, sure. Live together, okay, why not? Children, maybe someday. But married? Where had that come from? Yet it felt right.

This morning as I was doing my exercises the phone rang. It was Niels. He said he and Susannah had decided to get married. I assumed they were planning to do so today or tomorrow and I gave my tentative blessing, provided he stopped smoking ... Then I realized Susannah wanted me to offer to have an old-fashioned, formal family and friends' wedding here. I told her no way and she seemed sad and disillusioned. I am not an industrial product to be used when needed. She is not a virgin, white gown, Catholic walking down the aisle. (November 12, 1990)

Mom wanted nothing to do with our wedding plans. "Niels smokes," she'd say to anyone who asked. "Susannah is selfish." In her diaries, I am a daughter who nags her mother for money and obligates her to forward mail and organize sending the furniture stored in Dallas. As I read, if I am not careful, I end up disliking the me she describes.

I wonder if it is wise to refuse to share more with Susannah. Maybe I should allow her a less penurious and starving student kind of life. But she has been out of Berkeley five years. She has chosen that life, mainly following lovers of one nationality or another. I don't understand nor approve. (January 7, 1990)

Money is a tricky topic when family love is twisted. Poverty has its tender formulas. Privilege has its own. I know now that many families treat their children with openness, supporting them financially when they can and encouraging independence, too.

"Keep finances separate from emotions by talking about it with your kids. Don't keep things a secret," my financial advisor said a few years ago. I still think that sounds smart.

Back then; my mother rightly intuited I was not separate from her emotionally, so she kept a sticky connection of favors and obligations. She wanted me to connect to her emotionally, and I gladly accepted any financial kindnesses. The notion grew, exponentially, that love was there when money was there. Then love became money.

Though I truly didn't care that I lived in a sweet Oxford house with no heat that required making a coal fire in the fireplace each winter morning, nor how many times I trod the Barclay Bank walk of shame after my debit card was swallowed by the ATM as I dipped into overdraft, I also enjoyed her luxuries. Especially travel. We both mourned the loss of our closeness.

The family fold is bringing pressure to bear on me to go to Susannah's wedding .... still want me to do the dutiful Mother thing and go. I won't because Susannah has hurt me for so many years with her dislike of me and her abuse of herself. (February 14, 1991)

Now, as I stood there in the foyer of the chapel where I would wed, my hair made suddenly festive, my hand slipping through Niels's arm preparing to step toward the front of the chapel, I looked around. I was still hoping she would be there. That she'd be sitting in the back pew behind all my cousins. That she'd fly in just in time and pretend she had never written me a letter that said: "My extreme discomfort about marriage ceremonies, my adamant feelings about smokers and my insight that you'll relax and enjoy being a bride much more if I am not there, compels me to tell you and Niels not to expect me."

I knew she was stating her truth. But still, I hoped. I was her only child. She was my only mother. I hoped until the very last second.

Even after rice was thrown over our heads, and the roses were given to all the guests and we headed in a messy procession down Walton Crescent to the Lebanese restaurant, I caught myself looking around for her. Maybe her plane had been late. Maybe she'd arrive for dinner. I watched my grandfather and my cousins closely for signs they knew something. It was at the late-night party that it finally hit me. The relatives had gone home, and friends had shed their ties and pulled unmatched chairs into our little side garden. Jokes traveled back and forth.

In a quiet moment, Niels put his hand on mine, our rings flashing so new. He smiled gently. He understood all the layers of the day.

"She really didn't come," he acknowledged quietly.

At least my husband knew me. That must be a good sign.

She wrote in her diary that day:

Today is the wedding day of my daughter and I am far from her in miles to reflect the distancing she has done as adult from mother. She was such a wonderful child. Motherhood

was my finest enterprise and I was as proud of my daughter
as I was of myself. But it was all fake—come to find out my
daughter resented me for reasons still unclear and she took
strength and heart in the fact of making her own life and
personality away from me—out of touch. I remember that
same pride and strength when I freed myself from Alan. Niels
called and very gently said: "You will always be welcome with
us." (June 21, 1991)

I read this and immediately feel a familiar guilt. First, *my poor
mother, abandoned by her beloved daughter.* Then, *wait!* She equates
my growing up into an independent adult with herself ending a violent
marriage. She projects into me the identity of the suffering victim she
had once been. What a mess.

I wish we could have unraveled it together. It adds up to such un-
necessary heartbreak.

She never apologized. Not once. Not even when I dared to bring
it up in person years later.

"You wouldn't have wanted me there," she said.

"Yes, I did want you there."

"Why?" was her answer.

"Because you're my mother! And I love you, and I wanted you at
my wedding."

She shrugged, turning her attention to the pages of the magazine
she had been holding. Conversation over. I again was left feeling that
I was a huckster trying to sell her on myself, like my father must have
once tried to sell her that *this time* he would stop drinking.

What were the real reasons she never came to our wedding? For
years, cousins and friends asked me what I thought. Was she unable to
see my father again? Was she hiding a depression? Was she too vain to
be Mother of the Bride? Her diary gives some clues. There seems to be
an underlying complaint:

I am a motherless child and a childless mother. I feel dispirit-
ed and I miss Mother and Susannah. It would be nice to talk
to them and feel a support that goes deeper than causes or
politics. So many times in the rush and business of the days
which are full and interesting I stop to assess if I'd prefer never
to have been born and the answer, "Yes," always comes back—
not a suicidal, tortured yes, just a factual acknowledgement
that life is so disappointing and death is not a big deal in the
face of that realization. (October 6, 1990)

But looking at it now, I think that isn't enough of an explanation.
She wasn't one to act on her private complaints. Her public life was
too vivid for depressed suicide. No, now I believe that she stayed away
because my marriage to Niels symbolized that I was not choosing her.

It left a hole in my heart for years.

A Call in the Night

1994

THE PHONE WAS RINGING. Two times, three times. *Ugh. Maybe it would stop.*

"Hey, wake up. Aren't you going to answer it?" Niels nudged my thigh under the thick down quilt.

I didn't want to get up. I didn't even want to open my eyes. I could tell it was deepest, darkest dark. In March in northern Germany, it wouldn't be light for hours. The phone kept ringing. Four times. Five times. I maneuvered my baby belly to snuggle into Niels's back.

"No, it is just my father. I don't want to answer it."

In the three years since our wedding, my father had been trying to make good on his fatherhood. Perhaps as a result of *est,* or his years out of contact in the Florida Keys, he had been reaching out regularly to both my mother and me.

> Alan called me this evening and said he would like to come out so we could "spend some time together." He said he had a "continuing attachment" for me. I am fairly certain he was drunk! (March 15, 1992)

The following year, coordinated with our vacation from Hamburg in San Francisco, Dad had flown west, rented a sailboat and taken all of us out on the Bay, including my mother. A photograph of that day shows him squinting into the sun, bloated once-handsome cheeks drawn into a sort of smile sitting in the stern next to her, her thin hand holding onto a large black sunhat, her face in the shadows.

I remember that moment. I felt the breeze in my hair and moved with the canting of the boat. I tried to brand the scene into memory. It was the first time they had been together since my childhood. I kept expecting tension, but they were calm and friendly, almost like strangers.

> It was a beautiful day and fine brisk sail. Susannah and Niels were handy and good crew. And I just settled back and relaxed. I'm glad Alan came. (May 23, 1993)

My father had also visited us in Hamburg once before we were married. It was before the Wall came down, and we had taken a train trip to East Berlin. When I write those words, they sound like a loving father's effort to reconnect and I feel ashamed that I resented him so much. My mother's mantra for twenty years had been to warn me that my deadbeat father would show up someday on my doorstep hungry and penniless.

She often questioned: "Will you have the strength to turn him away?" She feared a sense of loyalty would dictate I care for him. How *would* I respond?

But my father had rallied at age sixty. He secured an editing job for the U.S. Actuarial Society and specialized in predictions about the development of Alzheimer's in the general population. Money was tight, but as always, he had a lovely intelligent woman in his life, this time named Patty. He rented a tiny basement studio in a well-heeled Washington, D.C. neighborhood.

Conversations with my father in person had often been meaningful. Especially during my years as a reporter in Dallas, when he returned from teaching sailing in the Florida Keys, when he was deep into *est,* and had learned a new vocabulary. We exchanged complicated letters and even more complicated phone calls.

As long as alcohol was not a topic, he was insightful and interested in life questions. A good listener. Even when the language he used was circumlocutory. But what I remember most from his trip to Germany was the sour gin smell of his skin and the hole in the bottom of his shoe that allowed the weather to seep into his sock. He would not (could not?) buy a new pair of shoes, and I was afraid to wound his pride by insisting. When we took a walk through the touristy Reeperbahn red-light district, nudie-bar gatekeepers tried to entice him away from us.

"Hey, sir, stop bothering that nice young couple. We have something for you in here." They thought my father was a dirty old man. *Cringe.*

Was I too dismissive of him that trip? Maybe I had just needed a little more time to be angry.

Now, I cuddled into Niels's back after finally hearing the last of the rings from the telephone. The only person who ever called in the middle of the night was my father, slurring his words and wanting to talk. He was looking forward to grandfather life and was grateful for our renewed communication. I usually ended up being polite, nodding along.

I sighed. I'd call him back tomorrow. And went back to sleep.

The next morning, Patty called. The sun was out. Our cat Luna was meowing for food. Niels was brushing his teeth in the bathroom.

"*Hallo, Kennedy hier,*" I answered in the German style.

A moment's wait. "Susannah, this is Patty."

"Patty! Oh, hi. How are you?"

"Your father had a stroke last night," she blurted out. Silence.

I didn't know what was appropriate to say.

"Is he okay?" *Was she calling from the hospital?*

"No, he is dead."

I walked the few steps to sit straight-backed on the bed, my hand resting against my beautiful pregnant belly. Patty said she had not heard from him, he hadn't answered his phone. She had contacted the super for a key. They had found him in his room this morning. "He died in the night."

The ringing of the phone in the dark. The ringing.

I had dismissed him, like a lady picking her way through the homeless people under a bridge. An imagined man's outstretched hand accused me.

Niels joined me on the bed, his arm tight around my shoulders, hearing something was wrong. I hung up. "He called and I didn't answer. Had he been trying to tell me something? What if he had been asking for help?"

> Susannah ... called with a voice of doom to say that Alan had died in his sleep in Washington. ... I am struck by the force of my relief that he died easily and also with the realization that his death has been on my mind for 30 years. When Susannah was an infant I longed to be a righteous young widow; in these later years I just hoped he would not live as a guilty burden assumed or declined by Susannah. ...Surely my life's high and lows have been defined by that person. He spared me the lonely widow fate. I have been on my own for so long now. (March 12, 1994)

She suggested I didn't really need to attend the funeral. I had every excuse, being eight months pregnant and all. I didn't owe him anything. But for me there was no option.

"Of course, I will go. He's my father, Mom."

She offered to pay for our plane tickets. Despite our history of uneasy pushes and pulls around money, I was surprised. "Oh, okay, well that's very generous. Thank you." We hadn't given a thought to financing the tickets. It was clear we would fly to Washington even if we had to draw on credit.

Talks with Susannah. They will fly to Washington on Tuesday. Alan's funeral will take place on Friday. I will pay for their
Lufthansa tickets and am gratified that they neither asked nor
waited for that offer before making the travel plans. They will
stay with the Jacksons and the body will be cremated and ashes scattered on the Chesapeake where Alan loved to sail. The
fact that all of these decisions seem perfect and easily arrived at
makes me feel less apprehensive that the toll will be too heavy
for Susannah's pregnancy. Niels's father called and I could hear
his concern echoing mine. Niels is so good to go, too. Time off
is hard on his career I suppose. (March 13, 1994)

Niels and I flew to Washington, D.C., my legs wrapped in support
stockings to ease the long plane ride. We stayed with the same kind
cousins who had taken me in after I had run away from a visit to my
father's house as a teenager, flying plates and angry stepmother voice
the final last straw.

The funeral home director wasn't happy that I chose the simplest
unvarnished pine coffin. *Was I sure? Wouldn't I reconsider?* No. I was
not going to spend any extra money on him. A half-hour later, as next
of kin, with Niels and Patty as support, I followed the solemn man with
bad breath to the bare room where my father lay in his plain wooden
box; skin a new kind of pale.

It was the first time I'd seen a dead body. I looked only long enough
to nod, "Yes, that's him."

My father's forehead was scraped. Patty gasped when she saw it.

"That scrape wasn't there when I found him," she cried.

I didn't want to contemplate what that meant. Had someone
dropped him? Thrown him around?

The memorial arrangements were organized by Patty and my father's St. Mark's congregation. A lot of people came. Lots of friends
he'd made in Washington. First cousins I'd never met. My family that
I did not know. All were concerned about the strain on my pregnancy.

But I felt strong. I took naps. I wore a Japanese black dress with flowy, wrap-around bands of silk. My baby would be fine. I was stalwart and mighty and handling it all. I was holding myself together.

Kennedy cousins I did not know asked about my mother, looking around as if to see her tall profile somewhere in the crowd. My mother's aunts Eleanor, Kay, and Great Uncle Richard came. They claimed they were doing research for their own funerals. I suspect they wanted to lend me their presence. I was grateful.

> Eleanor called. Somehow I got the impression she thought I should attend Alan's funeral. I lack vocabulary both emotional and social to explain the release afforded to a battered wife when the batterer is no more. Eleanor has been emotionally warped all her life—father, husband, sons always derided and dominated her. She fought back via dithering and driving them quasi nuts. But she loved. That's where we differ. (March 14, 1994)

It strikes me that I did not once denounce that my mother wasn't there that day. Alan had been a volatile husband and a difficult ex-husband. I didn't know then exactly how brutal he had been but I knew she had no duty to honor his memory. It is only now, while reading about it all again, that I realize she might have attended for me.

The memorial service was unlike any I have ever witnessed. One by one, friends from his many years in Washington stood and told stories. They cried and sometimes yelled. Stories of alcohol, tempers, stories of change and obdurate refusal to change. Stories of meaning and insight and deep connection. My first cousin Jim whom I did not know, a gracious Air Force colonel and military strategist, held a deeply evocative, intelligent, and empathetic eulogy, tears streaming down his face. Strands of snot were not wiped away.

He told my father's tragic story: "I'd never seen such intelligence." A little boy born too late to a mother who could not care, whiskey nourishment sought too young, men at the manor's mahogany bar, then managing editor of the Princeton newspaper, dropping out, the Korean War, Columbia, Phi Beta Kappa, fluency in Mandarin Chinese, foreign correspondent, India, medical journalism, divorce and a second marriage and divorce, *est,* teaching sailing in the Keys, transitional men's shelter in D.C. before his job at the American Academy of Actuaries provided rent for a studio apartment, then resurrection of a kind.

> I received a long and detailed letter from Kay. She described how loved Alan was and how sad Susannah was at the funeral ceremonies. I wish she had not written. (March 25, 1994)

We scattered his ashes on the Chesapeake Bay, Niels and I and a bunch of new cousins. Flowers floated away from the private dock on the dusky coastal ripples.

Niels and I spent the next day sorting through my father's belongings in his tiny dusty room with its twin bed, two-burner hotplate, and Klimt print on the bathroom door. I packed all his books to be shipped to Germany, the Chinese books I couldn't decipher, the bound books belonging to my grandparents, the sailing instructions, the *Men's Sexual Health,* the Eastern poetry and novels. I couldn't bear to give them away. Books were what my father had left me. Books and original iron railroad nails and a wooden trunk.

That is, I thought that was all he'd left me, until the appointment to pick up the contents of his desk at the actuarial office, where a Human Resources functionary informed me I would be receiving a check for $90,000. Suddenly, the world turned upside down. The man who had been born to millions and died almost penniless had worked for those last years to pay for a life insurance policy with me named as beneficiary. In relatively poor health, he must have felt he owed me something, maybe all those years of late child support. I was stupefied, and then giddy. It was a lot of money for me. At the end of our week, we splurged to rent a car and took a road trip to the

Hamptons, so Niels could see where Alan had grown up, where I had spent a few early summers in those violent New York years, where my unknown family was buried.

Baby Bauch

1994

BEFORE PATTY'S FATEFUL PHONE CALL, I had been writing my dissertation, working as a Business English teacher, and experiencing the German version of preparation for motherhood. Niels and I had moved back to Germany when my London fieldwork was finished so he could complete the rest of his residency in psychiatry and neurology and start his education in psychoanalysis. I was teaching in-house Business English in various companies around Hamburg while I wrote up my doctoral dissertation on Arabic-language television. I liked my job. It was easy money and a simple distraction from research.

Twice a week at 3 p.m. on the second floor of the Schneider Versand, a 500-employee printing and distribution company, I unpacked my games and worksheets and tried to bring the ten office managers and secretaries a little closer to fluency. That afternoon, my pregnant belly round under my long beige sweater, my German students began to ask me questions about the baby. Didn't I miss my family? Where would we live? Did I have other children?

I made a grammar game out of the family theme.

"Does Peter have ten children?" I jokingly asked Annette to start off the circle.

Annette laughed and turned to Peter to ask, "Do you have ten children?" Her eventual answer, "No, he do not have 10 children," gave away her difficulties, always stumbling on the negative.

Suddenly, Simona's arm shot up into the air, shocking me with its dark nest of underarm hair, like an unexpected glimpse of her privates. "I have two children. I never live far from my family," Simona said. "We do *so* much together. Weekend. Dinners."

The class jumped in, talking now in German, describing their own families.

I answered their questions. "No, I don't have brothers and sisters. No, I don't live near my mother." I didn't even bat an eye. "But that's okay. I don't want to live in the United States."

Simona paused. Her eyes didn't waver as she considered my words. She seemed to pity me. I recognized the look from the Middle East and Italy. From cultures with strong family ties. My glamorous independence suddenly wilted under this gaze and left me feeling puzzled and sad. I wanted a family more like theirs than mine.

"We will miss you when you stop teaching us," Annette added suddenly.

I was confused. "I'm not leaving."

"But you will have the baby."

I hesitated, quizzical. "I'm going to take six months off, but then I'll be right back here to teach you." I said it matter-of-factly, intending to reassure them. But I registered their surprise. Dismay, really.

A stillness came over the room. "What do you mean?" Simona asked.

I had assumed they were resentful about losing me as a teacher, that they would be relieved I would get the business of baby-mothering over quickly to be back in the classroom. I hadn't yet realized a cultural divide was yawning in front of us. Instead of admiration for my choices, they felt sorry for me having a baby without a family close by. Instead of applauding my shorter maternity leave; they were disturbed to think I would come back so quickly. What was wrong with me that I would not take all the time I could to mother my baby?

On the S-Bahn ride back home, all these perspectives swirled as

I watched the green trees zooming by the window. My mother had stayed home with me, not even sending me to preschool in Manhattan, preferring quiet mornings and afternoons in the park and playdates with other mothers. Now, after reading her diaries, I realize she did this because she loved my company but also because she didn't want lonely hours at home. She had never supported the American go-back-to-work-right-away philosophy. Famously, my childhood friend Agnes had returned to her office at three weeks postpartum and had already been working on a laptop on her Illinois maternity ward. My mother had never approved of multi-tasking or "having it all."

"That's not going to work out well for anyone," she would say.

Motherhood for my generation of educated women seemed like a conscious choice, not something that just happened to us. Or was all this thinking and worrying just my personal drama, child of the parents I had?

> My first glimpse of Susannah, the nurse brought her to me early in the morning of September 19. Her eyes were open and she was not crying. She reminded me of Alan's mother somehow. I held her with an unforgettable combination of tenderness, terror and eagerness. I knew everything had changed in our lives, but I had no clear idea why. I still loved Alan and had faith in him then, but his mood swings and alcoholism were highlighted during my 10 days at Holy Family Hospital. His visits there ended several times with me in tears and him storming out for reasons unknown or forgotten. I came home with Susannah alone in a taxi. Swami and Sarah settled me and Susannah in. She did fine. I had a horrendous headache for another 10 days if I rose from a prone position as I always did to accompany Alan at the dining table. Sarah was so competent and Alan was often proud and loving. So motherhood was bliss sometimes. (May 12, 2002)

As I approached my due date, what I knew for sure was that my mother was not going to be there. Inspired by the compelling stories I was hearing in the midwife-run Geburtshaus, of pregnant Hamburg women and their sisters and mothers joyous to be at the birth, I had gathered up my nerve one day and asked Mom if she would like to be present.

She snickered. "You won't want me there. I'm going to do you a favor and let you have the first weeks together. Then I'll come and help."

So, there it was. No female magical connection. No mother-daughter togetherness.

Was I a little relieved? Perhaps. I was already on the front lines of a no-doctor natural birth skirmish with Niels. My mother wouldn't have helped my cause. The idea that one could create a birthing atmosphere, sheltered and honoring, had never been part of my mother's story about what it was to be a woman.

I wanted something else.

In Dallas in the late 1980s, my boss, Bob, the *Dallas Times Herald* city editor, had tossed a query onto my desk. It was a reference to Texas midwifery politics, and he said I should go interview "some lady who had had her baby at home."

Home births? Okay. *Old-fashioned hippie chick? Something out of the Middle Ages?*

The woman I interviewed turned out to be educated and articulate, living in a home with columns and silk taffeta curtains. She wasn't what I had expected. Holding her newborn baby over her shoulder, in between cuddling a toddler, she talked cogently about midwife politics, adding: "Birth is so fantastic at home. Even almost sexual."

Those words sounded preposterous, yet the speaker was so sane as she gazed at me, and her older children and husband were so present, I tucked the home birth idea into my future like a secret password in a treasure box. If I ever got to that point, that is what I would want.

Pregnant in Hamburg, I had found a gynecologist who supported midwife-framed births. I had convinced Niels to enroll in a course at the Geburtshaus, and I signed up for prenatal care through their midwives. Every time we climbed the steps to the quaint old repository in Ottensen, and we placed our boots on the shoe shelves and pushed open the door to the cozy waiting area, with its special smell of Weleda drops and lavender, I was enveloped by calm and a feeling the world was all in its right order.

"*Geburt ist keine Krankheit*," was my favorite saying. *Birth is not an illness.*

For Niels, with his mainstream medical doctor background, these months were a challenge—trained in medical school only in basic hospital obstetrics focusing on risk pregnancies, he had to learn to trust in me, in the professional expertise of midwifery, and in our unborn child that he or she would find the way out safely.

Those midwife months were rich with Kundalini pregnancy yoga, oils to prepare the tissues, teas to influence the nervous system, learning *Ohs* and *Ahs* to sing in labor to relax the cervix. I soaked these things up as naturally as I would later savor the scent of my baby's beautiful skin. German *Mutterschutz* (enforced paid maternity leave) started six weeks before the official due date and lasted two months after the birth. Every woman I knew took it. Those weeks, which extended a little farther for me since I did not go back to work after my father's funeral, felt like a gift, ordered to stop working. I was given a chance to dream and to rest.

"Yes, the German system almost forces women to prepare for the birth," I told an amazed American friend one day. She had worked up until her waters broke, had had an unfriendly hospital birth with strange nurses after a shift change, and had struggled at home to breastfeed with no support. I told her I would receive daily midwife visits in the *Wochenbett* (postnatal weeks) and would have three years' unpaid maternity leave with guaranteed job security if I wanted.

There was a sniff of displeasure from her, as if the German way was too indulgent. There must be something wrong with it. Who would want to stay home for three years?

It was my next taste of parenting culture clashes.

"This is both kind of pre-feminist and like a hint of the promised land of good mothering," I wrote.

My midwife encouraged Niels and me to spend fun time together in the weeks before the birth and get lots of sleep while we still could. "You are allowed to end the conversation if someone starts forcing their horror birth story onto you, you know," she said. "You should stay calm and surround yourself with peaceful things."

* * *

A month after Julian was born, peacefully in the Geburtshaus, my mother arrived in Hamburg. She was a terrific grandmother, a natural with babies, an expert at establishing order in our chaotic hours—nurse, sleep, play, nurse, sleep, play. After a few days, she pronounced our mother-daughter relationship reborn.

> She looks worn and fat but so happy and proud and seems happy I am here. We sat in the lovely big garden with flowers growing in happy profusion and when Julian woke I took him outside, too, and Luna came to purr and brush along my legs and Niels fixed a wonderful pasta supper which we ate on the terrace. My lord it was dreamlike in its genuine European-American family ambience. Julian nursed and gurgled and fussed by turns and we three talked of him mostly. (July 3, 1994)

I remember being grateful for some peace between us and surprised at how relaxed it felt. We were a good team. It reminded me of our years traveling together when I was young. As if we were back to the natural order of things. In a way, I guess we were. She was again the parent guiding the child. Together we took turns holding Julian when he cried. I learned to divide the days into feeding, sleeping and playing phases. She accompanied me on those first nerve-racking between-feeding excursions to the farmer's market, returning through the Blankenese park with a baby carriage laden with fruit and vegetables.

Unfortunately, we clashed on other child development issues. For my grandmother Gummy, leaving a baby to cry had been considered good training. Breastfeeding was considered messy and difficult, and mothers were to return to their pre-pregnancy shapes and lifestyles as soon as possible. For my mother, too, a baby was to be shaped and disciplined to fit the lives of the parents. She had breastfed me for four months on the strict orders of the doctor in New Delhi, but after my initial immunity had been ensured, she told me she was happy to stop. She didn't understand the modern German preference for nursing for at least a year.

"Don't you want to have your life back?" she asked me once, astonished that I was not weaning.

Hers was partly an unreflected passing on of how austerely she herself had been raised, and partly it was a result of her own unease with messy things in the anthropological sense, things that don't stay in their ordered place, but ooze over the lines to other categories.

I had learned by then that crying is a baby's primary method of communication. Cultures where babies cried little were cultures where babies were carried. Presence is what babies needed, skin contact, a full stomach and comfort.

My mother did not agree.

Susannah is convinced that babies cannot be spoiled and that they respond to unalloyed physical cosseting by developing into self-confident and capable children. I have my doubts. Surely Julian is ultra demanding now—not content on his own ever really and only going to his crib after being rocked to sleep. (November 27, 1994)

One afternoon, she turned to Niels and said ruefully, "In India, they never allowed Susannah to cry."

She and my father had had a staff of servants in New Delhi, including a live-in *ayah* for me, Sarah, who had slept in my room and brought me to my mother for nursing in the night. Sarah had not believed in letting babies cry. She held me and carried me and kept me company all through that monumental first year of life when babies absorb what it is to be human through the responses of their caregivers. I suspect that my fundamental trust in being happy in my own skin I owe in great part to a woman in a photo with a beautiful smile who sang to me in Hindi and who I never saw again. Had Jane been my only mother during that time, I wonder how I would have turned out.

I don't believe Jane had meant to be callous toward me in India, just as I don't believe she thought it callous to later spank me and growl: "Stop crying or I'll give you something to cry about!" I believe she loved me, but that she also lived precariously, that she wasn't interested in how a parent's behavior molds their child. I also suspect now that she was lonely and that the social life of embassy parties helped her escape my father's rages. Living in fear of violence is not a postnatal experience any woman deserves.

The summer Julian was born, my mother wrote many diary entries bemoaning my figure, so many in fact that I had to retreat to photo albums to reassure myself I looked normal.

> What happened to vanity? ... This is not the time for honesty, but the stereotype of the fat mama at home with children while father has mistresses and is "out at the cafes" a lot impinges here. (July 11, 1994)

Sure, I had full nursing breasts, and I didn't care much about makeup and hairstyle six weeks postpartum. The photos from those weeks don't show me at my most put-together. To me, I look young and beautiful, a little tired, but that is how it should be. For her, it seemed to be a return to the "I am a foal and you are a calf" theme, pregnancy version.

Weight in pregnancy is a tricky topic in our culture. I have watched thin friends struggle to consume enough calories to produce breast milk and maintain strength during those first baby months. I've watched pregnant friends gain a lot of weight and others barely gain any weight at all. I've observed some women hide their bellies from the world, even at eight months, and others display round and beautiful bumps at five months. There are so many stories, so many journeys.

For me, the story of motherhood went hand in hand with learning to feel alive and powerful, to give birth naturally, trust my body, to learn its secrets. I learned to slow my days down, to pay attention to the color of the seasons, to enjoy decorating for holidays and organizing my home. Niels and most of our friends in Germany loved to cook, so food and drink became intertwined, too, with the vocabularies of sensual pleasure. Meals were always around a big table. Withholding and asceticism were not signs of discipline, but rather signs of inattention to life. It was rich and delicious.

Still, there were genetic factors at play—body types, gut microbiomes digesting certain foods best, and baseline temperaments. I realize now that while almost all my German friends—including Niels—remained naturally thin through the years like my mother, my genetics meant I gained thirty pounds despite eating the same foods and doing sports. My mother couldn't stand it.

> It hurts my motherly pride to look upon my once slender blonde daughter now that she is turning 40. But I keep my own silence and wait in vain for anyone to notice the transformation and divine my sadness in this regard. I will probably wait forever as "big and proud" is in now, a reaction to the Twiggy thin mystique. (August 4, 2003)

As I read the diaries, I find entry after entry complaining about me, almost as if she were obsessed. Why was she so concerned with how I looked? So invasive in her judgments? Certainly, a significant disconnection between my mother and me had always been my father's genetics, in her view a guillotine ready to drop at any time. Maybe it wasn't his alcoholism; maybe it was his stocky bones that I had inherited. The angular model body was one my mother had maintained with almost no effort. She expected me to imitate it, if not naturally like her, then through sacrifice and abnegation.

At the time, I tried to ignore her jibes. I was healthy, Niels and I loved each other, and our children were thriving. Then I read my mother's comments about our one-year-old Julian, who would grow up to become a splendid athlete:

> The beauty of Julian just stops my heart. Susannah was so right in her child rearing techniques. One can let a baby eat all he wants and his baby fat is just that and disappears into nothingness when all the energy of mobility takes over. (July 16, 1995)

She even stigmatizes a little baby's body. I begin to suspect there is something else at play. I recall a withering comment from a cousin about my grandmother Gummy.

"Adrienne served us the thinnest sliver of cake you have ever seen."

I recall hearing a story about my mother refusing to eat enough as a child, becoming a worry for Gummy, perhaps in connection with Helen's illness.

"Eat, Jane, eat!" my cousin-aunt mimicked my grandmother saying. Could food have been a tool of control in Jane's childhood?

Maybe there is something I wasn't seeing that only now is coming into view.

Eyes Dripping Like Ice Cream

1997

SMOKING HAD ALWAYS BEEN A FLASHPOINT of conflict with my mother. "Niels smokes," was the reason she proclaimed for refusing our wedding. I, too, had smoked off and on in my twenties, usually off. I wasn't stupid. I knew it was a bad habit. But at the time, most of my reporter and traveler circles smoked. I once insisted to a disapproving non-smoker in California: "You don't get it. This isn't a trailer park trash kind of smoking. My kind of smoking is a cool European thing."

Indeed, glamorous is what I felt as I slipped that silver Zippo lighter out of my leather jacket pocket and heard that satisfying *schunk clink* as the hinge flipped. I loved the rush of that first cigarette puff. *Mmmm*. Me as enigma. Grown-up. One of the bad boys.

Except that on the stage that really mattered—my psychology—I was the actress forever rehearsing in the wings. I had always hidden my smoking from my mother. If she happened to smell the smoke on our clothes, I allowed her suspicions to fall upon Niels rather than me. My mother and I were both complicit in this spectacle. If you don't talk about it, it doesn't really exist. But the diaries have surprised me. I thought I was smarter at deception on our visits.

> When I drove to 11:30 mass the car was full of cigarette smell and butts were in the ashtray, some with lipstick. I feel so disillusioned I can't even talk about it. Niels cooked a wonderful dinner for us. ... Susannah and I are so estranged. Niels is helpful—as helpful as a smoker and non-supporter of my daughter can be. (July 8, 1990)

In therapy, smoking had been a main vessel of my self-criticism. In the midst of all that I had been working through—becoming a mother myself, my father's death, struggles with my dissertation, adapting to German culture and language—I felt I was making progress on living more authentically. Yet about smoking I was a charlatan. Having quit with no trouble while I was pregnant, I had started again after Julian stopped nursing, as he began to walk. I was back working on my dissertation, and the Zippo lighter was an emblem of independent thinking amid diapers and German playground gossip.

I guess others in this intense phase of a woman's life might have gone out dancing, have given their babies to nannies, or gone back to work full-time. This was how I stayed grown up in a world of babies. I didn't think my mother would understand any of these considerations, so I didn't tell her.

But by August 1997, pretending to my mother had become a vise. She and I had managed a joyful familiar two weeks in Hamburg. I was confident we would be able to sustain the fight that would come.

The day before she was to leave, I sat with her in the hillside garden and took a deep breath. "Mom, I have something to tell you," I said.

She went still as a statue.

"You know Niels and I smoke, don't you?"

Her eyes focused ever so slowly on the horizon. A cacophony of birdsong surrounded us. A child screeched in another garden across the path.

"No, I didn't know." She remained still.

Shit. Shit. It was too late. I'd opened Pandora's Box. A crack. I'd stuff my words back inside. Too late. *Don't be a coward. Go on. Be strong.*

"Mom?" I said.

Julian hopped down the stairs with a bucket for the sandbox. "Looka what I found!"

My mother turned to him. "Let's collect some of the small plums that have fallen from the tree."

I remained on the bench for a few more minutes. They were chatting easily together, a three-year-old's nattering and a doting grandmother's responses. All seemed well. Relief. Finally, the worst was out. It wasn't so bad. She seemed fine.

Her diary said otherwise:

> My heart is leaden as Susannah said: "You know we smoke, don't you?" In fact I didn't know that, only sensed a burden in my presence, particularly this vacation.... Peculiar energy and delight in confronting me thusly. I am full of contempt for both of them. (August 2, 1997)

Later, looking down from the balcony, hanging up the wet clothes on the clothesline, I saw that although Julian was puttering around the sandbox, my mother was sitting very still on the wooden bench looking down the hill to the river. I watched him do his dervish dance of putter and run, then check whether his Nonna was paying attention, then putter and run. Suddenly he stopped and walked over to her, climbed into her lap in that unfettered way children have—as if the lap belongs wholly to them. Something was going on. I watched. His curly head was no longer bouncing unconcerned. He was still, drawn into what she was telling him. My heart froze. She was telling him something bad about me.

> Julian seemed interested in my tears on the last afternoon in the lower garden. "Why are your eyes dripping like ice cream, Nonna?' I guess he does not know that adults cry. I take relief in this. (August 5, 1997)

As they returned to the house, I recognized resignation in her down-turned eyes and half-smile. I knew that posture. But Julian bounced around as always. Niels came home. We went through the motions of our last evening, having dinner, sitting out on the balcony. She walked alone back to her hotel along the safe cobblestoned streets as she did every night. She said she found it enchanting. She was leaving for London the next day and to make the leave-taking fun for Julian, we watched the ship slip ponderously away from the harbor dock and then drove to a lighthouse along the river and waved again. As the ship sailed past, I spotted a lone woman at the stern, scarf flowing in the wind.

> The parting was dramatic and probably memorable for Julian as he waved merrily first from the dock and then from the Blanke-nese lighthouse as my ship sailed away down the Elbe. Susannah was videotaping and Niels waved, too. (August 2, 1997)

I knew none of this then, except for an intuition that told me my mother had said goodbye too calmly. That summer my cousin Bree got married on the lush family homestead in rural Pennsylvania. It would end up being the last big family wedding for years—until the one we were anticipating when Mom told me her suicide plans. So it turned out that we all met again two weeks after that smoking conversation. When he spied her on the lawn, Julian ran up to her, joyful at seeing his loving Nonna in the crowd. She was stiff in her greeting. Surrounded by relatives, leaning down, she gave him a kiss. But I saw something was amiss. So did Julian. Children are discerning. They see through everything. Julian changed his mood. He retreated to lean against our legs, to observe her from a place of safety, unsettled by her strangeness.

> The change in Julian's demeanor haunts me—so fearful and clinging to Papa or Mama, so unerring in his perceptions that I am toxic to his mother. Where did that merry, friendly little

cherub go? Time and distance, the strength of my character and convictions will sustain me. (August 17, 1997)

What hurts most when I read this is being reminded of those days. How distant she was to her grandson when they had just been cavorting together a few weeks prior. How was my sweet little boy to understand what had happened? How could anyone? The cousins noticed, gathered together to share jokes and their own cigarettes.

"I told her I smoked," drew only confusion.

"Is that all?"

For my mother, that was all there was.

A sense of things happening for the last time. Inside I have sort of dropped dead and long for my San Francisco compartment again. ... I don't know what I am but I will cope and smile. (August 16, 1997)

As I read, I am devastated at her views of my lovely joyful three-year-old. "That cold Montrose child who shunned me," she writes. Her words hurt way down deep inside. *Shunned*?! A young child does not shun.

But a mother does.

So clear. If I were to cry now it would be with jagged harsh tears. I don't cry. I concentrate on breathing and read more.

She writes she cannot sleep when she returns to San Francisco. It takes weeks for her to get back on track, to achieve her aloneness, her balance.

In the midst of Princess Diana's funeral news, Susannah called. I realize how much I want nothing to do with her by the effort it took to hold a brief and friendly conversation. She said: "I love you." How absurd. Alan always said that after he had gotten drunk and given me a black eye or split lip. I am sure Susannah suffers as he did. They both talk to my shell. My self has gone away. (September 6, 1997)

So began a period of two years when she discontinued contact. At first, I tried a few phone calls. But it was as if I were talking to a disinterested stranger, someone who had nothing to say in response to my questions. There was no spark. Three days a week I again took the S-Bahn to lie on a simple beige couch with a view into a green garden, my analyst a witness to it all behind me. Friends who were themselves analysts and therapists shook their heads in dismay. My mother's behavior made no sense.

At Christmas time, she sent a package of clothes. Her presents were always just the right size.

"Do you want to call Nonna and thank her?" I asked Julian. I held my breath and dialed the number. No answer.

"She went to Hawaii for Christmas," my grandfather told me the next day. He wasn't happy about the estrangement either.

In January, Julian and I tried again.

Again, we dialed the number. "Hi Nonna," went Julian's sweet little voice.

"Hello," she responded. I could tell her voice was strained. "Did you have a good Christmas?"

She used to ask him lots of questions: "How is your Papa's motorcycle," "Is kitty cat Luna still purring so loudly?" This time there was a dull disinterest.

I felt hurt for my little boy.

Soon he didn't want to talk anymore.

Niels and I considered whether she was depressed. She was withdrawn with us but her regular life was going along as always. She was busy and social.

Geoffrey Chaucer Company came to third period today. They were first rate, did the *Monk's Tale*. Three people, great costumes and original music. The kids paid $1.00 head and were most engaged. I think I succeeded in bringing literature alive for them via this performance. At least I hope so."
(December 4, 1997)

Family saw she seemed sad but said they were helpless. Just as with our wedding in 1991, nobody had a way into the sorrow that she did not name.

> This is the day Mother died 24 years ago. ... Susannah was 10 then. Whenever I want to hate her now I stop and require myself to recall what a joy she was to me as a child. She was there for me when I needed her most. She was smart, sweet and slim and she made me so proud. ...How devastated Mother would've been to realize all that beautiful and perfect childhood behavior resulted in a resentful and self-destructive grown granddaughter. (February 17, 1998)

Though I don't recall it, I apparently wrote her a letter in February, asking her to be in touch with three-year-old Julian, who played her homemade tape of family dog stories over and over. Her diary says:

> Oh my God, that little boy should not have to deal with me and the conflict I carry like a virus. (February 20, 1998)

She swam and taught and spent time with friends. By the end of April, she writes she had recovered her balance.

> I had a revelation today... I like myself. I take solace in my faith, relief in my financial independence, pride in my fitness and health, enjoyment from my friends and fulfillment from my job.... I pray Susannah protects Julian from harm but I wash my emotional hands of her and him. (April 22, 1998)

In August 1998, I called her to let her know we had had another beautiful boy, also with midwives in the Geburtshaus. All had gone well. We were back at home by breakfast. She wrote:

> Susannah called to say she had a baby boy August 2. She sounded

> peaceful and happy. I am full of relief ... I could hear the newborn
> baby sounds as she spoke, but my arms do not ache to hold him as
> they did for Julian.... August 2 is the exact year ago Susannah said
> "you know we smoke, don't you?" (August 4, 1998)

Observing these estrangement years, I am ashamed to realize I was
so hungry for the warm part of my mother—the one who played Go
Fish, that knew intuitively exactly what sized clothes to buy the children
for their Christmas box, recorded her own books on tape so they could
hear her voice, who brought them to the ballet and listened to them
read—that I may have done the worst thing I can imagine. By searching
for the good in her, I may have harmed my children with the bad.

Being now as old as she was then, I see there are other ways of per-
ceiving one's adult child. In those years Niels and I had built a thriving
little family. We lived in a pretty neighborhood. I was working on my
dissertation. He was working as a doctor. We enjoyed each other's company and when we disagreed, we did so without violence. I think all
this made her lonely, and instead of supporting us she undermined us.
I planned a trip to San Francisco so she could meet Dylan. I was tired
of shrugging in response to Julian's questions.

"No, Nonna won't visit this summer."

I suffered under the estrangement. If I tried one more time, maybe I'd find a way. I see now that that is the eternal fate of the child of a
mother like mine. We are the bridge-builders, always trying to reach out
to them. There is no other option. If we accept their cut, we lose them.

> When I phoned Westridge, Dad mentioned that Susannah,
> Niels and sons have told of a plan to come here to San Fran-
> cisco in March. I am unstrung on several levels. Too expensive,
> too hostile, too much trouble for me.... I feel only dread. (De-
> cember 21, 1998)

Now, knowing all that has passed since those years, I am ashamed.

I may have fallen into a trap of my own making. Or maybe it was inevitable. Over the years, I tried hard to refrain from judging her in front of the children. I tried to leave room for them to love her. I chose to believe her façade and to dismiss the rejection. Would it have been better for the children if we had just stayed away?

The Pilgrim's Gait

2018

TWO STEPS FORWARD, ONE STEP BACK.

It took me a few minutes to ease my way into the rhythm of the Pilgrim's Gait. I'd never walked like this before. Ungainly. It's very slow. Two steps forward, one step back. The German evening was chilly and dark. Inside the 800-year-old Kloster Luna, we were all wearing coats. Large thick yellow candles flickered onto the rough terracotta monastery tiles. I looked ahead but could barely make out the corner where the procession turned right, down the adjoining side of the covered medieval square.

Two steps forward, one step back. Acoustic guitar, louder on the forward steps, softer backwards. The shoulders of the man in front of me rose and fell as he moved. *Pilgerschritt*, it's called. I'd been invited to participate by friends. I was learning a lot of new things. I gradually found my ease with the rhythm, backward and forward until we were all one line, moving together. It was peaceful. But it seemed a counterproductive method of covering distance if you were a pilgrim. Wouldn't it be better to put one foot steadily in front of the other?

* * *

This week has felt like that Pilgrim's Gait. Two steps forward, one step back. I am visiting an old friend of my mother's, one of the friends that had dared—occasionally—to challenge my mother's mothering.

"Oh, Jane, leave her alone. She's a teenager. She's supposed to sleep late," I remember Beth saying once. She was also one of those friends that always seemed to adore my mother, laughing with her, listening to her stories. They had fun together. I was often jealous. I also basked in the reflected glory of being my "unique" mother's perfect daughter. But then Mom would leave Beth's presence and turn the tables. She would tell me of Beth's addictions and misbehaviors, weaknesses, and troubles. My envy of Beth would recede. My mother was the sane one after all. Lucky me.

Here we are, thirty years later, sitting together in her living room. My mother had always boasted she was living the best life. But my mother ended her life and isn't here anymore. And we are. Who is winning now?

I read Beth a few pages from the book I am writing about the diaries. Afterward she stays quiet. There are tears in Beth's eyes.

"Jane was always such a character. She didn't let anyone tell her how to live her life and I guess I kind of liked it that way. I always viewed her as a true friend. But by dying how she did, well, I have to admit it felt like a betrayal."

I relish this moment. Two steps forward. Maybe my story will be heard.

Beth laughingly tells me a tidbit about my grandmother. "In college, after dinner at your grandparents' house, we were always hungry. We'd go by the A&W Root Beer stand for a burger to fill up." Hmm. I conjure up a memory of dinner at Gummy's, a plate with a small piece of chicken, half a baked potato and three sliced carrots. I recall that other story about the thinnest sliver of cake.

A few minutes later, Beth's other guests arrive and she goes into entertainment mode.

"I have another story to tell you. When I was in grad school my housemate used to grow magic mushrooms," Beth said, beginning her colorful story, her guests primed to laugh. "I don't know what to think about ecstasy and all those things kids nowadays take, but boy, do I remember those times. Have you ever been to the Cascade mountains? One summer I drove up there with my boyfriend and they were just passing them out at the campsite. I had a saucepan full of them. One for you, one for me. One for the next person, one for me. Well, you can imagine how I felt when we took off to climb the rocks. You know those mountain goats that can leap from rock to rock? I did that, I swear." She is laughing hysterically at her memory. I'm amazed she did such things back then.

No wonder she loved my mother so much. Such talent, both of them, for telling tales and papering over emotional gaps. When Jane took the stage, Beth could rest.

I remember this dynamic at my mother's side, and I witness it again this evening. After another hour of this type of atmosphere, the guests are looking dazed. Especially since Beth's stories are mostly about her children, two of whom I knew had been in rehab addiction programs and in and out of halfway houses.

"Glen is such a good son. He's doing so well. He is the top student in his community college class. Oh, my gosh, he was such a good athlete in high school, almost made it to State in the high jump." The guests have long stopped reacting. All but me. I still smile and nod and laugh.

This feels familiar. This was always my role in my mother's groups. I was the audience.

One step back.

Is this what true matriarchs do? They hold dinner parties and entertain? Tell glowing stories? Gloss over the addictions and abuse and depressions? It is as if Beth's adulation becomes more vivid the more troubled the character in the story actually is, the more secrets Beth knows. Is that what keeps families together? I think of my great-aunt Fran and my cousin Liz. I love to go to their houses, sit around their tables. Do they do that? Do they tell only the positive? Am I drawn to them because I am hungry for something more than the food?

Maybe that is what an elemental mother figure is supposed to do. Tell the most positive story. Maybe it is exactly this that I must learn. Candor undermines; whitewashing holds together.

I'm not sure I can do that. I hate pretending.

Meanwhile, I read and write. I try to piece together the story. Between diary readings, I open shoeboxes of my old letters, kept loosely over all these years. I read some from the early 1980s. I had left home. I was at college. But I was still a child. *Dear Mommy.* The letters make me wince as I read them now.

> I really miss you! Your phone call helped so much. ...Right now, I'm feeling scared about my life ... It is a feeling of being in limbo, not having any direction. (My letter, September 29, 1982, when I was nineteen)

My children call in between, during these days of reading. Julian puzzles out whether to go to law school. Should he have said yes to being recruited to that Swiss professional soccer team? Will his ankle hold out? Dylan puzzles out his college life, hasn't found his tribe, his people. Should he transfer? Leah auditions for a high school musical.

She texts me, "It didn't go well. I'm crying in the bathroom."

Maybe it is more like three steps back today.

Are they looking to me for advice, or just to listen? Should I become a Beth, bringing people together under the polish of a glowing story? Is there another way? Can I be authentic and truthful, too?

* * *

I have been reading the diaries for nine months now. Taking notes, dictating longer passages, crafting my interpretations of the reading, composing pieces to share at workshops. The little journal books have gone from a soldier's order in white bankers boxes to a laissez-faire jumble. Now quartered in two cardboard cartons, they have fallen out of line. A tad disrespectful, but also liberating. Sticky notes remind me of pages to return to later. They have a lived-in feel, less frightening.

A diary is always a text that approximates a life, and even that is only through the lens of the diarist. A private rendition of a version of what we choose to show to the world. Up until now, her words have paralleled what I knew or felt about her life. But I am reading into the 1990s after my first children were born, and suddenly it feels like I've wandered into quicksand, my rain boots filling up. I'm scared of sinking.

Maybe it isn't quicksand. Maybe we are both walking a cliff trail, and she ventures out too far to the precipice and I spend all my time worrying whether she'll fall, checking her balance, picking my own way along the gravel. We advance forward on this thirty-year path, but she takes my energy. She wants to trip, by accident on purpose, and tumble into the abyss. Yet she stands so tall and walks so strongly. It couldn't really be true, could it?

At the beginning, I try diligently, thinking she has wandered to the edge of the cliff in error. The diaries are often candid and show she knows exactly what she is doing. For twenty years, we played this game. I try again now to be her solid rock, as I've always tried to be, the one to calm her down. But I realize that I am losing the fight, both times—the first as I lived through it, the second as I relive it now in the reading.

I'm anxious. I wake at 5 a.m. with my heart pounding. I am afraid this diary project will kill me, give me cancer, make my heart sick. I don't want that. Above all, I want to live. I want to live a better life than she did. I *am* actually living a better life. I must trust this.

These mid-1990s are her years of becoming a grandmother, with occasional bursts of love and enthusiasm that I take as representative of her whole. Yet I sense she is concealing something. The reading is getting slower and my muscles are stiffened with my internal responses. The process feels leaden. It isn't boring; it is dark. I have to work doubly hard to maintain my distance from her words so they don't overwhelm me. I consider quitting.

In the diaries during these years, my mother has reached her fifties.

Now I think perhaps she was going through menopause, though the subject is elusive. In fact, she only mentions that rite of passage twice. Once, she wrote in her diary at age fifty-five: "Lord knows I'm glad I have reached the safe sexual harbors of menopause and advanced years." The second time, in her seventies, she mentions it to me in person, suddenly stopping in the midst of her exercises on the floor of the living room.

"Let me tell you. The seventies are awful. The fifties and sixties were easy; even menopause went by almost unnoticed."

In her fifties she was still beautiful and teaching high school and holding court at dinner parties. She had won her landmark case against the school district for back pay and reinstatement of tenure, which meant she had more financial security. Her emboldened letters to the editor on district politics appeared frequently in the *San Francisco Chronicle*. She self-published her book *Lanky Honky Bitch*. She took up other causes, such as the rising pay gap between managers and workers.

Esteemed or disliked both inside and out of the classroom, my mother remained a force to contend with. She grew increasingly irritated with people, repeating to me opinionated statements she made to others of which she was especially proud: "You'll never be promoted if you dress like a hooker," or "Your son will never get his life together if you keep doing his laundry."

"Oh, Jane!" People would laugh, either appalled or delighted because she often said what they were thinking.

She mourned her anemic relationship with her brother, and she seems to have given up hope of finding a new love, settling, once again, but infrequently in her fifties into the familiar companionship of married James.

What I meant to say about James is this. He usually says, "I love you," but he loves no one really. He has always been a male chauvinist and closed as WASP snobs often are. But his looks and "haughty particulars" have always appealed to me. Most of all, his loyalty to me after I ended our love affair all those years ago and his evident pain and incredulity then still move me. We like each other in our lives—cold and loveless as they are, and so we cherish the insincere *I love yous* as they echo hollow down the years. (November 20, 1993)

These years also coincided with my years of anthropology and therapy and midwives and Waldorf ways of mothering. My world was expanding and challenging and full of grace, the main drag on my mood being my endless dissertation on a media and technology subject I cared little about, which took me ten years to complete.

Looking back upon that time now, I see that in her presence I was a lesser me, always recalibrating. I'd try again to establish contact, think of questions she could answer happily, gossip about family that she and I could share and laugh about. But there was a deep underlying unhappiness that colored our time alone when the children were not distracting us. And resentment, too.

I have reread the last couple of pages which are self-righteous and self-pitying. As if I have no faults at all in the way life has played out for me. As if Susannah, Steven, Phyllis, Caitlin, Alan are all to blame because they don't like me. Why do I have such difficulty in seeing my bad parts, the tactless, controlling and judgmental ones? Working to overcome the humiliation of growing grotesquely tall produced terrible thick skin and the ability to ignore others...Who cares anymore if a woman is a giant? (February 13, 2002)

By the late 1990s, Mom began to fill pages in her diary with details of famous people's deaths, like those of Jackie Kennedy Onassis and Richard Nixon. In the 2000s, she began spending more and more time with people who were dying—acquaintances, and sometimes strangers.

I hung out with old people today and wouldn't have it any other way. I learn keen lessons of zest and bravery from them and enhance my research that life is progressively not worth living for me after 75—healthy or not. (January 25, 2002)

One day in San Francisco, we were in her bedroom together. I was lying next to her on her bed watching the news.

"Do you want to see something?"

I nodded, thinking she was going to show me a picture or a ring in her jewelry box.

She lifted up her shirt to expose her flat belly and long left side covered with dark raised blemishes. She looked shy, as if she were showing me something shameful.

Unprepared, I looked away quickly.

"Ew, Mom."

"I know." She let go of the fabric.

I was not prepared for her intimacy. We were long past the years when she would choose bras and fasten stockings to go out on a date while I watched curiously from her bed.

Nonplussed, embarrassed, I was speechless.

Did she have a hundred melanomas, a result of her years of devoted sunbathing? Maybe. I know the only doctor she saw regularly in her last decades was a dermatologist. She refused every other kind of check-up. I never saw those marks again. But I thought about them occasionally. Worrying, wondering. Was it something I would have? Is it something she wanted to share with me? Did she have cancer? Is this why she was always flirting with the "won't grow old" theme?

When she was in her sixties, I finally decided to stop speculating and simply ask. I had just carried a big load of warm towels and sheets up from the co-op laundry room in the basement. It was a ritual we had always enjoyed together, folding clothes. It seemed like a cozy moment.

"I have a question, Mom. What were those marks on your stomach?"

"What marks?"

"Once you showed me your stomach and there were lots of dark things on your skin," I said a little shyly. "I didn't ask then what they were. But I've been thinking about them."

She picked up a large white towel and folded it in thirds lengthwise and then in thirds again so it would slot perfectly into her linen closet.

"What are you talking about? I don't remember having any marks on my skin," she said, her tone even.

Ahh. This was familiar. I had ventured to ask a sensitive question. She evaded the question like a black belt, denial by avoidance. There was nothing in her response that would lead me to a follow-up question.

As usual, I stayed silent.

I grabbed a twin sheet, feeling awkward. *Should I ask again? Had I made it up?*

It was a missed opportunity. I see where I learned to be quiet in awkward non-response instead of following through with another question in pursuit of truth. It is why I wasn't a good investigative reporter. Right here, with the silence of my mother's response. She gave no "Why do you ask?" to follow up. Nothing to relieve the awkward silence of me having introduced something she either did not genuinely remember or did not now want to talk about.

> Today the papers carry articles about the medical profession admitting that mammograms, colonoscopies etc. for symptomless people are unnecessary—perhaps harmful. The industrial medical complex sure has brainwashed hordes of people. (February 18, 2002).

It was also a missed opportunity because criticism of mainstream medicine was something we shared, something that might have offered us common ground. I was learning more and more about integrative medicine. In Germany, homeopathy and anthroposophical medicine were practiced by doctors with traditional Western medical degrees. Eventually, I would also start using Traditional Chinese Medicine and acupuncture. A future yoga teacher would have a medical Ayurvedic background. There was so much to learn that I might have shared with my mother, which would certainly have enhanced her quality of life. But she wasn't interested, much as she wasn't interested in therapy and self-reflection.

In 2012, she developed hip pain. "My complaints are banal compared with those described to me in the course of First Responder interviews. However, for the past two years, arthritis, back and hand pain have interfered with my energy and stamina," she writes in a note I found in her files. I encouraged her to go to an osteopath, someone who would perhaps also take a full history and by doing so give her a feeling of being seen and cared for.

When I followed up on my suggestion, she said: "Marie mentioned her chiropractor. I went to him and he wrenched me around some, but I didn't care for it."

"Mom," I said, exasperated. "I know in San Francisco you'll find excellent alternative medicine if you ask around. Acupuncture, for example, or something else. You just have to keep looking."

"We'll see."

She replaced her over-the-shoulder purse with a small suitcase on wheels and continued walking the San Francisco hills. She walked everywhere, did stretching and gymnastics religiously and swam an hour a day. Right until the end, she was the most active of her friends and family.

* * *

In this phase of the reading, I am feeling very needy. I don't like her version of Susannah at that time in our lives. One night I have a dream about a long tunnel and Good Samaritans whispering, "I'm sorry," "Excuse me," "Sorry," as they wake grisly, passed-out people piled on top of one another, trying to set them up in the middle so that they can breathe, and so that we walkers can have a clear path. In my dream

I do not want to be one of the helpers though my conscience tells me I should. I want to walk through without hindrance. I'm angry and shocked at my annoyance. I wake at 4:18 a.m. Adrenalin must have caused my heart to give an extra beat. Blood rushes too fast to my brain.

I'm anxious. Afraid.

How many more years of the diary are left?

Home and Distance

2008

IN LATE NOVEMBER 2008, I attended the annual American Anthropological Association conference, this time not presenting a paper but gathering inspiration for Motherlands, a website I was developing about mothering and raising children in a foreign culture. Living in Germany, raising children in two languages and cultures, had renewed my awareness of my sense of home. My doctoral research had started it off—all those hours of watching Arab cartoons and soap operas with Syrian families in England. Home culture transmitted via the screen.

The wish to maintain one's home language seemed to be something shared by many foreign parents abroad and they tackled it in different ways. Some, like the Syrians I knew in London, embedded themselves in an Arabic-speaking community and celebrated access to satellite television. Some, like my Israeli friends, sent their children to Hebrew school on the weekends. My Peruvian friend had a nanny who spoke Spanish at home with the children. Those I knew who rejected their home language, like the mother from Shanghai I met who spoke only error-filled German with her children, always seemed to be parenting with something missing. Their children would never know their own parent deeply if unable to listen to them in their native tongue. The added reality that they were growing up in a completely different culture to their parents made the chasm even wider.

In our case, Niels and I were committed to fostering a bilingual household. We hosted au pairs who spoke English. We made regular road trips to the U.S., alighting in one relative or friend's house after another, peeking into the peculiar Americanisms of family life, getting inspiration. Sometimes we remained thankful Germany offered what seemed a healthier lifestyle, with more outdoor play and less media; other times I wished my children could be exposed to more of the American generosity of spirit and expansive self.

Each American visit was new. As each time the children were older, seeing and being seen with new eyes.

One Easter, we were gathered at my mother's apartment. She had invited her brother, and two other families, those of a colleague, Kaaren, and our cousin Brianna.

"Let's have a game of Scrabble," my mother announced. I caught Julian rolling his eyes. A sophomore in the International Baccalaureate program, the last thing he wanted was more vocabulary on holiday.

Dylan called, "What's Scrabble?" Knowing Dylan, he might give this thing a chance, whatever it was. But he would follow his brother's lead. Leah, then only seven, bopped around, oblivious in the living room, playing with my old Breyer horses.

"I have to warn everyone. I'm a master Scrabbler," Brianna laughed. Jill and Bob lifted their eyebrows.

Kaaren whooped. "*Yes,* let's do it." She loved words. She was an English teacher.

I tried to bridge the lack of enthusiasm from my boys, who were remaining steadfastly far away on the big sofa. "I don't think our kids have ever played the game," I said. At the mention of "game," Dylan and Julian finally wandered into the dining room where Brianna was setting up the fanciest Scrabble board I'd ever seen. It swiveled on a turntable.

"Ok, let's play. Come on, guys." I remembered meeting with the Donovan cousins as a child, their endless rounds of cards, 20 Questions, and Fictionary, which entailed making up definitions for bizarre words picked out of an ancient five-inch-thick unabridged dictionary, witty creations and much hooting and laughter. A joy in togetherness around something literary. The use of language. I yearned for that for our children. I was happy they were getting a taste of it now. Our trips were often like that, an expansion of our reality and also perhaps asking a lot of all of us, to not be of one culture, but of two.

In 2006, we came up with the idea of taking a sabbatical year in San Francisco. I was lonely in northern Germany, missing my extended family. I felt I had taken everything I could from the culture around me: biodynamic food, rituals, punctuality, psychoanalysis, homeopathy and Waldorf. I had a few dear friends. But I could see the rigid part of Germanness taking its toll on all of us. The responsibilities for Niels. The provincialism on me. Expectations and discipline becoming too embedded in the children. Where was love and freedom? Silliness and romanticism? Hedonism and eccentricity? I wanted that whiff of freedom, that flash of joy that could spread across a face without being squashed by an inner critic.

We assumed my mother would be delighted to have her grandchildren nearby, as she had seemed sad the last time we left after a vacation in California:

> I studied my beloved family... Julian lost in his own thoughts, superior, handsome, reserved, but also very loving and helpful with his family as the oldest child should be. Dylan, exuberant and observant with many questions and happy enthusiasm for the moment. Leah, dare I imagine sad that I will be gone from her life after finding she loved me a little. Susannah, calmly efficient and happy, as I am, that her beautiful offspring have had a good time, no injuries, no sickness, and now full of joyful anticipation returning to Papa and all they relish in Nindorf.

The idea of a year in the USA empowers her and I hope it comes to pass. (July 31, 2006)

But it turned out she couldn't sustain that message.

Our communication, when I returned to Germany and she was at home in California, became an unexplainable roller coaster. I often sat still after talks on the phone with her, looking out the window, feeling like one of those Energizer Bunnies on which somebody had suddenly pulled the plug.

On this particular day in our farmhouse, in the distance, I watched as a neighbor came to gather her horses from the field, the smallest black pony snorting and tossing its head. A car wound its way up the one-lane road. I could hear chit chatting in the kitchen as everyone continued preparing dinner. I just stayed still. Eventually, I woke from my trance. Light was dimmer. Dusk was approaching. I forced myself to rise, pull myself together, like a wild animal in an African documentary coming out of anesthesia. I joined my family in the kitchen.

"Hey, who is setting the table tonight?" I asked.

It wasn't until after everyone was in bed that I had a chance to tell Niels we weren't going to be welcome in San Francisco after all.

Our plans for a year—for me to be back in the U.S., for our children to go to school in English, for Niels to have a desperately needed break from work—were dashed. We were both surprised. We had planned and saved for Niels' sabbatical year so carefully. It had seemed like such a natural thing. For Jane it would have meant having a whole year with her grandchildren nearby after fourteen years so far away across the world.

"Don't do it—for Niels' sake," she had said. "He can't close his practice. Don't bring Roxy. It will be torture for the good dog. You don't love her. Just like you don't love me."

All her *don'ts* drifted through my mind in the next weeks. It was as if she was in a world alone. As if Niels and I hadn't considered this sabbatical idea from every angle—financial, career, education. It would be a huge undertaking, to find a house exchange, organize schools for all three children, wind down his patient practice, organize pet details.

"Don't you think, Mom, that we have considered all these questions, from all sides? That we wouldn't do it if we didn't believe it would be worth doing?"

Eventually, like a mouse that plays dead but then revives to race to a crack in the wall, I woke up angry. Damn it, if she didn't want us, then we would find a new place to make ourselves an American home. If not San Francisco, then somewhere else.

In the end, we decided on Santa Cruz, California. It had the schools we needed, and it was close to the ocean, which Niels loved. I figured the ninety-minute driving distance was right. It would allow sharing in the wider extended family birthdays and baseball games or stage shows, which would in turn lead to an easing of our underlying tension.

She was unnerved. She accepted we would come, but began to agitate in another way, especially against our bringing our family dog to California.

"She will hate it. It is cruel to put her on a plane," she scolded.

"Yes, it probably isn't a nice experience. But Mom, it would also be cruel to leave her with strangers for a year."

"Well, then just give her away forever to a nice new family. You'll find one if you ask."

A knife again in my heart. "How could we give her away, Mom? She loves us, and we love her."

"No, you don't."

I could never prepare myself for these sudden stabs. Her sweeping judgements had the effect of making counter arguments appear defensive and weak. I was forced to insist, "Yes, we *do* love our dog." I felt like a five-year-old engaged in a *yes-no* fight.

I tried to look objectively at her words. For another family, it might have been possible to find our dog a good home with people who never traveled. Roxy might have been happy with them. It might have been possible. But it would have been like giving one of our children away.

Roxy loved us. We loved her. She was one of our pack.

No, Niels and I were raising the kind of family that would remain together. Whatever comes, we would experience it as a whole.

We spent the academic year in Santa Cruz, the children in kindergarten, fourth grade and ninth grade. We rented out our house. Roxy came with us. We saw my mother more often. It did, in fact, lead to an easing of tensions for a while. But it turned out she was planning out a path for herself that did not include us, and which was already interfering with my attempts to get closer.

Final Exit

2009

WHEN SHE WAS A LITTLE GIRL, Leah, born at home in our farmhouse, loved singing and creating stories, imitating puppet shows with their landscapes of wooden arches and driftwood trees, hills made of silk scarves, and hand-made mini-dolls, felt horses. Her books were filled with fairy gardens and root children. She even gently picked up spiders and freed them with her fingers.

One day, coming home from her Santa Cruz kindergarten during our sabbatical, she related with great reverence how she and a group of friends had found a bee buzzing slowly in the tall grass at the edge of the playground.

"We called to the teacher, 'There's a little broken bee.'"

Teacher Robin had picked up on their mood and eased the little creature onto a nest and sung a little song with them, until it buzzed away on its continuing flower journey.

"Mama, it flew away. We saved it."

Leah was thrilled with their rescue. It fit so perfectly into the beauty of the world around her. She was five. She wanted to rescue everything.

When my mother came to visit on Friday of that week, I figured Leah would tell her Nonna about the bee, as the story had been sitting joyfully in her for days. Our bookshelves were full of *The Adventures of Grandfather Frog* and *Peter Rabbit,* books my mother had sent us over the years, rough around the edges, some 100 years old. Nonna usually loved easing the children into literature, reciting rhymes and old stories.

So it was with only half an ear that I listened to their interaction in the back seat on the way home from the bus station.

"How are you, sweetie? How was your week?" she asked Leah.

Sure enough, I overheard my daughter in a happy little voice relating the story of the rescue of the garden bee.

But instead of the expected resonance, I heard, "That bee didn't deserve to live."

Mom's voice was spitting, a tone I knew. Extra emphasis when stating something she anticipated would cause shock. "I would have stomped my foot right down on it. I hate bees."

Silence.

Leah, the mile-a-minute talker, sat absolutely still behind me. *What should I say? Should I say anything at all?*

"Mom!" I managed. "That's not nice."

A rough, devilish laugh erupted. "Who said that I was nice?"

I hurt for Leah. *What the hell!*

Sure, Mom had always been afraid of bees. She became hysterical, jumping away, waving her hat, "Bad bee." She had a highly effective death technique: fill water in a spray bottle, squirt their wings until they can't fly, then kill them.

But in this case Mom wasn't angry at the bee for living. She was angry with Leah for caring about it, for living in a world where bees mattered.

By the time she was in her sixties and I in my early forties, my mother and I had learned to laugh together as long as we didn't talk about our relationship. We were most at ease when we exchanged news about family: Jake's newest play, Karl's run-in with the law, Fran's death-bed nursing of Great Uncle Dick. I had learned to interact with her in a way that kept the relationship from completely fading away. I knew by then that she would let me go entirely if I insisted on more closeness than she could tolerate.

She had become an outspoken advocate for the right to die on one's own terms. Laws had eased. There were headlines and political spokesmen like Dr. Kevorkian in the news. She monologued about the topic so often that most of her friends and family began to tune her out, not wanting to hear the strident tone and not knowing the reason for the emotional intensity.

"Yes, Jane, we know how you feel."

This wasn't just politics; this was personal. No one then knew about Helen in the attic, or Gummy's pills.

> As music transports my emotions, almost always I confront my wish to die while I am still a whole person. ... The USA deconstructs around shootings, removal of life support, abortion, but seems oblivious to the death and destruction of war, poverty and domestic abuse.... When one reaches 75 or 80 the most empowering thing a person can do is die with dignity and dispatch. (March 24, 2005)

In December 1991, my grandfather at age eighty-four had fallen and broken his hip while taking care of his horse. My mother had been plunged into despair, a kind of dreadful driving-the-hearse-before-the-body-is-cold kind of despair. She canceled her Italy trip for Christmas.

"I brought some beer and we watched TV and spoke nothing of all the things in our hearts," she wrote in her diary.

To me, in Germany, she had lamented on the phone about his bedpans, a walker and a Kaiser hospital bed. "It is just killing me to see him like that. He is despondent, hopeless."

"Well, Mom, I'm guessing he will get better, right? It is just a hip, and that seems to be a pretty common surgery."

"Phyllis says she's fine," she scoffed. "She's 'perfectly happy'. How can she give 100 percent to a man who barely acknowledges her?" Her voice was angry. "It's a psychic steel trap."

It was her trap, but she claimed it was everyone else's. *They* were the ones hiding behind "doing just fine."

In her diary, she described searching for an active solution, calling up memories of her mother's last days.

> I went to a Hemlock meeting at a beautiful Episcopal church on Gough. But I got no help with getting the name of a physician who can prescribe barbiturates like Seconol or Nembutal. I do not have the responsibility to kill Daddy as I did Mother because he has not asked me and is still lucid in mind, so I must just bear this horrifying reprise of Helen. (December 16, 1991)

To kill Daddy as I did Mother.
This horrifying reprise of Helen.

As I read those words, I am once again next to her, aware of the smooth skin on her forearm, driving the highway, eating dinner at our glass table overlooking the bay, cloth napkin folded to the left in its silver ring, or lying on her bed watching the Sonny and Cher show. She had always been thinking these thoughts, I realized. *To kill Daddy as I did Mother. A reprise of Helen.* It feels cold. I am frightened. Maybe I am getting a hint of an abyss here.

My grandfather recovered and lived another nine years of a somewhat stiffer but mobile daily life, to die suddenly of a stroke at age 93. It may be true that his last decade was a less fluid one, no more riding horses, fewer symphonies, no more long walks. I cannot judge whether it was a good decade for him.

But I am grateful he lived, that he was there. He welcomed me and Niels and our children and became my home base after my mother withdrew. For him, I created our long-distance family films, snippets of German daily life as the children grew. Had my mother had her wish, he would have been long gone by that time. For her, any frailty was Helen.

* * *

One sunny day during our sabbatical year, my mother and I were drinking tea on the window seat and we both caught sight of a neighbor carrying Trader Joe bags up his steep front Victorian stairs.

"Did I tell you about the Smiths?" she said.

"No, how are they?" I remembered a lunch at their house a few years back in their beautifully designed dining room. It had felt traditional and cozy and full of flowers.

"Violet is now bedridden and unable to eat alone. Dan patiently feeds her. Poor man." She looked genuinely stricken, as if she were describing someone she herself had to take care of. "He seems so beaten down. But his scruples preclude him doing what he should be doing."

I recognized her tone. I knew where this was headed.

"He keeps going on and on, instead of allowing her to die," she continued.

This was a topic I wanted to avoid. "Yes, it is a very sad situation. Hard. I don't have a solution."

She slid off the seat. "There is something I want to show you."

She beckoned me to one of the white wooden bookcases in the hall. "I've become involved in an organization I feel very strongly about."

Her body posture was strange, stiff. As if she were floating upright toward the books. It reminded me of the time she told me she had named her friend Peggy to be her health care representative because she didn't trust me to withhold treatment if needed.

Pulling out a yellow paperback, she turned it toward me, hesitating, half-offering it up. *Final Exit* by Derek Humphrey. I took in the two words, looked away. I tugged at my long shirt.

"Oh." I suspected what it meant. Some weird cult of the dead. Linda Blair's head spinning in *The Exorcist* came to mind. I hated horror films.

I switched from the left to right foot. I couldn't even concentrate long enough to absorb the subtitle, "The Practicalities of Self-Deliverance and Assisted Suicide for the Dying." I just heard her passion.

"This is a network of people who help those who are dying end their life on their own terms." I focused on her lips telling me all of this.

"Yeah, yeah. I know, Mom. We all know how you feel. You've talked about Dr. Kevorkian for years."

"This is just in case, you know. I'm in good health. But there is nothing I am more afraid of than lying somewhere wasting away. You hear me?"

"Yes, Mom. I know."

It reminded me of those after-school specials I'd watched in middle school instead of doing homework. The ones about a girl molested by her father. Nobody would know until he'd suddenly be arrested and friends and family would be shocked. "What, he was such a nice neighbor, a kind husband." I had always been fascinated by that. Would they *really* not have known? It was spellbinding in a creepy way. Just like now.

Here I was doing exactly what I suspected those friends had been doing. I was looking away despite the clues. We always had the clues. But Jane's life-long love affair with death seemed like the proverbial cyanide pill spies carried hidden in their mouths. It was psychological protection in case they were caught. We figured Mom would live into her nineties. We figured she would nag on about suicide as a safety net from illness because it made her feel better to imagine control over the ending. We didn't think she would actually do it.

According to the diaries, she got involved with Final Exit in 2004, having tried other groups earlier like the Hemlock Society. Others talked of her views on death as part of her eccentricity. "What a character Jane is!" It was just another provocative topic in another provocative Jane conversation. We all knew she hated Proposition 13, felt the San Francisco school board was corrupt, and went to shareholder meetings to protest corporate greed. And we all knew she talked often of "pulling the plug." It was one of a long litany of her harangues.

Final Exit began to haunt the in-between spaces in our talks. I felt an increasing tamping down in her, like a gardener smoothing earth for the winter. But I chose not to discuss it. I didn't want to engage in its morality: Is it right to take someone's life, and when? I was afraid any real talk would lead to estrangement again. I was no longer in Professor Gregor's class at Berkeley debating such ethical puzzles for the pleasure of it. I was giving all I had to raising my children to love their lives as I had never been encouraged to do. Her talk of death was an anvil, pulling at me wherever I went. It wasn't just that I might be held legally culpable by knowing about her activities. It was also just downright creepy.

> Leah and I went for an early cable car ride, then we three drove over to Chestnut Street so Susannah could check out Apple laptops. ... I came home, did a Final Exit intake interview and loaded the car for the block sale tomorrow. (August 22, 2008)

It was like the dirty work was sandwiched into a catalog of banal activities and thus became less tainted. Or that she saw her end-of-life death work as equally banal, which was also creepy.

Final Exit seemed to be a semi-underground organization, operating in the gray zone of hospice and changing medical ethics. In California it would not be legal until 2016 to lend someone help in ending their own life, and then only with appropriate legal documentation. I had no trouble agreeing with my mother that there were health situations that warranted assistance to die, just as we do for our animals. Niels' uncle Hans had died of ALS a few years before. I retained a vivid picture of what the end had entailed for his family. Assisted suicide seems appropriate in such situations.

But as I'm reading, I really don't want to know about this side of Mom. In my imagination, she was becoming an Angel of Death, moving unseen through city streets, alighting at the bedsides of the infirm with her creepy concoction of helium bags, pipes and opiates. The bag goes over the head, the helium is connected with a pipe, the pills bring sleep. At the edge of those thoughts floated wisps of my grandmother's last months, and the new knowledge gained from reading the diary that my mother had secretly fed her the life-ending pills. It was high melodrama kept under wraps. I had no words for a conversation she never sought.

Her involvement with the group feels like a perversion of grandmotherhood, a dirty hidden life. Like those German children who discovered that their fathers had once been Nazi commandants. They would find out after his death, when going through papers. Usually, it turned out the family always somehow *knew*.

The diaries show that she spent six months in negotiations with Final Exit to be assigned an exit guide for what was called her *transition*. Her pages show lots of activity.

> It is the end of a powerful and emotionally taxing day. We learned how to help someone die and leave no trace that it was suicide by helium gas. The experts instruct the novices. Plenty of time for Q&A and hands-on trials. I am tired and strangely lonely, wishing for home and the sweet comfort of usual routine. At the same time I am grateful for the knowledge that a conclusion of my own life is within my own reach now. (November 10, 2007)

This diary entry was seven years before her final act. She rehearsed for a long time. The diaries increasingly catalog what she refers to as the BODs, the *Better off Deads*. These were acquaintances who were feeble and old, as well as friends and neighbors who were hospitalized. Soups, rides to doctors' appointments, accompaniments to the symphony, advice on live-in care bills, all this she seems to relish while she continues her own daily regimen of swimming a mile, yoga, and gymnastics.

A few months before her suicide, she receives the news that Final Exit would not provide an exit guide for her plans on ending her life. She had no diagnosed illness. Final Exit was already being charged as part of a case in Minnesota. They did not want to be held accountable.

She is alone.

James

2012

"JAMES DIED," MY MOTHER SAID QUIETLY, after a short pause in our phone conversation.

Our talks on the phone between Germany and San Francisco since our sabbatical felt uneasy, forced. This pronouncement came into the conversation almost like a shy offering, her tone hesitant and heightened. It took me a few seconds to recognize the name, but I changed tack in my next words carefully, automatically, as I might do after any announcement of death.

I remembered then the James she meant, the elegant patrician man with the Roman nose and blue, blue eyes, my mother's elicit lover. This was before I read the diaries. I hadn't thought of him in years, and even those few thoughts had been poisoned by derision. My mother had always dismissed the notion of true love to me and had chastised me for the feelings I admitted to having for my teenage boyfriends.

She had also expected me to lie for her constantly. "No, she's not home," "No, she's away for the weekend"—as her many suitors called and she juggled her dates, one man coming for cocktails, another later to take her to the symphony. James had been one of those men. He was never a three-dimensional figure in my life. Rather he was kept carefully controlled on the sidelines. If I had suspected anything deep, she had denied it. He was singular only because his name had continued to appear very occasionally in her conversations for longer than the others, after I had gone to college and even after my own children were born.

But I heard her voice on the phone that day and felt the trembling. "Oh, I'm sorry to hear that. Were you still seeing him?"

"No, he was with his family," she answered. I didn't sense her need to let the conversation linger, nor did she insist. We went on to other things.

In reading the diaries, I wondered if I would discover something I never knew about my mother, something that would explain her strange years of a lonely and busy life, and then her peculiar death. Maybe a secret child before me, a shame vastly deep, a hidden illness? It would almost be liberating to find something like that.

But what I have found instead is love with a married man. In her diaries are outpourings of love and affection, of doubt and secrecy, descriptions of cautious platonic, guilt-laden meetings over two years, and then the development over more years of a daily and reciprocal secret relationship, hour-long snatched phone conversations, mutual yearnings and protestations, "a love of a lifetime," she wrote.

My understanding of the dimensions of her hidden life has crept up on me only gradually as I've read, gathering momentum as her entries have grown ever more voluble, romantic, cathartic, or remorseful. Her language is often melodramatic: "I pledged him to secret keeping and I prayed for an exemption from the pain from the emotional holocaust which the sharp edge of that sword can so easily bring to several of us." But it is also clear by the variety of descriptions over a long period of time that they were deeply and genuinely in love. I believe this love lasted decades.

In the midst of my reading this morning, when I suddenly remember those quiet words spoken to me on the phone, I am sad, as if I had overlooked a special gift from someone who never gives gifts. I feel guilty. I am that child again at Christmas, prying open green and gold wrappings to find an ugly blouse I'd never wanted.

"If you don't like it, just tell me," she'd said. Maybe she saw the look on my face. But I could never tell her. I was trapped by the image of her carving time out of her busy days to shop for it. It was proof my mother loved me. I would wear the shirt.

With my mother's "James died," I was suddenly made aware of her isolation. I suspect there was no one but me who had ever known about the two of them. I was the one person she could tell who would give her experience resonance, who might have honored an inner world of passion never allowed into the public light. But I wasn't able to hold that moment, to hold her, because I didn't know. She never allowed me to know. She was so alone.

It breaks my heart.

Then it makes me furious.

Once again, I am the one paying attention to her emotions, allowing her to breathe and bringing her to life in the world. Her diaries make clear she kept him in his marriage. He would have left his wife for her. James and my mother might have had a chance. For a few minutes, I imagine my life if there had been a Grandpa James at Nonna's side for our children. She would have softened, not been so brittle. She would not have obsessed so much about illness and dependence. She would not have killed herself.

But it never happened that way. Her approach to James seemed designed to keep her distant from any man. Being with James would have meant surrendering control. Or becoming emotionally dependent, vulnerable. His unhappy marriage was safer. Emotional distance enshrined. With that anger, I also realize her hypocrisy. All those years of calling me promiscuous, "not a virgin" when I married, and here she had been the other woman in an affair for decades.

I was so dependent on her. Every kind gesture felt like confirmation of life itself, like a baby bird receiving a worm from its mother. It isn't the worm; it is the fact that the mother returns at all.

I must have felt her emptiness even then.

Pick Her

2018

RETURNING HERE TO SANTA CRUZ after the tumult of Mom's death
and the decision to move back to the United States permanently, I
felt the openness of the first days of a school year again. The morning following Labor Day in September had always been the start of a
brand-new life when I was young: a new classroom, a new teacher, a
new group of kids, sometimes a new school. I remember waking with
an excited, bubbly feeling in my stomach. I was nervous. But mostly I
was full of anticipation. What would this new year bring?

In my twenties, I kept to this rhythm. Though it wasn't Labor Day
and wasn't every year, I moved quite often. Each time, I was full of anticipation. What would this place bring? The moves were also a chance
to look at myself, to decide to dress a new way, or dim or flare certain
of my traits. It was as if I were being given a blank slate upon which to
record my new experiences.

Now here we were heading to the Seabright area. We would have new
neighbors, new connections, colors and lines and textures. It was a time to
understand how my life could take a different path than my mother's.

After a while, Niels and I became acquainted with Rima, who had
a particularly artsy garden that we passed on our daily dog walks. Rima

was short, with wiry gray hair, fit and active. She talked continuously. She gave us the scoop on her street. "Over there, in that white house, live Tracy and Jim," she told us one day after inviting us over for tea. "They're expecting their second baby in August. Next door to me, who knows. I never see them, just hear their dog sometimes. Over on this side, Zack just moved back in. He and his wife lived over the hill, renting out this place, but I guess they decided to come back. Terrific, 'cuz the guys who rented, whew, they sure could party."

She told us a lot about her grown daughter and her parents. "I thought about moving, you know. I'm an Elder Care person now, my parents are both still living—in a place in Palo Alto. I have to go over there every few days. Let me tell you, I tell my daughter, if I get to a certain age, I'm just going to kill myself. Just give me a shot or give me a bunch of pills."

She laughed with a short bark.

I laughed, too. Like a woman laughing at her boss's penis jokes in the office.

I took a breath and steadied myself. Easy, she doesn't know your history. People toss around phrases like this without meaning them literally. I shifted from my right to left hip against the small sofa. Should I interrupt her? *She'll never really know you if you are not honest.* Eh, who cares about her? Just stay quiet. My stomach felt queasy.

Niels and I exchanged a look.

It was a moment suspended, like a rain droplet gathering weight at the end of a twig. Would I release the story?

I didn't. The moment passed. She continued to talk. I half-listened until it was finally a decent time to go home. I felt haunted by her statement. Sure, it might have been a joke. But *if* more and more women are beginning to speak about end-of-life suicide, maybe my mother *was* in the vanguard? Maybe I'm wrong to feel so angry and abandoned. This off-balance mood lasted until my tea on Tuesday with Nancy, my next-door neighbor.

She and I had met a few times over the past months. Almost eighty, she was also short and sprightly and loved to cook. She talked a lot, too, but differently. She hesitated in the middle of sentences, as if she were searching for words, agreeable to abandoning the sentence midway.

"What have you been doing the past few weeks?" I asked.

She looked excited. "Well, I have actually been doing something really interesting." She paused. "I have begun to sing for hospice. Do you know about that?"

I did. It terrified me. I had first heard about hospice singing four years ago. I had wanted to hide and cover my ears with my hands.

I forced myself to smile. "Oh?"

She talked about her experience accompanying two women with Alzheimer's in their end stage care. Her group went every few days to sing for them at their bedsides.

"Doesn't it scare you?" I asked.

Pausing to look into the distance, she said, "It doesn't, funny enough." In that second, my breath slowed. I sat deeper into the couch.

I loved that she understood the fear behind my question and didn't dismiss it. Rather, she seemed to be contemplating her own emotions and how she got herself into this unexpected place of singing people to the other side.

"It feels more like an honor," she said after a while. "Like an experience of awe. Like it is awesome. That's a stupid word though. Hard to explain."

As she told me about the group, I felt, instead of dread, a little bit of room to breathe. I remembered research on certain African tribes that sang at the births of babies, how the women were held and carried by the camaraderie and power of the female voices. That had inspired me in my birthing years.

Listening, my thoughts got jumbled up in how lonely most Westerners are, left alone in these vital life rituals, birthing and dying in the absence of community, according to a hospital schedule.

I think that was what scared my mother most. She was alone, renaming her aloneness as "independence," bearing it aloft as if she were carrying the Statue of Liberty's torch herself. But by being alone and strong, she rejected connection.

I cannot shake this view of her.

I am struck by the paths that have opened up in front of me. These two new women in my life, both intelligent and educated, are beckoning to me so differently. Rima, with her feisty wit and sardonic laugh, draws me to her. I'm almost powerless to resist her tough charm. I see now how I've been automatically drawn to women who have my mother's defenses, repeating a pattern I know from birth. Ready contact that seems like genuine interest but is not true contact at all.

It still takes a huge amount of strength to resist my mother's pull, as if she is a moon and I am the tide. But slowly, I am changing. Slowly, it feels like I'm cultivating a healthy adult wisdom that comes not from mocking emotions but welcoming them and sitting with them and keeping them company.

Nancy's courage to muster lovely notes in the presence of death seems like a promise of hope. This is good. Maybe I won't have to end up like my mother after all.

Almost Done

2018

MY MOTHER NEVER TOOK ANY REGULAR MEDICINES, was never hospitalized, nor diagnosed with a disease. She rejected mammograms, colonoscopies, and plastic surgery. She was firm in her decisions. She ate well and exercised and was blessed with good genes. She observed in her friends that testing brought more suffering than good.

After her death, many people questioned me, "Did she have a terminal illness after all? Could that be an explanation for her decision?" I thought back to those weird moles on her skin. I thought about her refusal to engage in Western medicine's business of diagnostics. Was something bad hiding inside of her?

But no, her autopsy was clean. There was no physical ailment that drove her to choose suicide. I refused to read the autopsy report, afraid of what I might find, creeped out by the very idea of some technicians in the bowels of the morgue pulling her apart. Niels was a doctor. He was used to such things. When he related the contents to me, I was relieved. Jane had been exonerated in her determination not to take all those diagnostic tests. I was glad not to give fodder to all the family and friends who were waiting with *I told you sos.*

But in the end, what did her victory get her? She was right in a world fueled by what can go wrong. She remained an oddball rather than an inspiration. The strain of remaining true to her convictions, mixed in with her fear of losing control, in the end became too much for her. What does this leave for me, except to continue to tell the story and slowly find her toxic power over me released?

She left the diaries for me, and chose deliberately to do so. Her last weeks were filled with purging and organizing. She made lists. She labeled. She could have taken them to the dump or burned them in her fireplace. She didn't. Am I glad she left them? That I've spent the last year working through her words, learning secrets, remembering my own life afresh?

I have always been convinced it is better to know as much of the picture as possible in order to truly puzzle out its meaning. In the Indian parable of the blind men and the elephant, one touches a side and feels a wall, one touches a tusk and feels a spear, one touches a leg and feels a tree. They quarrel bitterly over the truth of their findings because they cannot see the whole. This has been my one chance to look at different parts of Jane, to hope to understand more of myself.

I don't think that is what she intended. At the beginning, I suspected she wanted to leave them as her final statement to the world. To prove her own narrative correct. But now I think differently. Especially when considering her harsh and often relentless private criticism of me, I think now that she left me the diaries to nail the coffin shut.

Leave me, she would say. Don't think about me. Don't look back.

As for her effect on others, she intended to inspire them, to trumpet, "don't grow old," "exit life's stage way before you have to." She wanted to be seen as heroic, if not in life, then in death. But I cannot feel anywhere in her circles that this has happened. Her suicide in the prime of older life seems to have had a splintering effect, leaving hurt and bewilderment. A hole that cannot be properly grieved.

Had she been terminally ill or suffering great pain, I think many, including me, would have accompanied her choice to die with dignity, on her own terms, when and where she wished. There is a reason the end-of-life movement is gaining political influence now.

But my mother was active and healthy. Death became a violent act. We all felt it.

The diaries have shown that it was as if she carried too many secrets for too long. As if she were exhausted from the struggle to be the Jane she showed the world. Her obsession with death robbed her of joy she might have felt over so many years and has tinged the lives of everyone who loved her.

If I hear echoes of admiration for what she did, they come from people who never knew her. People who are suffering, or who worry about being lonely themselves. Their imaginations alight with the details of her death. "Wow, I kind of admire that," they say.

At first, I was irritated. Didn't they see how much damage her death has caused? But I have learned to remain distant. I know that they know nothing of my life, or hers, that they are simply giving voice to their own thoughts and fears about how to encounter the ending of life in them. Our culture gives little room for sanguine discussions of birth and death.

I wish I had my Great Aunt Fran's belief in heaven. But even then, I don't think my mother would be there. I remember feeling the strange-but-true whoosh of Mom's spirit as it circled me on the parking lot hill, behind the concert church, when I heard about her death. That still day, invaded by wind, the sky roiling. An arc. It was so clear, and then it was gone.

I remember the absolute silence in me that followed her death. No dreams. No visions. No feeling her spirit was hanging about. An absence that seemed bigger than just my grief. It felt more like she had paid her dues to whatever energy controls such things. She had entered into a bargain of caring for the ill, the *Better Off Deads*, so she could be utterly released.

She's nowhere now. Slipped through a dark hole in the universe.

* * *

A few weeks after her suicide, I was invited to take part in the New Moon group again. Women's energy would be good right now, I agreed. I joined their greeting circle, holding hands under the beautiful fruit trees in my friend's backyard. Eden, with thick curly gray hair down to her waist and red-layered clothes looking very much the hippie healer, spoke a calm Native American prayer. At first, I relished the lines, repeating with the circle:

"Oh, spirit of the East, the winds"

The words sounded so beautiful, affirming.

"Oh, Spirit of the West, the land of the setting Sun—

We call on you and ask for your wisdom and blessing here with us today."

This hopeful, peaceful prayer. We all held hands, were quiet.

"We call on our ancestors to join us in this circle, to bless us with their presence."

My voice stilled. A terrible unease filled me. These words felt wrong. *So* wrong.

My mother would not want to be brought back.

And I didn't want her here.

The Aerie

2019

I AM UP IN THE AERIE, or that's what it feels like on the window seat
of my mother's apartment overlooking the Bay. It is five years after her
death. Oversized pillows of many pale designs form a frame to my
perch as I settle into the feet-outstretched spot I've known since I was
ten. Whitecaps in the distance indicate a stiff breeze. A sailboat whips
along. A ferry plods toward Alcatraz. A group of Asian tourists pose
on the street far below the window, kneeling so their photos capture
the length of Coit Tower in the background. A Tesla sneaks up the
hill without a sound, causing the posers to giggle and scatter to the
opposite sidewalks.

I am filled with melancholy. This was the place my mother spent
her last days, planned her self-execution. Li Fen, her cleaning woman,
whispered to me at the memorial, "Your mama, she not sleep well. She
sleep in living room."

That sentence caused my stomach to clench. What had been
haunting her? I pictured tears on her cheeks, her mind inundated with
memories of deaths she had visited, accompanied, in preparation for
her own. I shook inside. What does it mean to be born to a woman
who practiced her own death ritual on others? What is her legacy?

Did she even do all the things my imagination envisions?

Her early-1900 molded-ceilinged, sun-filled, white-walled apartment with the stupendous view has been officially transferred to my name. I am its owner. It is a truly beautiful apartment, and stylish and elegant, nestled against a green pathway on Russian Hill. It is a rare gem. Its hardwood floors and pivot picture windows evoke pearls and symphonies and dinner parties; friends from abroad who have visited me here know more about me through the apartment than was shown through my Waldorf-mama life. I liked possessing a key to a world that tells such a strong story about my roots. I might have merged with it, become easy with it.

But I hate it now. I cannot stay here. I try, each time we visit the city. I try to enjoy it the way I once did. When I shared it with my boyfriends and adult friends, when I brought everyone important in my life to my mother's world, when I proudly embellished my children's American experience with this central San Franciscan home-away-from-home. How could I be so lucky as to inherit such an architectural treasure and then reject it?

I remember the early years here, when I was still at Sherman Elementary School, when my mother barely got permission from the co-op board of directors to buy the two-bedroom. She had been a divorcée, a single mother, in the early 1970s, unheard of and a threat. I had to be quiet, respectful, always well-behaved. "Never give the neighbors a chance to complain," she warned. In the years when I'd bring my own children here, I felt proud and afraid at once. For weeks before each trip from Europe with Julian, Dylan and then Leah in their toddler years, I had wrestled with nightmare visions. In these visions, my young child, used to climbing and jumping everywhere, would climb onto this same very sturdy 8 by 5 foot window seat, jump up and down in euphoric kid delight, then lose their balance and crash through the windows down the five-story drop to the cement below. It was persistent, this fear that my small children would die here.

No running in the hallway, no loud music, no parties. These were companions of my youth and the youth of my children when we visited their grandmother. We made it through. We were quiet. We benefited from the rarified view. Yet, Niels and I had chosen to live in the countryside, where our children could scream at the top of their lungs and climb trees and get dirty and yell *"Jaaaaaa!"* at a soccer goal by their favorite team, even late into the night. But now our children are almost grown, and I am looking toward another phase in life. Should it be set in this place? A city jewel. What luck I have.

"Why not smudge the apartment?" a new friend suggested. I chuckled and waved my hands.

"Oh, I have smudged, and sung, and swept, and banged wood and misted. I have done all I could think of."

The rituals did help a little. That circle of women showed me what it meant to come together. And freed me to invite friends to use the apartment, to give their own DNA blessing to the bedrooms and kitchen. Co-op rules forbid us renting it out to strangers. Then Julian and Shelbi had moved in, bringing a new generational juju, sex, and joy to the air. They had loved living here, but they didn't love it so much that they planned their lives to stay. It would be relegated to a temporary place in their history together, a stage on their own life's journey.

So here I am, again on the window seat, again contemplating why I don't feel at ease and yet can't give it up. Should we move in once Leah goes to college? Should we sell it?

"We could buy a different place with the money," Niels says.

"But it wouldn't be this amazing place," I respond. I'm still stuck within these walls.

One night Niels asks, as we sit at the dining room table high above the Bay, "Would you be happy here if something happened to me, and you would live here alone?" I picture myself in my eighties, ambling around the apartment, a glass of wine in front of me as now, perhaps having watered flowers and done yoga in the mornings as my mother routinely did. Perhaps also lying awake at night alone with my anxieties just like she had done.

My reaction is immediate and violent.

"No—*no!*"

My hands rise in the air, I shake them savagely, pushing away the image. *No.*

This was her sacred space and even that wasn't enough to save her from herself.

The D Word

2019

MY MOTHER'S FRIEND ABIGAIL stands before me with startled eyes. I can see she is struggling, like a child contemplating a convoluted math problem. "I just don't understand. She was so beautiful and active, all that yoga she did." I wait for the question I guess is coming. "Do you think she was," slower voice, hesitant, "Depressed?"

When Jane's friends first began tentatively asking that question, in the days following her suicide, I had shrugged. No, my mother had not been depressed. She had just had her first root canal done, she picketed every week with Occupy Wall Street, had season tickets to the symphony, swam, and listened to NPR on the kitchen radio while she was making dinner. She had been an active, healthy seventy-five-year-old. She just didn't want to live anymore. She'd spoken for years of being Death's Joan of Arc, inspiring by example. Thorny she was, yes. Difficult. But not depressed.

As Abigail stands before me, though, I feel something tighten, somewhere in my muscles outside of conscious reach. Maybe I had it all wrong. Had we all been duped? Seduced by our wish to see her as she presented herself, convenience over truth? The only clinically depressed person I had known was Dr. Sargent, a retired, kindly neighbor in our courtyard complex. He and his wife had invited us once into their beautiful home. At age fourteen, I hadn't paid too much attention. Certainly, I hadn't thought much about him since. But, standing in front of Abigail, with this tension in the air and that searching question, I suddenly remember a frisson existing around Dr. Sargent's name. Something had happened.

I clicked into having seen the doctor once, somehow thinner and frailer, gazing at me with blank eyes, or maybe it was his daughter who had greeted me, guiding him from the car to red steps in a way that communicated incapacity. In that second, I registered that he had dwindled. Something was wrong. I had asked my mother about him and all I remember is the explanation, "Depressed." Just a word, not even one I really understood, but I felt a chill. A shiver. Then, somehow, Dr. Sargent was dead and there was no other explanation. Just the D-word hanging in the air. This absence of information from forty years before leaves me chilled now as Abigail's eyes search mine.

No, my mother had not been depressed in the way that Dr. Sargent had been depressed. She had not died from an inability to command life. But I see now she died from something more muted and almost more tragic, because it was preventable. Like a sailor who ignores the rules of the emotional sea, she pushed away her underworld, the tides and seaweeds, rocks and craters, and died from the effort to stay on top. She had all the means necessary to have helped herself live a different life, one in which she wasn't so alone, but she chose not to pursue those paths. The anger I feel is mostly about this. I would have liked to have a better mother longer. Not necessarily my real mother longer, for the add-on years would surely have been strained. But a better mother, who wanted to be with us and her grandchildren. For more years. Yes.

So many times, Niels and I offered to listen, to talk to her, sensing a budding hesitation as she became both tougher and more brittle with age. She was an expert at starting chummy conversations and ending them.

"Niels, do you find the type of patients has changed now that you moved your practice to the new neighborhood?" she'd ask, settling onto the sofa as if for a long chat, eyes interested, attention tuned. At some point she always asked about his patients.

"No, not really," he'd say. "My patients travel from all over Hamburg to my practice."

Lots of people asked Niels about such things. Usually, it was a prelude to some sort of roundabout question about therapy for themselves or a friend.

"What do your patients talk about?" she'd ask. *How crazy are they?* She seemed to be querying.

"My patients are people like you and me," he'd say, zeroing in on what seemed like the underlying skittish question.

She'd consider this for a minute. It seemed like an opening to a larger conversation.

Then Jane would suddenly change. "You know what, I need to start dinner," she'd say. That would be it.

One afternoon we were in the living room in our German farmhouse, peeling potatoes for dinner, a Bruce Springsteen ballad on the stereo.

"Nice music," Mom said, seeming to dip into the contented mood of the room. She paused. "But how can you stand the sadness of it?"

A few more lyrics passed through the air before Niels gave her his answer. A way forward. "It's important to allow for some sadness, if it's there."

I could almost see her back straightening as she turned away. "Not for me," she quipped. A lightening turn of mood, then a scoff. "Who would want to open that can of worms?"

My mother's philosophy was compartmentalization. In other words, *not* feeling. Niels and I, people who had worked very hard to learn to mix narratives and emotions together, were the softies, silly fools, like poets at a conference of prison guards.

The worst was that I played along with her charade. I wanted a mother in my life, a grandmother for my children. I wanted the good parts of her but wasn't yet able to clearly identify where the good began and ended. Niels played the game, too, because I asked him to, and because when she was nice, she was very, very nice. Generous. Witty.

Thoughtful. Lively. Yet we were always holding an umbrella overhead on a tightrope, hoping we could manage a balancing act of enjoying her company without getting hurt. We knew already from the smoking conversation when Julian was little that there were only two choices: Play along or have no mother at all.

One summer, Mom visited us in Germany and went with me to Dylan's Waldorf kindergarten festival. I could feel she was out of sorts and thought it would cheer her up to share the beautiful blue-sky gathering, parents whooping in outside games with their children, four-year-olds with cotton clothes and simple, hand-made toys. She took it all in, standing by my side. I assumed she felt as expanded as I did. Until she exhaled.

"They have no idea what awaits them, all these happy children," she said.

As if through black magic, pride flipped to foreboding in my heart, the scene in front of us changing. I no longer saw my son and his friends happy and playing. Raised strong for their future. Now I saw bleakness. We were raising our children to teeter on a cliff, unprepared for the storms to come. All my early-childhood anthropology research was tossed out the window. I think above all she was angry at me for raising my children with hope.

The thing about parents is that they will always be with us. It isn't about "getting over" our difficult mothers or fathers, despite magazine advice and what some quick self-help programs say. It is about absorbing them and moving on, encountering them as we do, in some form, in every man and woman we meet. I had envisioned the process of reading the diaries as circular. Something beginning with my birth and ending with my rebirth into some sort of woman-beyond-her-mother. But mother and daughter dances are not circles. They are spirals. I learned that from my midwife. They move away from each other and back to meet again. Each age is its own encounter. Reading about my childhood has brought me awful moments of anxiety, when I felt that my boundaries to stable mental health were porous.

I understood for the first time what Niels has always said: "Human beings are fragile creatures."

I had always been strong. Until I began to learn how to feel.

Reading the diaries has also brought me closer to my mother, in sympathy with her childhood, marked by sadness and given no words, and then her life as a Catholic housewife in 1960s Manhattan, married to a violent alcoholic, in a time when divorce was not an accepted option. It has surprised me, how her diaries twist my sympathies yet again, giving me evidence that though she wrote occasional loving words about me, she spent almost all her time thinking about herself. Surely a mother's first loyalty should be to her child. She did not leave my father at the first outburst of rage, way before I was born. She left me alone with him. She pretended. Then she rejected me when I grew up to walk my own path.

In childhood, the spiral is close in diameter. At middle age, farther apart. But I see that the coil doesn't end. I have met my mother in new ways during this reading of her words. We will meet again, probably when I am seventy-five, the age when she chose to leave the stage. I will be confronted again with her reasons for suicide, but at a time when there is more of my own life that has been lived than is to come.

This book has dominated my life for two years. Niels missed me. Leah missed me. Every day took longer than I thought. Sleep was often full of bad dreams, worries about illness and death. Restlessness. Heart beating. Nerve sensations. *Stop worrying. There's nothing.* On those days, I was glad the night was over. Afraid the book would make me ill. I have often danced around anxiety. I'm tired. But I'm stronger, too.

My friend Lizzie complained to me recently: "You're not as flowy as you were."

No, I'm not as *flowy*. I'm not as interested in the New Moon group or prayer huts or trying on new identities. As I leave my writing nook today, my eyes survey all the papers, diaries, and letters deposited around the room. Physical remnants of my great-grandfather, my grandparents, my mother and father, what three generations have left for me.

I poke my head into Niels' office.

"Want to take a walk?" I suggest. The wild beach beckons.

I want to talk about selling the apartment. I can finally do that now. And about visiting our new grandchild. Julian and Shelbi are expecting a baby next month. They are planning a home birth. I will be right there to help in those first days.

Niels and I have so much to be thankful for.

Maybe we'll build a bonfire later.

Enjoy more about

Reading Jane

Meet the Author

Check out author appearances

Explore special features

About the Author

SUSANNAH KENNEDY, DPhil is a former journalist and has a doctorate in social anthropology. She was born in India, grew up in New York City and San Francisco, studied at Berkeley and Oxford and later, with her German psychoanalyst husband, raised three children in a thatched-roof farmhouse in the northern German countryside. She integrated motherhood and village life with phases of academia as an adjunct professor, a freelance writer, and a researcher on birth and child development. Her mother's suicide and its aftermath then brought her back to California in 2017, when she began melding creative nonfiction with the anthropological lens. She has been published in *The Summerset Review, Evening Street Review, Halfway Down the Stairs, (mac)ro(mic),* and *Wilderness House Literary Review.* She and her husband now live on the coast north of San Francisco.

Acknowledgements

I'd like to thank my husband most of all, who has been a patient witness to the many years of my emancipation from "my mother and me." Without his wisdom, insight and sense of fun, I could not have walked this reading path. Also, I thank Julian, Dylan, and Leah—may they feel seen and loved and may they have benefitted from the journey that got me here. And, especially to Leah, who was young when the events that start this book occurred, and has been the most affected, I wish it hadn't had to be this way.

I would like to thank my writing mentor and teacher Laura Davis, whose Thursday writing group and quarterly retreats in the Santa Cruz mountains eased the transition from panic about the diaries to curiosity to the chapters that became this book. Also, a thank you goes to Sue Campbell for her book marketing workshops, and Elizabeth Percer and Ann Randolph for additional writing workshops. Thank you to Jenefer Shute for her help with an early draft and Betsy Graziani Fasbinder for insightful and decisive editing that turned it into the final narrative. And a huge thank you to the indomitable Julia Park Tracey and Vicki DeArmon at Sibylline Press, who inspired a new kind of publishing model and offered me the opportunity to soar with them.

For the indispensable physical training which balanced the seated life of computer work day after day for two years, I am grateful to Wendy

Willis and Stephanie Berard. For medical support and bodily calm, so vital to being able to work through traumatic material, thank you to acupuncturist Tracy Cone, and massage therapist Jennifer Eisele. For moral support throughout the writing process, my gratitude goes to Susan Buckley, David Bodanis, Maure Quilter and Mary Deir Donovan, who extended a serendipitous bridge to the world of publishing when I was in need of a spark.

I've been lucky to find supportive maternal figures at important life intersections. Thank you to Palma Trionfo for her mama role at my wedding, to Dr. Ursula Ostendorf for helping me understand my inner worlds, and to midwife and author Margarita Klein whose wisdom opened the path to what babies and young mothers really need. Lastly, there are many friends who have walked this mother-daughter journey with me, and strangely, some of the most important ones are only in the wings of this story. Know, please, that I remember you, learned from you and value your time in my life.

Book Group Questions

Reading Jane: A Daughter's Memoir
by Susannah Kennedy

1. How do you feel about Jane's decision to end her life at 75? Do you think she made the right decision? Do you think she considered the fallout from her decision?

2. What do you think of Jane's version of Susannah's life, as told through her diaries? Do you think she told the truth?

3. What do you think of Susannah's decision to read the diaries? Did reading the diaries affect Susannah's ultimate opinion of her mother?

4. How would you describe the mother-daughter bond or relationship between Jane and Susannah? Between Jane and her own mother? Between Susannah and her daughter?

5. How are female relationships portrayed in Jane's diaries—positively or negatively?

6. How do Susannah's life choices differ from her mother's? How is therapy (including the insights given through Susannah's husband) helpful to the mother-daughter relationship depicted here?

7. What surprises or shocks did you learn from the diaries that would have made you stop reading? Do you keep a diary or journal? Are you leaving surprises for your reader/child/heir? Will you save your diaries to be read after you pass?

Sibylline Press is proud to publish the brilliant work of women authors over 50. We are a woman-owned publishing company and, like our authors, represent women of a certain age. In our first season we have three outstanding fiction (historical fiction and mystery) and three incredible memoirs to share with readers of all ages.

HISTORICAL FICTION

The Bereaved: A Novel
By Julia Park Tracey

Paperback ISBN: 978-1-7367954-2-2
5 3/8 x 8 3/4 | 274 pages | $18
ePub ISBN: 978-1-9605730-0-1 | $12.60

Based on the author's research into her grandfather's past as an adopted child, and the surprising discovery of his family of origin and how he came to be adopted, Julia Park Tracey has created a mesmerizing work of historical fiction illuminating the darkest side of the Orphan Train.

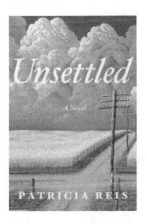

Unsettled: A Novel
By Patricia Reis

Paperback ISBN: 978-1-7367954-8-4
5 3/8 x 8 3/4 | 378 pages | $19
ePUB ISBN: 978-1-960573-05-6 | $13.30

In this lyrical historical fiction with alternating points of view, a repressed woman begins an ancestral quest through the prairies of Iowa, awakening family secrets and herself, while in the late 1800s, a repressed ancestor, Tante Kate, creates those secrets.

MYSTERY

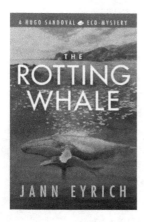

The Rotting Whale: A Hugo Sandoval Eco-Mystery
By Jann Eyrich

Paperback ISBN: 978-1-7367954-3-9
5 3/8 x 8 3/8 | 212 pages | $17
ePub ISBN: 978-1-960573-03-2 | $11.90

In this first case in the new Hugo Sandoval Eco-Mystery series, an old-school San Francisco building inspector with his trademark Borsalino fedora, must reluctantly venture outside his beloved city and find his sea legs before he can solve the mystery of how a 90-ton blue whale became stranded, twice, in a remote inlet off the North Coast.

MORE TITLES IN THIS ECO-MYSTERY SERIES TO COME:
Spring '24: *The Blind Key* | ISBN: 978-1-7367954-5-3
Fall '24: *The Singing Lighthouse* | ISBN: 978-1-7367954-6-0

MEMOIR

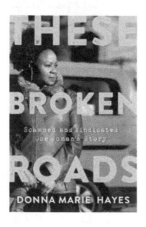

These Broken Roads: Scammed and Vindicated, One Woman's Story
By Donna Marie Hayes

Tradepaper ISBN: 978-1-7367954-4-6
5 3/8 x 8 3/8 | 226 pages | $17
ePUB ISBN: 978-1-960573-04-9 | $11.90

In this gripping and honest memoir, Jamaican immigrant Donna Marie Hayes recounts how at the peak of her American success in New York City, she is scammed and robbed of her life's savings by the "love of her life" met on an online dating site and how she vindicates herself to overcome a lifetime of bad choices.

Maeve Rising: Coming Out Trans in Corporate America
By Maeve DuVally

Paperback ISBN: 978-1-7367954-1-5
5 3/8 x 8 3/8 | 284 pages | $18
ePub ISBN: 978-1-960573-01-8 | $12.60

In this searingly honest LBGQT+ memoir, Maeve DuVally tells the story of coming out transgender in one of the most high-profile financial institutions in America, Goldman Sachs.

Reading Jane: A Daughter's Memoir
By Susannah Kennedy

Paperback ISBN: 978-1-7367954-7-7
5 3/8 x 8 3/8 | 306 pages | $19
ePub ISBN: 978-1-960573-02-5 | $13.30

After the calculated suicide of her domineering and narcissistic mother, Susannah Kennedy grapples with the ties between mothers and daughters and the choices parents make in this gripping memoir that shows what freedom looks like when we choose to examine the uncomfortable past.

For more information about **Sibylline Press** and our authors, please visit us at **www.sibyllinepress.com**